T0271950

Routledge Revivals

Free-thought in the Social Sciences

This *Routledge Revival* sees the reissue of a seminal work by British economist, sociologist and academic John A. Hobson, elucidating his views on a variety of topics, drawn from across the social sciences. He makes particular reference to the struggle between the disinterested urge of the social scientist and the interests and other motive forces which tend to influence and mould his processes of inquiry. The work is split into three parts, focussing upon free-thinking, economics and political ethics respectively.

Free-thought in the Social Sciences

J. A. Hobson

Routledge
Taylor & Francis Group

First published in 1926
by George Allen & Unwin Ltd

This edition first published in 2010 by Routledge
2 Park Square, Milton Park, Abingdon, Oxon, OX14 4RN

Simultaneously published in the USA and Canada
by Routledge
270 Madison Avenue, New York, NY 10016

Routledge is an imprint of the Taylor & Francis Group, an informa business

Publisher's Note
The publisher has gone to great lengths to ensure the quality of this reprint but
points out that some imperfections in the original copies may be apparent.

Disclaimer
The publisher has made every effort to trace copyright holders and welcomes
correspondence from those they have been unable to contact.

ISBN 13: 978-0-415-57856-1 (hbk)
ISBN 13: 978-0-203-85188-3 (ebk)

ISBN 10: 0-415-57856-6 (hbk)
ISBN 10: 0-203-85188-9 (ebk)

FREE-THOUGHT IN
THE SOCIAL SCIENCES

FREE-THOUGHT IN THE SOCIAL SCIENCES

BY

J. A. HOBSON

AUTHOR OF " ECONOMICS OF UNEMPLOYMENT "
" PROBLEMS OF A NEW WORLD," ETC.

LONDON : GEORGE ALLEN & UNWIN LTD.
RUSKIN HOUSE, 40 MUSEUM STREET, W.C. 1

First published in 1926

PREFACE

JUST fifty-two years ago Herbert Spencer, in his *Study of Sociology*, introduced to the educated classes of this country the novel conception that social organisation could be material for scientific study, and that laws of evolution could be discovered in the history of human institutions. A most impressive aspect of this study was its presentation of the conflicts which a disinterested worker in this field of knowledge had to carry on with the biases of custom, interest and passion, which at every step tended to divert the mind from the path of reason.

Two generations have passed. In universities and other centres of culture certain branches of social science, especially economics, anthropology, politics and ethics, have won substantial recognition, while a general consent is accorded to the belief that the ' reign of law ' extends to all departments of human behaviour. But the rapid progress made in some of these studies, and their claim to the establishment of laws, with a rightful authority for the direction of the social arts, especially of industry and government, make it desirable that reconsideration should be given to the limits set upon the intellectual integrity and accuracy of thinking in these studies. Modern psychology has revealed many subtle ways in which emotional interests and valuations secretly, but powerfully, intervene in the processes of seemingly disinterested observation, reasoning and judgment. The ' soft ' material, the defects of language, the intrusion of traditional or popular ideas or generalisations, the complex and delicately qualitative interactions between the mind of the student and the object of his study, all contribute to make it difficult for any social science to attain, or even approach, the measure of accuracy, consistency and objective truth rightly claimed for the more advanced physical sciences.

Associated with, and part cause of, these difficulties of the social sciences is the wide and obscure penumbra of popular opinions and beliefs that encircle and infect them. The mathematician, the physicist, the chemist, even the biologist, is not seriously hampered by the loose thoughts, sentiments, or language of the man in the street, or even in the pulpit. But the idols of the cave and market are everywhere obtrusive in social studies, and often impose their images and terms in ways extremely detrimental to exact and disinterested thinking.

My object in this book is to examine afresh the character of this struggle between the disinterested urge of the social scientist and the interests and other motive forces which tend to influence and mould his processes of inquiry, reasoning and formulation, having regard to the peculiar nature of the subject matter which he handles.

I fully recognise that the treatment of this subject in my book fails to justify the claims of its ambitious title. Inadequacy of intellectual equipment, as well as limitations of time and space, have prevented me from attempting to give an equal and orderly consideration to the various branches of social science. After some general discussion of the character, methods and difficulties which distinguish all social studies, I pass on to examine the actual struggles for disinterested thinking, not in a comprehensive survey of the progress of the social sciences (a task beyond my competence), but by illustrative studies, chiefly in the field of political economy and politics. Though there are reasons for regarding the evolution of economic theory as a particularly valuable testing-ground for the conflict between disinterested science and the interests, I recognise that other fields, especially in anthropology and social psychology, deserve far more cultivation than is represented in the slight excursions I have made into them.

My main purpose has been, by disclosing the nature of the dangers to which the social sciences are exposed by the inherent difficulties of their material and method, taken in conjunction with the *naïveté* and self-assurance of many of their practitioners, to achieve two objects. The first is to afford some explanation of the slowness of these sciences in producing any considerable body of larger truths, in the shape of generally accepted laws and principles; the second is to show how the vindication of free-thought, with its accompanying increase of intellectual productivity in these studies, is linked up with definite reforms of social structure needed to liberate these studies from the hampering conditions which have hitherto cramped and malformed them.

Portions of the material of this volume were used in lecture-classes last year at the Brookings Institute of Economics and Politics in Washington, where discussion was very helpful.

The greater part of Chapters II and III in Part II appeared in the September 1925 issue of the *American Political Science Quarterly* (Vol. XI, No. 3), under the title ' Neo-Classical Economics in Britain '.

Readers who possess no special training or interest in economic theory may prefer, in following the general trend of the argument, to omit the chapter of Part II entitled ' Marginalism ', which pursues a controversial topic of high importance but involving more technical equipment in economic science than do the other chapters.

In conclusion, I wish to express my deep indebtedness to my friends Professor L. T. Hobhouse and Mr. R. H. Tawney, not only for the formative influence which their writings have had upon the tenor of my argument, but also for the careful reading and valuable criticism they have given to the controversial matter of Part II. I would add a word of regret that the delay, occasioned in the publication of this book by a prolonged visit to America, disabled me from making certain additions and improvements in my treatment of political and industrial psychology, which my recent reading of Mr. H. J. Laski's *Grammar of Politics* and Mr. Delisle Burns's *Industry and Civilisation* would have prompted me to make.

HAMPSTEAD,
   October 1925.

CONTENTS

PART I

THE ART OF FREE-THINKING

CHAPTER I

THE DISINTERESTED PURSUIT OF KNOWLEDGE

§ How far and in what sense the pursuit of knowledge can be 'disinterested' are questions to which no easy and certain answer can be given. Each primary instinct of man, nutrition, reproduction, motor-activity, combativeness, defence, etc., proceeds by exploring and experimenting with some part of man's environment and so acquires a cunning and technique for its special purpose. Even when instincts appear to operate with automatic accuracy, it is difficult to suppose that this natural skill has not been bought by 'trial and error' or some rude process of experimentation. If, ignoring lower forms of vegetable and animal life, we confine our attention to man, his elaborate tactics, or behaviour, in hunting and other search for food, in courtship, combat, and other primary activities, seem to imply observation, memory, and reasoning directed to secure the means of a specific satisfaction.[1] It seems reasonable to hold that the beginnings of some at least of the physical and mental sciences are to be traced to these early fumblings after special bits of useful knowledge, useful in the sense of aiding some instinct or group of instincts to do its particular job more easily or more successfully. This specific search after knowledge cannot of course be described as 'disinterested', though the special interest it serves need not impair but rather assumes the soundness

[1] I.e. they are not wholly instinctive in the strictly biological sense

of the observation, memory, and reasoning upon evidence, which it employs.

But when the operation of these instinctive urges is thus raised to the level of consciousness and employs ' reasonable methods ', we can no longer regard the tactics as those of the specific instincts, each acting on its own, and using in its separate interest some purely private fund of energy. At some stage in organic evolution a general intelligence (or biological cunning) must come in, to co-ordinate and to control the operations of the various specific urges in the general interest of the whole organism and of the species. A highly centralised nervous system takes over in large measure the work formerly done by specialised local centres. This physiological centralisation is accompanied by a similar centralisation of intelligent control. The direction of a large part of the fund of organic energy is thus placed at the disposal of the control-board in the brain. As in the case of the separate instincts, so in the case of this general intelligence, a growing knowledge and skill arise from the employment of the surplus energy which remains after the ' costs of maintenance ' are defrayed. This surplus, absorbed, in the case of lower organisms, in the ' play ' or tactical cunning, or perhaps the decorative display of the special organs, passes through the more developed central control of the human brain, into the play, art, or ' science ' of the organism as a co-ordinated whole. The question how far science is ' disinterested ' thus emerges in a new form. So far as the intelligence of man and the fund of energy available for its operation are released from the control of the separate instinctive interests, and are put to the account of the central control, they may be said to have become ' disinterested '. But if the change only consists in the interest of the whole being substituted for the several interests of the parts, have we yet got what is meant by a disinterested pursuit of knowledge ?   If science is consciously directed to secure the general good of the human personality or of mankind, conceived in biological terms of survival and development, or in any other terms descriptive of human welfare, have we a fully disinterested science ? Or must that term be reserved exclusively for a pursuit of knowledge which, though indirectly and incidentally conducive to human welfare, takes for its direct and conscious aim knowledge as an end in itself, as the satisfaction of an intellectual curiosity which is in no sense the servant of the other special instincts. Or, perhaps, it is unnecessary to assume that this general curiosity, or drive for knowledge, belongs to the original outfit of man. It might be that, at first a separate and subservient part of the primitive instincts of nutrition, sex, defence, etc., it came, with the developing brain, to assert its independence of these particular controls and to set up as a purely intellectual interest on its own account. In either case it will rightly rank as ' disinterested ' in the double sense of being devoted directly and exclusively to the attainment of knowledge, and of operating free from the mandates of the special instincts that are its indirect and strictly unintended beneficiaries.

Whether this early fumbling of man, or other animals, with their material surrounding to find out what can be made of it in the way of interesting ' discoveries ' and combinations can rightly be defined in Mr. Veblen's language as ' idle curiosity ' may be doubted. Even Professor McDougall, who includes curiosity as a primary instinct, admits that an element of ' fear ' often enters in. It may well be that man's curiosity, as that of dogs or horses, tampers with strange material, partly in the interest of nutrition, partly of defence, and partly of some other specific instincts, motor-activity, a constructive, or building instinct, or the like. But there clearly comes a time when man turns his mind to the general work of understanding the world, moved by the satisfaction of the desire to do that work. It first begins to come to the child when he no longer tries whether an unfamiliar object put before him is ' good to eat ' or ' good to make a noise with ', but when he tries to ' find out what it is good for '. This ' idle curiosity ' must have emerged early in the life of man and may be taken as an efficient motive for the earliest forms of art, religion, and philosophy, though always qualified by the demands of certain strong special instincts, as those of nutrition and sex. But the age of science can hardly be said to have begun until this ' idle curiosity ' became more or less ' organised ' in direction. By a true, though exaggerated statement, this discovery of the scientific spirit is sometimes attributed to the genius of Greece, contrasted with the pragmatism of Egyptian or Roman civilisation. In Greece, it is said, we first encounter a number of free minds inspired by a passion for ascertaining the general truths, or laws, governing the operations of animate and inanimate Nature, and following knowledge ' for its own sake '. How far it can be true of any branch of intellectual inquiry that it can ever proceed wholly unaffected by the influence of the special instincts and interests may remain an unsettled question, though certain conditions of the intellectual life, to which later reference will be made, seem to indicate that no study is so abstract or remote from the passions of humanity as to boast complete ' disinterestedness '.

But in whatever way we interpret the disinterested pursuit of knowledge, its activity and the satisfaction that attaches to it must be taken as elements in the welfare of individuals and of mankind. Equally certain is it that this disinterested activity of the mind will be continually exposed to the violent assaults or the insidious machinations of particular instincts and interests, seeking to secure the authority and fruits of science for the promotion of their several ends, and to prevent the discovery and spread of truths or speculations likely to disturb any beliefs or institutions advantageous to their cause.

It is with the limits of ' disinterested ' culture, or conversely, with the biases to which it is liable by the operation of special instinctive urges, that we are concerned.

§ Now the measure and modes of such interferences will be dependent partly on the nature of the material in the sciences and arts and its relative adaptability to purposes of immediate utility by dominant interests.

The higher the abstraction in the sciences, the less ' feeling ' will attach to the material, and the less exposure there will be to unconscious bias in observation and reasoning. So Mathematics is the most disinterested, because it is the most abstract in material and in method. Among the physical sciences Astronomy is the most exact, because it goes least into its subject matter. Physics, Geology, Chemistry, are more susceptible to utilitarian motives. When Astronomy was Astrology, there was great temptation to ' tamper ' with objective facts. When strong mystical or gainful interests controlled Alchemy, much narrowing and distortion of Chemistry occurred, with a credulity and cooking of evidence. But where the material is static or inorganic, and admits precision of measurement, the biases of human interest are of very limited scope.

In the organic sciences, Botany, Biology, etc., not only do we encounter the elements of utilitarian selection for serviceable human ends, but there are two other sources of error or interest.

(1) The material is less susceptible of precise measurement, and not being static, is more refractory to observation and experiment, thus lending itself more easily to biased interpretations. *Organum sum nihil organici a me alienum puto.* The organic sciences, therefore, are of necessity

infected by the human interest, i.e. theories (emotionalised) about the nature and end of man seek supports from all organic sciences.

(2) The human interest is stronger, and the material is more susceptible to the moulding influence of this interest. When we enter directly the sciences of Man, body and mind, it becomes self-evident that what we would like to believe s liable to interfere at every point in the selection of nquiries and areas of attention, the formation of hypotheses, the observation and assessment of evidence, the reasoning upon the evidence. Human physiology and psychology, anthropology and history, even if they purport to concern themselves purely with facts of registered behaviour, cannot escape the constant play of passionate interests. The important judgments which these sciences yield to the arts of moral and social conduct cannot be regarded as evoked by rigorously objective inquiry in a dry light. The desire to sustain certain pre-conceived opinions and lines of conduct helps to direct the course of the scientific investigations, and so to form the conclusions which are then taken as 'disinterested' supports for these opinions and lines of conduct.

§ When we come to that study of the social sciences and arts which is our special theme, we shall find these disturbing influences at their maximum. This is because the material of these studies is softer, more plastic, and more complex, while the interests involved in the attainment of certain judgments and certain rules of conduct are more intense.

As we approach the interest-affected areas of knowledge, we encounter a middle sphere of semi-intellectualism, a mass of loosely related concepts and passion-laden opinions couched in language of popular appeal, which constitutes a public opinion, or a variety of conflicting public opinions. Politics, economics, ethics, sociology, philosophy, differ from the physical sciences in that they are surrounded by these popular opinions which they are compelled to use as part-material for their scientific treatment, and which, as we shall see, use them. Popular notions and interested opinions, couched in emotional rhetoric, have little influence on the sciences of physics and chemistry : while botany and biology have had difficulty in pursuing a disinterested course and keeping their light dry, their terminology and methods have lain too far from the path of popular thinking to be great sufferers. For, though certain specific needs of man and not a merely ' idle curiosity ' prompted those early questions and discoveries about man's environment that formed the rudiments of astronomy and physics, botany and biology, and have always kept a selective hand upon the sciences that sprang from those loose empirical studies, they have not much infected with interest and emotion the methods of these sciences.

But when we enter the sphere of the mental sciences, the case is very different. Rigorous ratiocination here seems impossible. This insusceptibility to exact measurement and to stability is particularly applicable to the most important classes of social facts. To certain elementary dispositions of men, the senses, the reflexes, memory, for example, it has been possible to apply laboratory tests which can yield exactly measured records. Not so with the prime facts in social psychology. " The facts of human nature which are of the greatest importance to the social psychologist are just those to which laboratory methods are least applicable. It is almost impossible to arrange a series of identical experiments to illustrate the working of patriotism or ambition or the property instinct or artistic and intellectual creativeness." [1] The material of a social science is soft, variable, and mixed with observer's feeling.

Under such conditions hard objective fact is non-existent,

[1] G. Wallas, *The Great Society*, p. 32.

and sound generalisation impossible. We believe what we wish to believe. " We may thus consider the first stage in human thought to be one of which the process of organising experience into common categories is incomplete, and the evidence for the truth of an idea is not yet separate from the quality which renders it pleasant. This is the stage characteristic of the most primitive peoples." [1] More of this primitive mind survives to-day in the beginnings of our social thinking than we care to admit. The notion of applying a strictly inductive reasoning to a primitive mass of objective facts, or phenomena, which by classification and a series of abstractions, shall discover truths or laws in an ascending scale of generality, building them up into the unified structure of a science rendered ever more exact by quantitative analysis, will not bear close consideration.

A purely ' idle curiosity ' fumbling about in a primitive deposit of human phenomena would get nowhere. A moral or social science cannot start with an inductive process. A social student, set to work at the face of some human deposit, must bring with him certain specific questions and hypotheses, if his study is to be fruitful. He must put some order into his mass of raw material, if he is to get more order out of it. A single illustration will suffice. A researcher set down in a slum district, confronted by an immensely intricate mass of human and environmental phenomena, would flounder hopelessly unless he came provided with a number of speculative questions, deduced from prior knowledge acquired elsewhere, bearing upon such issues as the measurement of overcrowding and its relations to infant mortality, family budgets and the relation of their composition to the different grades of family income, the part played by charity in supplementing real incomes, the contribution of the woman towards the family wage, the regularity of school attendance, and the percentage

[1] L. T. Hobhouse, *Development and Purpose*, p. 96.

of children getting secondary education, with a score or more of other questions derived by some preconceived social interest.

Thus we recognise that the very foundations of social science are laid in a pre-existing deposit of social interests, themselves infused with certain ideas of social betterment. In other words, social art precedes social science, and is in its turn nourished and informed by that science.

§ But it may well be said that, though these social interests underlie all processes of social science, they need not impair the disinterested conduct of the science. The selection of certain issues, as a basis for classification of phenomena and for inquiry, does not imply any bias in the rigour of the observation and the reasoning. The 'interests' which lay down the basis of inquiries are selective, but not injurious to the attainment of truth, nor need they blunt, distort, or otherwise impair, the scientific instruments employed.

This brings us to the need for a brief consideration of Reason, regarded as a scientific instrument, in its application to the social sciences. It is first desirable to distinguish Reason as regards the nature of the work it does, its reasoning. By whatever name we describe the reasoning processes, including attention, observation, classification, and the interrelated induction and deduction, much of it is evidently applied to furnish means to the satisfaction of the particular instincts, interests, and desires of man, the technique of the various arts of life. But, as we have seen, reason must be assigned another or perhaps two other distinguishable functions. It must exercise a central control over the whole fund of activities in the interest of the personality and of mankind (i.e. of a social personality); and, if a special instinct of curiosity be held to exist, directed to the pursuit of knowledge ' for its own sake ', that special interest must have its due provision in the general economy of the personality.

Now it is important to realise that in each of these functions, error is possible from two sources : (1) There may be false reasoning, due to the imperfect working of the instrument, or the refractory or obscure nature of the material. Or (2) there may be a falsification of the weights and measures, a faking of evidence, a cooking of results, due to the intrusion of motives alien to reason. The peculiar difficulty of the social sciences is their susceptibility to injury from both sources of error.

The social sciences, inclusive of psychology and philosophy (regarded as Scientia Scientiarum) differ, as we see, from the more exact sciences in that they find their prime material in the feelings, thoughts, judgments, and conduct of man. Now, in endeavouring to grip this material, in its nature mobile and incommensurable, so as to apply to it reasoning processes, they are confronted with a loose popular terminology, grown up for immediate practical uses, and with a large unordered body of popular feeling and opinion, loose generalisations from experience and tradition, often incorporated in the language of proverbial philosophy. Much sifted wisdom and shrewd common sense are doubtless contained in this popular conceptualism, but it hampers, heavily, the beginnings of the sciences. Consider, for example, how unfitted are such terms as ' politics ', ' economy ', ' soul ', ' society ', for exact instruments in the sciences whose ' title ' they prescribe. Everywhere the beginnings of these sciences are cumbered by a litter of these ' idols of the market ', popular concepts laden with diverse emotional contents, and couched in terms that have no fixed meaning even for the same user. Yet they cannot be shed. Attempts are made to define them, and to get the definitions accepted for scientific purposes. But largely in vain. Words like ' profit ', ' will ', ' Nature ', ' nationality ', ' instinct ', make it very difficult to get dry light or accurate thinking into the problems where they figure. Most even of the phraseology in which early abstract thinkers couch their thoughts, such as ' the natural rights of man ', ' equality of opportunity ', ' the product of labour ', ' Liberty, Fraternity, Equality ', has been a terrible impediment to disinterested science, not only by reason of its slipperiness, but because of the interested and often impassioned burdens it carries.

CHAPTER II

THE BIAS OF METAPHOR

§ But common thought and action influence and direct social sciences in another and a subtler fashion. All thinking of an abstract order involves the employment of words in a metaphorical sense. The nature of the metaphors employed depends upon the dominant trend of the interests and activities of the common people. The very atmosphere in which social problems are conceived and presented will be saturated with the feelings and thought-processes of this common life. Thus, quite independently of the subservience to close practical utilities often forced upon the sciences, there will be this strong tendency of the 'disinterested' science to take on the colouring of the activities prevalent in the society where it operates. In his opening chapter on *The Place of Science in Modern Education*, Mr. Veblen calls attention to the change brought about in the conception of causation by the passage of modern man from a peaceful agricultural type of society (where organic nature imposed its language and its ways of thought) to the predaceous feudal life of the Middle Ages, when

" The canons which guide the work of the idle curiosity are no longer those of generation, blood-relationship, and homely life, but rather those of graded dignity, authenticity, and dependence."

A theology emerges to support this earthly régime, and the early ' science ' of the State is strongly based upon the absolute validity of this idea of a predaceous society. How different are the fundamental concepts of social thinking when this type of life is superseded by modern industrialism where mechanical instruments and processes direct man's energies and mould his thinking.

"His canons of validity are made for him by the cultural situation ; they are habits of thought imposed on him by the scheme of life current in the community in which he lives ; and under modern conditions this scheme of life is largely machine made." [1]

It may well be, of course, that the intellectual and moral atmosphere of one phase may be intrinsically better adapted to clear and effective thinking than that of another. The more impersonal character of modern great industry, and the high 'rationality' which pervades its mechanical processes, have undoubtedly had an effect in making economic science colder and more exact in some departments of its thinking. But for the moment we are only concerned to note how the prevalent conditions of work and living give their special tone and character to the social sciences. This influence largely proceeds by way of metaphor. All thinking being conducted by use of words, much depends upon the words which get prestige from the dominant activities to which they first apply. We shall, therefore, expect to find mechanical metaphors playing a great part in our social sciences.

"These analogies between bodies natural and politic", writes Burke, "though they may sometimes illustrate arguments, furnish no argument of themselves." [2] Unfortunately the illustration is apt to carry the main force and appeal of the argument. Its chief effect is to suggest to the mind that the laws and relations of the material world are rightly applicable to the moral and political. This is no doubt inevitable. The real bite of words is on the hard

---

[1] Page 17.   [2] Letter to W. Elliott.

physical facts of life.   When, later on, thought is directed
to facts of the inner life, the tools invented for the earlier
process are alone available.   Nor are their deep defects at
first discernible.   For, with the language, the ways of
thought and feeling are carried over from the physical into
the moral world.   It is only later still, when the wide
divergencies between outer and inner life are realised, that
the injury inflicted upon the ' moral sciences ' is seen.   That
injury does not consist merely in the inadequacy of the
physical concepts applied by analogy to the inner life.   By
imposing false ideas of human nature, they poison at the
source all the sciences and arts of conduct.   What fatalism
is conveyed in the vision of

> " . . . a tide in the affairs of men
> Which taken at the flood leads on to fortune . . . ."

' Waiting on the tide of events ' furnishes the rationale of
a lazy and unprincipled opportunism.   ' Streams of tendencies ', ' Currents of thought ' suggest the impotence of
individual will.

The Constitution, regarded as a tree, changes slowly by
some internal laws of growth which cannot be safely interfered with by any Parliament or People !   Radical reform
is thus ruled out by metaphor.   Or the Constitution is a
stately edifice, built up by the skill and industry of many
generations of statesmen.   Renewals and repairs may from
time to time be needed, but structural alterations are
dangerous, and any attempt to tamper with foundations
will bring the ' edifice ' to ruin.

Or it is a ship, moving in a stormy ocean.   Don't interfere with the steersman.   Milton, arguing against frequent
Parliaments, puts both metaphors :

> " The Ship of the Commonwealth is always under sail ; they sit
> at the stern, and if they steer well, what need is there to change

them, it being rather dangerous ? Add to this, that the Grand Council is both Foundation and main Pillars of the whole State ; and to move Pillars and Foundation, not faulty, cannot be safe for the Building. I see not, therefore, how we can be advantaged by successive and transitory Parliaments ; but that they are much likelier continually to unsettle rather than to settle a free government, to breed Commotions, Changes, Novelties and Uncertainties, to bring neglect upon present Affairs and Opportunities, while all minds are suspense with expectation of a new Assembly, and the Assembly for a good space taken up with the new settling of itself." [1]

Or, in modern times, the Constitution is pre-eminently a piece of machinery, a thing of carefully adjusted parts and balances. Thrust a ramrod into this delicate machinery, you do irreparable mischief. Disturb the nice equipoise of its constituent parts, you bring it to a standstill. Great modern Constitution-mongers have been notoriously swayed in their policies by the mechanical conception of a Balance of Powers. The difficulties of securing those constitutional reforms which the altered conditions of American life require are manifestly due to the rigid Constitution, with its mechanical checks and balances, which the genius of Hamilton devised. But it is perhaps in conserving the relations between States that mechanical metaphors have wrought the greatest mischief. Here the policy of the Balance of Power, as the guiding principle in European politics, has more than once brought the world to the brink of ruin. And even yet the lesson of its play is not learnt by statesmen nourished on the old metaphors. Or, sometimes, again, States are conceived as celestial bodies moving in space by some laws of mutual attraction and repulsion. So Sir Edward Grey, in 1911, expressed in England's policy his fear lest " France should be drawn within the orbit of German diplomacy ".

§ It is, however, in the sphere of economic science and art

[1] *The Ready and Easy Way to Establish a Free Commonwealth.*

that the mechanical concepts are most potent. How should it be otherwise? The machine, power-driven, exact, elaborate, and efficient, is the most impressive fact in modern industry. The young mind gets its first glimpse of industrial order from the mechanical structure of a factory, workshop, or railway. As its conception of the meaning of business widens, this concept, with all its static rigour, is enlarged to cover the whole system of production and commerce. The ' laws ' of industry for production, exchange, and distribution of wealth, as conceived and formulated by the makers of the Classical Political Economy, were based on this conception of a great mechanical system with rigorous static adjustment of parts, and with automatically regulated flows of capital, labour, and money. Not only were the normal processes of supply and demand of goods and money conceived as mechanical processes, abstracted and divorced from the wills of men, but the unity and harmony of economic life were the expression of a mechanical view of the Human Nature involved in the economic processes. The whole calculus of the enlightened self-interest of individuals, operated by a pleasure and pain economy, which gave what seemed a rational justification to the theory, was itself only a projection of the machine-pictures from which the modern man takes his notion of order in the natural world.

When we come to closer grips with this economic teaching, we shall see more clearly how the sort of necessity, attached to the conception of natural laws, has been improperly imported into the economic world for definitely interested purposes. For the moment, however, we are concerned with a preliminary survey of the difficulties which mechanical metaphors have put upon clear thinking.

I have said that a chief effect of physical analogies is to secure a static view of the sciences and arts of conduct.

This, it may be urged, is surely modified by the intrusion of analogies from the organic sciences, involving an application of the dynamic concept of Evolution to social constitutions and conduct. Constitutions, economic systems, and other social forms, are represented now as growths, rather than as edifices or machines. Nay, the very arts of architecture and machinery, as distinct from their concrete embodiments, are themselves constantly evolving. Though the impressions of the older static images, drawn from the dead world of matter, cannot be effaced, their dominance is surely contested by the spread of evolutionary ideas and formulas.

This must be conceded, but it does not go far to secure the full liberation of the social sciences and arts from the thraldom of mechanics. Insensibly we always tend to revert to the familiar images of our earliest and strongest experiences of the physical world, the world of rivers, trees, houses, stars, and machines. It is true that persons are from the first more interesting. But their behaviour is so much more fluid and unintelligible that it is only the relatively fixed characters of their external personality that count with us, and when we begin to try to ' understand ' them, it is by the application of analogies from those parts of Nature which are fixed and best bide our early questions. Thus popular thinking, at any rate for town populations, has never come to be affected strongly by organic concepts and language.

Even where the evolutionary concepts have made their way into popular thinking and the rudimentary social sciences, they have come weighted by a fatal disability, due to the fact that evolution, alike in the inorganic and the organic physical sciences, leaves out of account the most vital factor in human conduct. Physical evolution is sometimes conceived as operated by a *vis a tergo*, sometimes by the magnetic pull of some ideal to be realised : sometimes

it is treated impartially as a mere process with an ' urge '
which is neither push nor pull.

§ Now analogies and formulas drawn from these physical
sciences are defective for use in the social sciences, in several
ways. First, they present a sort of determinism incongruous
with human experience, a blind pervasive pressure as the
causa causans in evolution. The idea of slow continuous and
regular movement, in conformity with ' law ', which in the
last resort is a mere description of this movement, adding
nothing in the way of explanation, is the leading concept
which popular thought has taken from physical evolution
to apply to social movements. The processes of change in
the physical world are slow and gradual. So must be the
processes of change in the intellectual and moral world.
Even the sort of ' Free Will ' realised by individuals in their
own conduct and career is denied to social processes pictured
as ' growths ' or ' streams of tendency '. Hence the organic
metaphors are weighted with conservatism. It is true
that evolutionary teaching does not present all change as
slow. Geology knows catastrophes. Modern biology leans
ever more heavily upon sudden conversions or mutations.
But though there have not been wanting thinkers who have
utilised this revolutionising concept for human politics, the
defects of the analogy are evident. Whether conceived as
catastrophes or as mutations, such phenomena neither
require nor easily admit the concept of a purposive control
and the ' creative ' or ' determinant ' power of the conscious
will of man. They are natural phenomena, determined by
past events in the history of the social systems, political,
economic, or other, to which the evolutionary concept is
applied. In other words, man must wait until events are
' ripe ' for the change. There is no proper place provided for
his intervention in ' ripening ' them. When an institution
is ' worn out ' it may crumble away ! If its adjustments

get out of gear, it will cease to work ! If it is overloaded, it may topple over ! As the inorganic analogies are applied to organic growths, and dominate our conceptions of them, so they are carried on into the realms of conduct. The Marxian conception of revolution is rightly exposed to this same criticism. If the capitalist system must grow to its limit of concentrated structure and power, and must then catastrophically break down, giving place to a proletarian socialism, why should socialists agitate and propagand, making unnecessary trouble for the minds of themselves and other people ? As soon as it is realised that the human will may purposely interfere as an effective agent in bringing about the change, we get outside the play of the ordinary evolutionary analogies into a sphere of conduct which is vague and unintelligible, precisely because language has never been prepared to meet its needs. For, though Ethics and Philosophy have for long ages played with doctrines of Free Will, their experiments have always been bowled over by potent analogies from spheres of action where Free Will has been ruled out. For popular and even scientific concepts of efficient causation have presented a figure of Human Nature too clumsy for any work of transforming human institutions, in ways that are at once quick, safe, and economical.

It is only as we come to understand the subtle, strong, and comprehensive grasp which analogies and metaphors have obtained over the social arts and sciences that we realise the difficulty of a ' disinterested ' culture in dealing with such subjects. In a world so replete with mechanical analogy and suggestion, social evolution itself appears as a mechanical process. Its concepts are instinctively exploited by the controllers of intellectual activities, with a bias for Conservatism and Vested Interests (intellectual and moral as well as material) partly in order to win acquiescence for the *status quo* or slow change, partly so as to suggest concepts of harmony and inevitable ' laws ' against which it is foolish, wrong, and futile to attempt to kick.[1]   The net effect is to deny the existence and operation of the creative power of the human will, by presenting Human Nature itself as a static being, responding to laws that are immutable in the same sense and degree as those which govern the operations of stars and plants.

[1] The very name ' State ' carries this bias to fixity.

CHAPTER III

DISINTERESTED SCIENCE AND THE INTERESTS

§ So far we have been concerned with general defects of the instruments of speech and thought, affecting first popular sentiment and opinion, and thence passing into the more formulated systems of the social arts and sciences.

It is evident, however, that these defects may be utilised, consciously or unconsciously, by individuals or groups 'interested' in moulding social theory. In doing this they will be impelled by a natural tact to conceal this utilisation, and to represent their thinking, and the scientific laws which flow from it, as disinterested processes of the mind.

Now in entering on our study of these exploitations and concealments, it is of the utmost importance to realise that the struggle for disinterested culture in the social sciences is in essence identical with what is commonly called 'the moral struggle' within the private conduct of each of us.

In both cases the effort of the co-ordinating principle, seeking the good of the whole, a personality or a society, meets in perpetual conflict the efforts of powerful instincts, or groups of allied instincts, within the individual personality or the society, claiming to dominate that system, so as to direct its activities to the realisation of its separate selfish ends.

Every thoughtful person knows from his own experience how this battle is waged and the weapons and tactics that are employed. Modern psychology has only given new evidence and closer formulation to happenings always known to wise men and women. How the powerful passions of love, hate, fear, admiration, envy, vanity, ambition, are able, either singly or in some close, narrow alliance, to seize the entire resources of a personality and direct its whole conduct for their particular satisfaction ; how in the pursuance of this purpose conflicting passions are suppressed or subjugated ; how the tyrant passions dress and conceal themselves in the cloak of fine sentiments and reason—such knowledge has passed into the proverbial stock of every civilised people. These arts of selection, suppression, sublimation, rationalisation, apparent in the ordinary private conduct of a personality, are practised with greater ease and freedom in social or co-operative conduct. It is common knowledge that a man, as politician, will do things for his party which he would refuse to do for his own personal ends. His ethical code, as member of a trade or profession, is usually lower or more elastic than his private personal code. No valid commandments qualify the ruthless selfishness of nationalism or patriotism. Under the cover of collectivity, the primitive passions, denied free scope for direct personal ends, find for themselves a legitimate, often a consecrated, channel.

War is the most explosive outbreak of the suppressed instincts. Politics is an incessant struggle upon the national and international planes between reason, as we have represented it, and the tyranny of primitive instincts. With the practical implications of this commonplace I am not here concerned, only with its bearing upon the thinking processes.

The ethics of personal conduct in the narrower relations of life formally acknowledge the reign of reason. Our codes of morals, laws, customs, are designed to curb our wild and selfish instincts from kicking over the traces, and even in some measure to stimulate altruism and co-operative conduct, in our ordinary dealings with our immediate neighbours. Thought, sentiment, and theory, are in these narrower fields of conduct kept fairly under the control of reason, so far as ideals, maxims, and professed principles are concerned. Defects and violations of these principles are admitted to be 'wrong', whether judged from some extra-human standard or from that of reason. So far, at any rate, as the main body of these ethical principles is concerned, there is no intellectual conflict to correspond with the practical conflict of the moral struggle within the individual breast. Though the rigour of the rule of reason and its too prohibitive control may sometimes be called in question, as in the revolt against puritanism, such excesses of righteousness, when they occur, are more of the nature of administrative vices than of faults in thought or theory.

It is when we turn from private morals to trade, political, or other social conduct, that we are confronted with the fact that the rules for such conduct frequently conflict with and outrage the principles accepted in the more intimate sphere of conduct. To make my meaning clear, I may remind readers that, whereas good private conduct involves the constant suppression of personal selfish aims, good economic conduct involves the fullest and keenest expression of these aims under the protecting cloak of a theory that such selfishness contributes to a final harmony of human welfare. 'Good' political conduct in the dealing of States with one another does not even 'rationalise' itself into a pretence of world-harmony. With certain slight, and in the last resort negligible, qualifications, it stands for a completely enlightened selfishness.

Now this contradiction in the arts of individual and social conduct finds its counterpart in the theory, or science, which takes these activities for its subject matter.

Everywhere 'idle curiosity', the impulse of intellectual exploration, seeks to apply the methods of accurate observation and dry reason to the discovery and formulation of rigorously scientific laws. Everywhere it is met, crossed, modified, or deflected by influences which proceed from secret founts of interest or desire. The plainest form of the struggle is with the narrower utilitarian demands that are always endeavouring to short-circuit the current of scientific effort, and divert it to some narrow immediate purpose of their own. This war between science and short-range utility is, of course, waged perpetually throughout the whole field of knowledge. The physical sciences have suffered much by the hasty demands, made upon them by the practical arts, to justify themselves by useful contributions to human comforts and conveniences. Persistently have they urged, first, that it is not their business to bring grist to the utilitarian mill, and, secondly, that the condition of their ' making good,' in the narrower utilitarian sense, is that they shall have complete freedom to work along ' disinterested ' lines. Such freedom, they profess, will ' pay ' better, even in a material way, than any direct subjection of science to ' useful ' ends. If ' idle curiosity ' has, on the whole, beaten the baser utilities in this struggle, it has done so by practising a certain cunning of defence which has enabled it to apply to disinterested work resources put at its disposal by utilitarians too ignorant to follow and to check its methods of research.

§ A far harder battle, however, confronts the disinterested student in the social sciences. For these sciences are exposed to a double attack.

Economics, politics, ethics, sociology, handle, at close quarters, material so full of vital interest and so inflammable that it is very difficult for students to preserve an attitude of scientific impartiality. Human themselves, their humanity continually tampers with their intellectual processes, bringing into secret play their personal or group passions, interests, and prejudices. How potent and insidious this interference is we shall recognise by later instances drawn from the fields of economics and politics. Here it must suffice to register a danger to which the physical sciences are far less exposed. Every man has business interests and a thousand contacts with political affairs. How can he hope to lay aside these interests and contacts when he puts on his scientific robe ? When these directly personal pressures are reinforced by the sentiments, interests, opinions, conventions, prevailing in the profession, social class, party, church, grade of culture, to which he ' belongs ', the possibilities of a completely disinterested pursuit of the social sciences appear still more dubious.

The wise old scholar's warning to the young student entering a career of research, " Beware, my son, lest you discover what you are in search of ", has its closest application in this intellectual field. For the looseness and inexactitude of these studies leaves them an easy prey to the ravages of the invader.

A very human situation emerges from the endeavours of social scientists to defend their intellectual virtue.

The attitude of the ignorant multitude towards the intellectual and the cultured has always been one of mixed contempt and suspicion. Not only the scholar and the scientist, but the priest, the artist, and in large degree the lawyer and the politician, have lain under this popular ban. Their activities are not ' real work ', have no real product or result. Yet somehow they procure a good living by doing nothing ! In this there is at once waste, wizardry, and dishonesty ! Sometimes contempt predominates, as towards the scholar, sometimes suspicion, as in the case of the chemist, astronomer, or other trafficker with dangerous, unknown powers. Only in recent times has popular education, coupled with the rich ransom of visible utilities flowing from the physical sciences, made these studies innocent and even respectable. But intellectuals working in other fields are still ridiculous to the red-bloods of all classes, for whom gainful employment, sport, and physical enjoyments, are the sole realities of life.

Among these intellectuals it is only natural that social scientists should concentrate upon themselves the largest volume of this popular mistrust. The man in the street has strong views about the politician : he thinks he knows what he is ' after '. Politics, as he sees it, is at best a party-game, often a dirty game for office, power, or business gains. What can such a man think of a super-politician, who claims to treat political institutions and activities as a field for intellectual cultivation ? The man in the workshop or the railway sees industry as a selfish scramble for profits or a living. What can he think of professors of political economy, with their theories of marginal utility and laws of value ?

Is it not natural that when the man in the street, or workshop, removes his eyes from his job, or ' the winners ', to survey these social scientists with their high dis-interested claims, he should also wonder what they are ' after ' ? In the ' intellectual ' thus assailed, this popular suspicion arouses, sometimes indignation, sometimes con-tempt. Conscious of his intellectual rectitude, he brushes aside such ignorant prejudices or treats them as testimonies to his superiority. Such popular misunderstanding seems ridiculous to him. But what if some shrewd common sense underlies those suspicions of the popular mind ? How if this assumption of immaculate disinterestedness is mere eyewash ? Why then the laugh is on our social philosopher, and his very conviction of his innocence, his *mens conscia recti*, is itself the core of humour in the situation. A mere quack, consciously faking his ' science ' for personal gain, is no object for ridicule. But the comic spirit has no finer field of frolic than a science whose devotees, genuinely believing themselves to be dominated by a single-minded zeal for knowledge, are yet exposed at every turn to the secret manipulations of the interests and passions against which they believe themselves immune.

We would not prejudge the case against the social sciences. We believe that most of their academic and other serious practitioners employ as much intellectual integrity as the nature of their subject matter and their intellectual instruments allow. Their resistance to most direct attempts of outside influences, political, economic, or other, to limit or distort their free reasoning processes, and make their research or their teaching servile to special interests or utilities, need not be questioned. Cowardly submissions to such interferences have been not uncommon, and we may refer later on to the open perils to which disinterested science is thereby exposed. But just now we are concerned with the more dangerous, because insidious, pressures that proceed from secret influences entering the mind of the student in these sciences.

I have spoken of the suspicions of the popular mind regarding the social sciences. But hardly less important in the psychology of the situation is the disparaging view of these studies which even now is held by addicts to the exacter sciences. Though economics has won a fairly secure and reputable place in the scale of academic studies, political science remains a shy fledgling, and sociology has, as yet, no formal recognition in the older British Universities.

Between the two fires of popular and academic suspicion it was to be expected that these studies would present a humorous vacillation between timidity and effrontery. Upon the whole they have inclined to brazen it out, laying claims to more rigour and exactitude of principles and method than they possess, and putting on a brave array of terminology and formulas to hide their half-conscious sense of their defects. The newcomer into any society is usually particular about his dress.   But if he has tact or humour, he will conceal this concern.   The failure of social scientists to observe this rule suggests that a defective sense of humour may attach to the very process of conducting a social science, or perhaps, even, to the acceptance of the notion that a social science is possible.

But, be this as it may, in this country and still more in America (where far more attention is given to these studies), the too rapid blossoming of erudite and esoteric terminology arouses some not unnatural suspicion, as if designed to bluff the intellectual public into an acceptance of the social sciences upon their own valuation.

CHAPTER IV

TABOOS IN THE SOCIAL SCIENCES

§ A CHIEF obstacle to the disinterested pursuit of the social sciences is the vital, not to say inflammatory, matter they contain. The fundamental institutions of society are hedged with a mysterious sanctity, that forbids the scrutiny of reason.

Religion, group loyalty or patriotism, property, the family, and certain concepts of personal morality, not merely surround themselves with taboos, but emit passionate fumes to blind the sight and confuse the brain of timorous scrutineers. The case of religion is notorious. No truly religious person will submit his deity or his worship to cold tests of the intellect. Industrious anthropologists may track each of the holy rites back to its origins in sympathetic or imitative magic. But they will not eradicate entirely the ' superstitious ' sentiment attaching to this magic, and to the primitive *Weltanschauung* of which it was a part. But the most conclusive testimony to the difficulty of a scientific study of religion is, not the emotional bias of the believer, but the counter-bias of the unbeliever, the *odium anti-theologicum*, so conspicuous in professing ' rationalists '. They are not to blame. An escape from prevailing sanctities, stamped by early association upon the tender mind, can only be achieved by an emotional struggle in which the combative instinct is engaged so strongly as to leave behind a sentiment of hostility and disgust, often intensified in passionate natures by well-founded fear lest the emotional escape be incomplete. Students of comparative religion, or of the higher criticism, will be well aware of the havoc made in the application of laws of evidence to matter laden with such passionate appeal.

But even more significant is the sentiment of sanctity when its veneration and taboos are applied to the concepts of country, property, or sex. The moral and legal supports of these concepts, and of the obligations they impose on conduct, are termed appropriately ' sanctions '. For into each of them is carried the same sentiment of awe or mysterious veneration that is realised with fuller consciousness in religious ceremonial and beliefs.

In order to exploit more advantageously this sentiment, political practitioners cultivate with care the divinity that doth hedge a king, or, when personal government has dwindled or been displaced, the close linkage of ' God and Country '. The elaboration of symbolic ritual in salutation of the flag, national holy-days, patriotic hymns and processions, and the running of history into sentimental moulds of national heroism, for the education of our children, is a semi-conscious endeavour to divert to patriotic purposes the fund of superstition liberated by the weakening of religious attachments. Where powerful religious feelings still survive they can be rallied round the sacred person of the King or the holy Fatherland. Where they decay, owing to the waning belief in another world, the State claims such reversionary rights to its emotional inheritance as it can make good in patriotic practices.

How patriotic passion not merely perverts the conduct of public affairs from the paths of sweet reasonableness, but conceals or transforms the truths about this conduct, is in abundant illustration, familiar to all serious students of history. Yet such truths constitute the raw material of political science. Even when they are laboriously dug out of their hiding-places, or restored from their defacement, the 'scientific' treatment accorded them is everywhere liable to the subjective valuations of historians or scientists who cannot wholly divest their minds of personal sentiments. The best, because the most truthful, histories are those which make no attempt to conceal these necessary biases. The pretence to a strictly scientific impartiality is both false and foolish. For the human sympathy involved in the perception, interpretation and valuation of events, acts, and characters is incompatible with the impartial attitude that is claimed. This is not uncommonly admitted as precluding a reliable history of very recent affairs. But it is applicable in a greater or less degree to the treatment of remote events, which cannot escape the back-stroke of a selection and valuation governed by the current ideas and feelings of to-day. Though the 'political scientist' may distinguish his calling from that of the historian, he can hardly escape the legacy of defects in historical records which must form the staple of his 'scientific' treatment.

But not only are 'my country', its King, its Constitution, sacred. The fundamental institutions of its legal and social order are also sacred. Property is peculiarly sacrosanct. It is hedged with legal, intellectual, and moral sanctions which make it more dangerous and more wicked to tamper with than any other institution. The genuinely religious awe attaching to the property concept could not be better illustrated than in the shiver that ran down the backbone of all good citizens the world over at the revelations of Bolshevism in Russia. It was not the cruelty and blood-shed, the forcible autocracy, or even the collapse of industry with its accompanying starvation and misery, that stirred this passionate abhorrence. It was the sudden raking up from the embers of a dateless past of the horror of 'the unclean thing'. The other feelings of pity and resentment entered in but as accessories to this central rush of inflamed horror. Normally we do not realise the emotional meaning we attach to such a concept or institution as Property. We are not obliged to realise it, and there is an intellectual economy in not doing so. But when it is subjected to a sudden challenge, the full force of the ' survival value ' which it has carried down the ages suddenly awakes in us. We feel that Property is holy, and its destroyers in Russia, or elsewhere—they and their remotest sympathisers, the professors of any doctrine, the advocates of any policy, that threatens any sort of recognised property—are sacrilegious monsters.

I have no desire to dispute the survival value, and, therefore, the natural necessity of this sentiment, but how are the sciences of politics and economics going to conduct their processes with cold scientific rigour on the crust of a volcano like this ?

§ There remains, however, one matter perhaps even more intractable to scientific treatment than property, namely sex and the social relations into which it enters. To sexual activity and selection, with resulting parenthood, is assigned the chief part in organic evolution, the individual survival being regarded primarily as a means to survival of a species. In sex mentality, conscious and unconscious, psychology, therefore, finds the most potent of human urges. To sociology the family is not merely one among many social institutions, it is the nest and nursery of those restraints and provisions which are the source and condition of all larger and higher modes of group life. For though, as some anthropologists hold, tribal groups may have preceded definite family life, the tender emotion, fostered in the narrow circle of the family, is a far more powerful educator of self-restraint, altruism, and co-operation, the springs of social conduct, than any of the thinner and more diffuse feeling of gregariousness. Precisely because sex and parenthood are the most potent and intractable of urges,

the practices and institutions designed to their utilisation
and control are compelled to work by strong regulations
and repressions.

Making all allowance for those diversions or transmuta-
tions of sex-passion into art, sport, religion, called sublimation of the instinct, a continual warfare is waged between
the crude demands for sex-satisfaction and the interests of
social order.   Especially is this the case in communities or
classes, where social order is sought to be enforced by strict
taboos, involving tight curbs on thought and speech as well
as conduct, Nature here comes to the aid of the suppressed
instinct by ranging on its side curiosity and the related
interest of intrigue.   When strong natural promptings are
present, the sense of shame and moral reprobation by
which law, morals, and customs, have striven to enforce
their taboo adds zest to temptation.   This is so well recognised among intelligent persons that organised attempts are
made to remove the veil of reticence which helps to shed a
glamour upon sex.   The error of Puritanism consists partly
in misconceiving sex feeling as an enemy to society, partly
in supposing that forcible modes of suppression can be
effectual.   There can be no better security for social
order than the provision of economic and other arrangements compatible with a freer satisfaction of sex-feeling,
not only in its sublimated but in its primary expression.
It is, indeed, significant that a strong and widespread
interest among social students is being directed to the
related problems of quantity and quality of population,
and to the economic, political, racial, and moral issues
involved in birth-control and eugenics.

The most striking of all testimonies, however, to the
explosive and disturbing influence of sex is afforded by the
recent science of psychology.   I allude here not so much to
the fact that schools of professional psychologists have
gathered round sex as the chief centre of activity and

interest in the psychical study of man. More significant
for my present purpose is the enormous and quite popular
réclame which this study has obtained. The fact that
everywhere huge numbers of otherwise unintellectual men
and women are chattering psycho-analysis, in clubs, drawing-
rooms and improvised study circles, and are dabbling in its
literature and practices, furnishes a striking revelation of
the difficulties of an impartial scientific treatment of any
social problem into which sex enters as a factor. For it is
quite evident that it is no purely ' disinterested culture '
that attracts most of these devotees, but the lure of sex
itself, masquerading as a scientific interest. This is as
evident in the denunciation of what for convenience may be
called Freudism as in its acceptance. Everywhere, upon
both sides, the note of passion is discernible under the
coolest parades of discussion. The assailants of the study
exhibit (in trying to conceal it) the same sex-sensitiveness
as the devotees themselves.

When, therefore, we reflect that none of these studies can
exclude this inflammable material from its treatment, and
that, for any comprehensive sociology, sex urges and activities and the institutions they help to mould and sustain, are
of prime importance, we are driven to smile at the *naïveté*
of a social science boasting reason as its sole arbiter. It is
not merely that instinctive emotions and valuations prevail
in the social arts, but that they deflect the balance of reason
in the social sciences.

CHAPTER V

PERSONAL AND ECONOMIC BIASES

§ One considerable topic remains for brief discussion before we can enter the study of the special sciences selected for application of this general analysis. In considering the dangers and difficulties that beset the ' disinterested ' scientist from the nature of the materials, instruments, and methods he employs, we have not yet taken directly into account certain factors commonly designated ' the personal equation '. In all sciences allowances are made for differences in accuracy of observation and record. If sufficient observations or experiments are available, the limits of such errors may be measured and an average reached in cases where quantitative error alone is involved. Even qualitative errors, if they are numerous and small, may be cancelled out without much loss to scientific accuracy. But where it is a matter, not of physical or intellectual inexactitudes, but of personal bias, due to valuations based on feeling, the personal equation is much more troublesome.

That everybody's views, opinions, judgments, are liable to be influenced, or even dominated, by personal feeling or interest, without any deliberate intellectual dishonesty, is notorious. Even the crudest of political careerists is usually able to believe that the cause he supports is reasonable and in the public interest, and that he is moved by those considerations in the support he gives. Psychology has almost wiped out hypocrisy. Sincerity is a matter of

degree. It is very difficult for most men to conceive the
possibility, much less to be convinced, that the satisfaction
of any of their strong desires, not inhibited by some definite
social taboo, should be illegitimate. So potent is the urge
of the sacred instincts safeguarding the citadel of Personality
that it is well-nigh impossible to prevent most men from
finding reasons for believing anything they want very badly
to believe. Now nobody would contend that the graver
intellectual pursuits are quite immune against these disturbing personal motives. Wherever Science touches, even
indirectly, any prized element of *my* Personality, *my* safety,
or salvation, *my* property, *my* self-importance, powerful
emotions rush to the defence, challenging the right or
reason of the critic or assailant. We have already recognised how impossible it is to preserve an atmosphere of
calm ' disinterested ' inquiry into the existence of a deity,
human immortality, the monogamous family, or communism. Though philosophers and scientists may not
bang the door to reason with the intolerance of the platform politician or the popular preacher, their own personal
feelings and interests, working less consciously, will surely
intervene at every stage of a scientific inquiry. When
man's most sacred interests and beliefs were held to be
threatened by free-thought in astronomy or chemistry, the
heaviest penalty was, not the outer persecution, but the
secret inner ban on freedom of hypothesis and reasoning in
his own mind and among the thinking few. If the doctrine
of Heliocentricism seemed likely to involve the collapse of
the whole fabric of Catholic Theology, with its scheme of
personal salvation, was not this secret fear certain to affect
the dryness of the light in which such a controversy was
conducted ? There are many alive to-day who remember
the obstacles to the disinterested study of geology
and physics, due to the fear lest new evolutionary doctrines should injure the vested interests of comfortable

beliefs.[1] Biology to-day is rife with inflammable material. But the heat does not originate in the material itself : it is pumped into it by the excited feelings of the students whose reasoning is affected by their vested intellectual interests.

§ But, as in the case of the collective biases with which we dealt in our last chapter, so here the private personal biases are more formidable in the social than in the physical sciences. The full force of what I may term the vital or instinctive prejudices is not realised until they are tracked down to their sources in the sacred personality of individuals. Patriotism becomes most real and intense when it is identified with *my* country ; the institution of property in the last resort derives its sacredness from the blind, fierce sentiment of *my* possession. In the Western world, at any rate, the root of all religion is *my* salvation.

The gregarious instinct, sublimated and refined by the evolution of the tender emotion, and operating through numerous modes of human co-operation, doubtless qualifies or expands the ego, so as to mingle the feeling for my good with a widening sympathy for the good of others. But it is idle to pretend that a peculiar sacredness does not attach to a man's regard for his own personality, in ways that must affect and deflect the free play of idle curiosity, or disinterested science. His passionate desire to have a reasonable support for certain political, economic, and other social creeds, is bound to interfere with his pursuit of these sciences.

Nor is this interference confined to tendencies to find reasons for maintaining our political opinions or our economic interests. There is another less recognised sentiment of very subtle influence in the moulding of scientific thought. ' Idle curiosity ', or a genuinely scientific activity, may lead

[1] The recent growth of the Fundamentalist agitation in America is a striking instance of the crude intervention of vested religious interest in scientific education.

a man to the discovery of some new fact or law which seems to him to have great importance. The interest of possession then comes into play. This fact, or law, or theory, becomes his peculiar property. He has discovered it, and it belongs to him. In a word, it is identified with his sacred personality. It differs, of course, from material property in having no limit of quantity. Others may hold, or accept, this knowledge without entrenching on his property. Nay, on certain conditions, every extension of its holding raises its subjective value to him, the discoverer. But it remains in a peculiar sense his property. Perhaps even his sacred name becomes attached to it, and it becomes the Jones Nebular hypothesis, or the Smith-Robinson theory of radio-activity, or the Malthusian law of population. The last of these examples, indeed, best realises the needs of illustration. For readers of the life and works of Malthus will see how this intense pride of intellectual property may cut into a thinker's sense of intellectual proportion, disable him from seeing any flaw in his intellectual jewel, and lead him to the most desperate devices for its defence and aggrandisement. There are few men with the high intellectual integrity of J. S. Mill able to discern the faults in one of their central positions and willing to scrap it, as he did his Wage-Fund theory. When one of our prized intellectual possessions is attacked or threatened, there is an instinctive rally of our emotion of self-esteem to its defence. If a hole is found in our defence, we rush to fill it up with any specious arguments which may be to hand. If such material is lacking, we ignore the hole or plead its insignificance.

Nor is it necessary to the operation of this bias that we should be the original discoverer of the particular ' truth '. If we are in a sufficiently small minority in holding an intellectual position our self-esteem is similarly, though perhaps less intensely, involved. How we came by this opinion, indeed, is of little relevance. We may have picked it up, not to support some interest or prejudice, as often happens, but out of sheer contentious-ness, in order to assert our superior knowledge or intelligence or to ' put down ' some objectionable dogmatist. But once taken up it becomes ours. Having once befriended it, we become attached to it. It is attacked again in some other company, and we defend it. Others come to recognise it as ' our ' opinion. The more peculiar, paradoxical, and improbable it is, the more is our self-esteem engaged in its defence. We realise ourselves as part-owners of an intel-lectual property for which we will fight to protect it against destruction or depreciation. The social sciences in their early growth necessarily suffer more than the older and exacter sciences from this cause. For in the social sciences, in their present inchoate form, there is far more scope for specious discoveries, for radical transformation of methods, and for the formulation of new laws carrying large and critical judgments upon social behaviour.

It may doubtless be urged that in this consideration of intellectual property the chief bias lies, not in the discovery of the new facts or laws, but in the propensity to defend them after they are discovered. Indeed, the personal prestige attached to discovery may be regarded as a strong aid to the instinct of exploration, and to the labour involved in verifying an interesting hypothesis. In the exacter sciences this personal pride is kept under a pretty close control of reason, because of the rigour of the tests to which each fresh claim of a discoverer is sure to be subjected. But in the social sciences it is easier for the explorer both to persuade himself of the novelty and importance of some fresh presentation of his material, and to contend with any hostile criticism that may be brought to bear upon it.

§ Under such conditions the emotion or sentiment of self-

4

esteem and self-aggrandisement, which in most men of intellectual ability is peculiarly intense and subtle in its operations, is liable to deflect the play of disinterested curiosity to an unusual extent, involving great intellectual waste, and a slow advance or a mis-development of social science.

Indeed, when this self-importance is harnessed to some other strong primary urge, such as sex, pugnacity, or fear, we have the making of a 'complex' of a dangerously devastating order. Fanaticism thus easily invades a social science. Wherever theory is in close contact with some passionate practice, the most reasonable thinkers lose their heads. Neo-Malthusianism and Eugenics, Diffusionism, the Freudian Wish, National Sovereignty, Pacifism, the Class War, Personal Immortality, concepts of high importance in psychology, economics, politics, ethics, religion, philosophy, can hardly be discussed even by serious thinkers except in an atmosphere clouded with the fumes of personal prejudice. The projector, or even the supporter, of some theory or hypothesis on one of these topics finds himself in a state of hot emotional excitement. For the instinct tapped by the topic joins forces with the challenge to intellectual self-esteem in the conduct of a difficult defence, and changes the discussion from a disinterested search for truth into a dialectical contest for personal victory. The preservation of some conventional civilities of controversy must not hide from us this dangerous truth. The *odium scientificum* is not less real and intense than formerly because conducted with more amenity of manners, and the methods of debate to which it will descend are not more reasonable. Everyone who has had long experience in difficult controversies upon important issues in a social science will be aware of this emotional excitement at the mere approach of the inflammatory topic, and the effort he has to make in order to appear sweetly reasonable in discussing it. This experience is not confined to holders of a fad or *idée fixe*. I have known several instances of men with exceptionally well-equipped and widely interested minds, sociologists or philosophers, who completely lose their heads when any one of half a dozen hot hypotheses is trailed before them. They will diverge from the main line of any discussion to pursue this hated fallacy or myth, following it into the intricacy of all its wicked implications, with a passion that exhibits all the well-known traits of hysteria. How far it is the direct instinctive interest of the matter itself, how far the challenged self-esteem, that accounts for these curious deflections from the path of reason, is a question that admits no easy answer. But in any consideration of disinterested science these ebullitions of the *sacro egoismo* cannot be left out of account.

Interested propagandism, chiefly unconscious, thus presses in at every turn. No small part of its cunning consists in the assumption of a strictly scientific method and a sweet reasonableness in controversy designed at once to establish intellectual authority and to conceal interested motives.

*   *   *   *   *

§ The dramatic interest of the struggle of the social sciences to preserve their intellectual integrity amid all the temptations of this wicked world is a theme for a new Book of Job. Consider the situation that has arisen. War and absolute Sovereignty, of which it is the forcible expression ; political oligarchies, avowed or masquerading as democracies ; law and convention everywhere partisan and obsolete but everywhere resisting change ; an economic system rooted in selfishness, injustice, waste, and oppression ; decaying religions with new superstitions sprouting from their refuse ; orthodox education and its vested intellectual interests everywhere on their defence ! In a word, every institution of the established order is put to the question.

In every department of social conduct, politics, industry, morals, religion, law, education, challenges are given in the name of free-thought and disinterested science. Psychology, claiming to unearth and reveal the real supports of accepted and authoritative doctrine in all branches of social conduct, brings them to the bar of reason and threatens them with ' revelation '.

The domain of political and economic rulers, the spiritual and intellectual orthodoxies and authorities, the secure and comfortable lives of the luxurious and leisured classes, the pleasant illusions of the herd-mind, so ' good ' in themselves and so serviceable to the ruling and possessing classes, all feel themselves menaced by free-thinking and free-speaking science.

It is too late, too dangerous, too difficult, to strangle science. It is better to patronise it, to feed it, to control and use it. Politics can be nationalised, economics classified, ethics theologised, education disciplined into fresh subjection. This can be done by a judicious combination of force, persuasion, bribery, cajolery, and cunning. Much attention has been directed to the cruder methods by which the wealthy business classes on the one hand, Government and the politicians on the other, sometimes interfere in the selection and rejection of teachers and of teaching in schools or colleges where they have reason to suspect ' unsound ' doctrines are propounded in Politics, History, or Economics. The methods formerly employed by the Prussian State, and the regulations passed in some State Legislatures in America for repressing heresies, political, economic, or religious, and ensuring loyalty and orthodoxy in all public schools, constitute so open an affront to ' science ' that men of more sensitive intelligence will everywhere show recalcitrance. The real perils are of a far subtler kind. There is in the genuinely scientific nature a special *naïveté* of which advantage can be taken. Just because he is unworldly, the scholar or scientist is peculiarly exposed to the wiles of the worldly. So long as he is allowed to believe that he has his head and can go where he likes, he will not see the reins or the driver. The innocence of many social teachers and students is both amusing and pathetic. A quite important factor, for example, in the conservatism of economists is their naïve admiration for the gifts and virtues of successful business men. Nor is it only the lords of industry and finance that command this worship. As Thackeray recognised in his *Book of Snobs*, there is in the academic atmosphere and its close intellectual life a special servility to ' the powers that be ', whether in Church or in State, or in any other elevated walk of life.

In some measure this deference comes from a physical timidity and low vitality that are selective factors in the scholarly career. There exists a secret envy, an instinctive worship of the sterile thinker for the fruitful doer, a testimony to a baulked instinct for active self-assertion. Mere thought is somehow felt to be a badge of inferiority even among those who profess the keenest pride in the life of culture. At the back of their minds is the gnawing feeling that " Those who can, do ; those who can't, teach ". To the ' red-blood ' (which nearly every scholar, scientist, and philosopher secretly aspires to be) the academic life spells impotence or failure.

This helps to put the free scientific impulse at a disadvantage when powerful outside interests bring their influence to bear upon the processes of research and teaching. The ' intellectual ' is terribly sensitive to the approval and disapproval of rulers and other authorities in the outside world. His strong personal sympathies are engaged in keeping the good opinion of successful practical men. The knowlege that he and his fellows and the intellectual life they conduct are not directly productive of economic values, and are in this sense ' parasitic ' on the practical life, feeds the sentiment of deference. His feeling for the dignity and importance of his intellectual function no doubt stands out more clearly in his ' consciousness ', but underneath, in the hidden recesses of his mind, this sense of weakness and inferiority rankles. Man is primarily a doer, not a thinker. ' *Im Anfang war die That* ', and the addiction to a close life of thought costs dear in terms of ultimate self-respect.

It is, therefore, seldom necessary for the rich donors and influential patrons of new Universities to impose penal conditions to secure their good will and support. The governors and the teaching faculty will meet them more than half-way in their demand for safe teaching in all subjects where unsafe teaching might cause offence in rich and influential quarters. In making these concessions they will not think or feel that they are cramping liberty of thought and utterance. For disturbing thought and teaching, especially in matters that touch practical affairs, will seem to them unscientific, alike as involving rash departures from attested truths, and as importing heated controversial feeling into the calm atmosphere of study ! Under such conditions it is easy to perceive that choice of subjects, teachers, textbooks, modes of teaching, direction and equipment of research, will be subject to a constant moulding by non-scientific pressures. It is not necessary to cite concrete instances of heresy-hunting or other rude interferences with intellectual liberty. The definite fear of losing a teaching post plays but a small part in sterilising the scientific impulse, as compared with the more constant and insidious breathing of this conservative atmosphere. The more blatant illustrations of the maxim that ' He who pays the piper calls the tune ' even help to screen the more delicate manipulations of the ' hidden hand '.

The graver perils to free-thought and scientific progress in the social sciences lie in this timid conservatism of their

professors and their genuine class sympathies and rever-
ences. They are not so much the intellectual mercenaries
of the vested interests as their volunteers.

§ In thus dwelling upon the special character of the
obstacles and interests that invade the social sciences, I
may have seemed to overstress these interferences and to
prejudge the victory in the struggle between the powers of
light and darkness. I may seem open to the fair retort :
" How is such an intellectual world as you describe, where
private interests and particular passions are so powerful,
compatible with the actual considerable progress of these
sciences ? "

Disinterested science must have some advantages so far
not disclosed or adequately estimated. This is true. If,
as I hold, the very existence of the elaborate structure of
civilisation is a testimony to the power of human reason,
some special virtue must reside in this central power of
rational control, enabling it to defeat the machinations of
the separatist instincts. Here we need not speculate upon
the nature of this reason, the central co-ordinative drive
towards a larger, fuller, more unified life. But that it
exists lies beyond dispute, and the scientific impulse belongs
to it. While, therefore, all the various interferences which
we have cited are real, and responsible for much waste and
damage in the social sciences, they cannot do more than
weaken, impede, and temporarily deflect the stream of
scientific endeavour.

But the recognition of this long-range economy of intellectual life must not blind us to the serious nature of the
present problem of freedom for the social sciences. Particular group-policies and interests, dignified by the ' ism '
suffix, Nationalism, Imperialism, Capitalism, Socialism,
Protectionism, and the like, desire to have the aid of ' disinterested ' intellectual authority, partly for their general

prestige and as a cloak for their interested purposes, partly, also, as an instrument of educational propaganda in the active pursuance of their policies.   The need for influencing the mind of great bodies of citizens in modern States, and the potency of scientific 'captions' for this purpose, are recent discoveries.   In other words, the exploitation of the social sciences has come to play a considerable part in the fine art of propaganda.   This abuse does not necessarily impugn the virtue of the sciences.   But where the interests and passions conducting the propaganda happen, as will often be the case, to be vested with influence on the governing or teaching staffs in schools and colleges, liberty of research, teaching and publication is sure to be injuriously affected.

A particularly dangerous conjuncture of circumstances has brought this issue to the fore.   So long as the social sciences were probing dull generalities, concerned mainly with the discovery of methods and principles remote from the actual play of current happenings, they were neither regarded as dangerous nor as serviceable to political or business practitioners.   The uneducated masses paid no heed to them.

But now behold a triple transformation of the situation. In every country a crop of critical social problems, fraught with literally vital value, has sprung up within a single generation, many of them quickened by the war.   The social sciences themselves, owing chiefly to the advances made in psychology and anthropology, have shown a growing disposition to concern themselves with these social problems, exploring them and even offering authoritative advice to the practitioners.   This is particularly the case with the problems of finance and business organisation, constitution-making, race, and population, education and penology, which are chief centres of social and intellectual disturbances.

The education of large masses of our populations has just

reached the level where specious scientific terminology and mysterious thaumaturgic ideas can be successfully exploited by adepts in propaganda.

This conjunction of needs and opportunities has put a clearer consciousness and more definite purpose into the outside pressures for the restraint and moulding of the social sciences. The very knowledge of the partisan inflammability of much of the matter which they handle will insensibly incline timid students and teachers to stick to orthodox safe doctrines and to go slow with new experiments and hypotheses, while others of a bolder nature may thereby be carried into rash excesses which will, in their turn, be exploited by conservative propagandists in justification of restraints upon liberty of teaching and publication. Nor will propaganda be confined to the special interests of the ruling and possessing classes. Reform has its propaganda, quite as reckless, interested, and unscrupulous, as the propaganda of reaction ! It is, however, less formidable as a bias to disinterested science, partly because of the weaker finance and social prestige behind it, partly because the wider popular interest it represents and seeks to make prevail is nearer to the dictates of ' right reason ' than the narrower interests upon whose influence we have chiefly dwelt. There are, however, as we shall see in our closer study of economic and political doctrines, certain key positions where loose rhetoric and impassioned demagogy have impressed themselves most injuriously upon the sciences.

The upshot of this discussion is the urgent need to realise the new intensity of the conflict waged on several fronts between the forces of disinterested reason and the special interests, economic, racial, national, class, sex, individual, in all the sciences which deal with the ideas, feelings, and activities concerned in the various departments of social conduct.

PART II

THE MAKING OF AN ECONOMIC SCIENCE

CHAPTER I

THE RISE OF POLITICAL ECONOMY

§ IF we agree that the function of Reason is to co-ordinate the activities of Man in the service of personal and social welfare, it becomes a mere matter of words whether we speak of Science, the chief organised process of Reason, as ' disinterested ' or not. The work of Science as a human activity, and its fruit of knowledge, can only have meaning or value in terms of humanity. This is not an idle qualification. It signifies that neither ' things in themselves ' (intrinsically unknowable) nor the whole floating mass of phenomena presented to human consciousness, is the subject matter of Science, but portions of that floating mass selected for attention and intellectual exploration. Whether the curiosity, which is the emotion lurking in these activities of attention and exploration, has a direct biological survival value or not is immaterial to this inquiry. Curiosity, directed to the unsorted mass of phenomena, shouts specific questions at them, selecting, rejecting, and arranging them, in order to extract answers to these questions. Generalisations, laws, hypotheses, do not, that is to say, proceed either by some self-revelation of phenomena, or by some equal and impartial treatment of them by the human mind, but by a method of approach and handling which is definitely ' interested ', in the sense of putting preconceived questions to which answers are sought. In this sense all Science is qualified by human interest. So when we speak of 'disinterested science' we mean, either that the answers to these questions are valued merely as knowledge, or that, if behind that knowledge lies the sense of the need to utilise it, that utility is conceived in terms of general human welfare, not in terms of some particular gain. Specific utilities must come as implications, or by-products, of Science, not as conscious ends or motives.

§ But one further concession may be made, of special importance to our inquiry. It may be held that a search for knowledge is genuinely 'scientific', although directed consciously to solve a practical problem of utility, provided that it is conducted with accuracy of observation, experiment, and reasoning. Much 'scientific' work of this kind is done in applied physics, chemistry, biology. No doubt it has intellectual dangers. A strong desire to overcome some obstruction, or to verify some directly gainful hypothesis, or to discover some new property or process, is liable to lead to biased observation or improper use of evidence. But this drive of practical utility is furnished with strong safeguards. However keenly I may desire to discover some new source or economy of mechanical power, the knowledge that my discovery will be submitted to certain and early tests will tend to keep my intellectual processes clear and sound.

But in the social sciences there are no equally valid tests and checks. An inquiry into the merits of some political, economic, or educational method or device, P.R., profit-sharing, prohibition, Montessori teaching, vaccination, indeterminate sentences, is liable to be vitiated at every step by selection, mis-valuation, or doping of evidence, due to the presence of a desire to prove a case, and the difficulty of conviction for error. Where deeply engrained habits of thought and sentiment are involved, as in the support or rejection of political, economic, or other social opinions on matters of urgency, an unlimited amount of such bias is likely to enter a professedly 'scientific' inquiry.

The distinction sometimes made between 'pure' and 'applied' has so much less application to the social sciences than to the physical that these considerations bear much more strongly on their general scientific character.

In a word, the social sciences and arts lie closer together, and all infections to which the latter are exposed are liable to influence the former.

§ These brief general observations may serve as a preface to a closer investigation of the development of the Science of Economics. I select for special treatment that branch of social science, partly because it is the most advanced, in the sense that most intellectual work has been put into its structure, partly because the problem of interested pressures is there more clearly posed than in other social sciences.

It will be most profitable to begin at what will seem to some the wrong end, viz. by a statement of the conception of Economic Science and Economic Art which will, I think, fairly represent the considered opinion of an increasing number of present-day economists.

The Art of Economics addresses itself to the arrangement of the human activities and conditions for attaining the welfare of humanity, so far as it is affected by transferable products widely desired and limited in quantity. The human, or welfare, value of these products consists in the surplus of satisfaction over dissatisfaction in the joint processes of production and consumption. A given stock of goods or services, which has 'cost' little in the net 'disutility' of its production, and yields the largest amount of net utility in its consumption, is a successful product of Economic Art.[1] Economic Science is concerned with the

---

[1] Some psychological economists consider that the utilitarian calculus is entirely discredited and needs to be replaced by some other standard of

discovery of the laws or principles of human nature and its environment which are discernible in these economic processes. Modern Psychology bids fair to transform the character of Economic Science by the new light it throws upon economic welfare.

The resolution of economic wealth, or real income, into terms of vital utility, or satisfaction, by setting subjective gain against subjective cost, alike in the production and the consumption of the real income, will be found to undercut the whole attempt at exact measurement of wealth. For the amount of welfare, represented by a given objective quantity of wealth, will vary widely and immeasurably with the nature and the distribution of the human activities that go to its production, and the nature and distribution of the consumption of the wealth. Since no two persons will be in precise agreement about the relative worth, or human value, of different activities and satisfactions which go to make up a standard of life for an individual or a society, economic welfare cannot mean precisely the same to any two persons, or, indeed, to any one person at any two times. Even if, therefore, we take actual current desiredness, not some ideal desirability, for our standard of measurement, we cannot hope to get any close correlation between economic wealth, as measured by money, and the human wealth to which it contributes. There is nothing peculiar in this discrepancy. It is inherent in all art valuation, which defies the attempt to express in quantities differences of quality. To this subject I shall return later. I only introduce it here in order to make clearer the limitations imposed on modern Economic Science. They do not invalidate the aids rendered by the science to the art. Science, for instance, can show that an equal distribution of a product must tend to produce a larger aggregate utility,

value. In an appendix to this chapter I offer a defence of the retention of a modified utilitarianism.

or satisfaction, in consumption, than an unequal distribution, and that, if a measurement of relative needs of consumers were possible, an unequal distribution, proportionate to these needs, would yield a still larger aggregate of satisfaction. It may even discover serviceable methods for gauging needs, and so for maximising the human welfare obtainable from a given income.

This is useful scientific work, even if its results have to be checked for economic application by consideration of the reactions upon incentives of production due to the changes of distribution that are proposed. In a word, modern Economic Science aims at providing a calculus of the amount of human welfare involved in, or arising from various quantities and methods of production and consumption. Human welfare, for such a science, may be understood in one of two alternative ways : (1) as assessed by current standards of desirability ; (2) as referred to some psycho-physical standard of vital valuation, that would be the current standard if men knew their ' good ' and followed it. This standard of ' objective human good ' would, however, vary according to the time perspective for its application, the extent and the intensity of the concern for the distant welfare of humanity.

Economic Art, in fact, vacillates between these two standards [1] and the science follows her lead, though with a preference for current standards.

The economic scientist will not have in his mind, as he pursues his scientific investigations, the particular nature of the contributions he may make towards the progress of the art. But, as we have seen, the way he approaches the

---

[1] The State, in its many interferences with industry, professes to apply hygienic and other social standards based on vital values other than, and generally higher than, those ordinarily practised in the current arts of industry, and ' better ' employers are concerned in the voluntary application of this higher standard, so far as cost and price conditions permit. The science, like the art of industry, thus straddles two divergent standards.

5

mass of his raw material, the order he imposes on it, will be determined not mainly (or exclusively) by a general curiosity, a general itch for intellectual order, but by specific questions and a specific order, which flow from the needs of the art.

Not how to escape this service of the art, but how to perform the service with the utmost fidelity to Reason, is the problem of disinterested Economic Science. For at every point the tendency of some specific personal or class passion or interest, to usurp the place of human welfare in the art, and to call upon the science to give its intellectual blessing to this usurpation, imperils the integrity of the scientific economist.

§ It is no reproach to Economic Science that it grew out of practical interest in particular economic problems, rather than out of a disinterested desire for knowledge or a general regard for Human Welfare in the economic order.

Though thinkers in the ancient world turned their attention sometimes towards agriculture, industry, and commerce, it cannot be said that they laid the foundations of an economic science. This is attributable mainly to their treatment of economic activities and products from the standpoint of the political or social order. Even Plato and Aristotle, in discussing what from the standpoint of science is the primary economic fact, division of labour, treated it almost exclusively as a basis of social classification. On the other hand, special studies of an economic nature, such as the technique of husbandry, the ethics of usury, the population question, the functions of money, came from philosophers, jurists, or practical business men. So long as this failure to take economic phenomena, in the sense of an economic system, as a subject for separate inquiry continued, no science could emerge. The basis of a science could only be reached, on the one hand by releasing Economics from its subordination to an inchoate political science, on the other, by a correlation of the special economic studies.

The beginnings of such a science were not possible until the Renaissance had brought about an adequate secularisation of the human intellect. Throughout the Middle Ages the influence of the Catholic Church upon economic life and thinking, alike by its practical morals and the operation of its canon law, hindered the realisation of industry as an autonomous province of the intellectual world. So long as the prevailing thought accepted the subordination of economic activities to the paramountcy, either of the State, as the arbiter of social order, or of the Church, as arbiter of moral order, a ' disinterested ' political economy remained impracticable.

Moreover, the conception of a general economic system was slow to dawn upon an intelligence confronted with so much local self-sufficiency as prevailed until the rise of modern capitalism. Even when local barriers to trade were breaking down under the economies of division of labour within the nation, while foreign trade was assuming large dimensions, the persistence of ideas and valuations belonging to the older political and spiritual rules was very stubborn. The mediaeval conception that war was the natural relation between States, and that a treasure was essential to success in war, combined to poison thought and policy on foreign trade long after the fostering of national industry had assumed a general primacy in policy. As is well known, it underlay the first conceptions of a national economic order, in the shape of a Mercantile System, a notion still responsible for the unreasonable concern for a favourable balance of trade, a preference for exports over imports, for raw imports over manufactured, and for other related follies of modern Protectionism. But, with all its bad inheritance from mediaeval times, Mercantilism may rightly lay claim to the title of the earliest Political Economy, upon the national plane.   Its leading theorists did attempt to envisage and represent the relations of interdependence between agriculture, manufactures, and commerce, internal and external, and to give some orderly account of the monetary system.   The growing importance given to foreign trade was itself a testimony to the fuller conception of the economic life of the world as a single system, though that conception was distorted into the narrow notion of a national economy operated in the joint interests of trading companies and State financiers.

Along with this gradual emergence of the conception of a single economic system, fed by able works in France, Italy, and Britain, there came a large variety of special studies upon particular economic problems of political, commercial, or social importance.   In the seventeenth and eighteenth centuries money, taxation, rural economy, population, and above all, foreign trade, drew forth a crop of scientific or controversial writings.

§ The Physiocrats were the first school of thought that endeavoured to draw together into a more disinterested scientific system these various lines of study.   Chiefly in France and in Italy their leading thinkers began to apply to economic life the rationalist method and the humanitarian passion which the eighteenth-century free-thought had brought to bear upon theology and politics with such shattering effect.   Their doctrine was not, of course, the pure product of dry reason.   To its moulding went a strong resentment against the shackles which an interfering State put upon liberty of industry and commerce, with the extortions and corruptions that were engendered therefrom. The sentimental Naturalism, of which Rousseau was the passionate spokesman, favoured an economic analysis that made agriculture the only truly productive occupation and the foundation of the economic order.   Quesnay's *Tableau*

Économique, purporting to show how, under a system of natural liberty, the products of the soil, the only source of wealth, would be distributed among the various classes of the community, first for manipulation by manufacturers, merchants, and transporters, and finally for consumption, may be regarded as the first attempt of scientific economists to construct a rational system. The fact that these economists were for the most part enthusiastic reformers must not be taken as negativing the value of their science. For their enthusiasm was disinterested, in the sense to which we have agreed, viz. it was directed to the establishment of an economic system favourable to the general welfare, as they conceived that welfare.

§ The lasting significance of this school of thought lay in its underlying faith in the principle of individual liberty in industry and commerce as the source and guaranty of national wealth and welfare.

It was the logic of this " simple system of natural liberty " that Adam Smith incorporated as a providential guide into his system, so far as it can be called a system. Its character and virtue consisted in the two qualities of comprehensiveness and impartiality, so far as this latter quality relates to matters of political and business interest. Though ethical judgments not infrequently intrude into his analysis of economic activities, while one practical reform of great moment, viz. Free Trade, may be said to have been a definitive motive in the writing of *The Wealth of Nations*, few will be disposed to question the verdict of Professor Cannan :

" There can be no doubt that he actually undertook his task with the desire of adding to the bounds of knowledge ".[1]

Unfortunately for Economic Science, the looseness of

[1] *Theories of Production and Distribution*, p. 384.

structure and the discursiveness which belonged to this attempt to bring large stores of information from various fields of knowledge, exposed Adam Smith's great work to grave abuses by later thinkers less imbued with his scientific spirit. It was a ' baggy' system, in that you could pick it up at various points, and it would fall into quite different shapes. For labour-men it furnishes an armoury of passages assigning labour as the original source of wealth, and condemning the excessive gains which merchants and manufacturers obtain at the expense alike of worker and consumer by their combinations to keep prices high and wages low. For radical land reformers there is a keen analysis of differential and monopoly rents, a plain admission that landlords " are the only one of the three orders whose revenue costs them neither labour nor care "[1] and a powerful condemnation of their selfish Corn Laws and other instruments of class protection.

On the other hand, the central influence given to " the funds destined for the maintenance of labour ", and the importance of profit, " which puts into motion the greater part of the useful labour of every society ", the importance assigned to ' saving' and to the ability of entrepreneurs, proved very serviceable to future theorists who chose to disregard Adam Smith's solemn warning against entrusting any law or regulation of commerce to " an order of men, whose interest is never with that of the public, who have generally an interest to deceive and even to oppress the public, and who, accordingly, have, upon many occasions, both deceived and oppressed it ".[2]

But while scientific impartiality may be said to be the keynote of *The Wealth of Nations,*

" The case of the early nineteenth-century economists is entirely different. With them, in the great majority of cases, practical aims were paramount, and the advancement of Science secondary."[3]

[1] Book i. ch. xi. [2] Vol. i. p. 230. [3] Cannan, p. 384.

These practical aims were, so far as the prevailing economic doctrines went, directed to two related ends, viz., the acquiescence in the existing order of economic life on the part of those portions of the population likely to become discontented and disposed to revolution, and the release of the new entrepreneurs and capitalists from the restrictions upon their profitable activities imposed by Corn Laws, Workmen's Combinations, the Law of Settlement, and all other present or threatened interferences with liberty of contract and of trade.

Building, in part, with blocks of theory and policy drawn from the liberal quarry of *The Wealth of Nations*, and worked up into more serviceable shape, the early builders of the Classical Political Economy set about their work of furnishing the new capitalists and entrepreneurs with an authoritative science that would justify the economic behaviour to which plain self-interest impelled them.

It is no part of my intention to discuss the several sources from which this once stately edifice of Classical Political Economy arose. But a just instinct led its authors to take for their foundation what has been rightly designated " the secret substance " of Smith's economic doctrines, by one who thus describes it :

" In his view Nature has made provision for social well-being by the principle of the human constitution which prompts every man to better his condition : the individual aims only at his private gain, but in doing so is ' led by an invisible hand ' to promote the public good, which was no part of his intention ; human institutions, by interfering with the action of this principle, defeat their own end ; but when all systems of preference and restraint are taken away ' the obvious and simple system of natural liberty ' establishes itself of its own accord ".[1]

§ Now this ' simple system of natural liberty ' affords an admirable example of the rationalisation of the acquisi-

[1] Ingram, *History of Political Economy*, p. 91.

tive instinct in the development of economic doctrine. Discovered by Adam Smith in his capacity of moral philosopher, as part of a broad providential design, it was applied as a principle of intellectual and moral harmony in the economic world, without any *arrière pensée* on his part. Writing, as he did, before the modern capitalist economy had disclosed its supremacy, he had no premonition of the service he was to render the coming generation of ' profiteers ', in providing them with an intellectual defence for their gainful policy of unrestricted competition and freedom of individual contract.

But when the new machine-lords were transforming the face of the country with their factory towns and their collieries, while export trade was expanding by leaps and bounds, and a new finance was springing up to direct the supplies of fluid capital, the value of this libertarian principle, alike for breaking down obstructions and for establishing confidence in the new economic order, became obvious to thoughtful business men, their politicians, and their philosophers.

To establish in all educated circles a firm belief that Nature and Providence were solidly backing the policy which Lancashire, the Tyne and Clyde, and the City, found profitable, was an object of considerable importance. For Britons, perhaps more than any other people, like to have a ' good ' reason for doing what they want to do. Now gritty and resourceful men in Lancashire, Glasgow, Leeds, and London wanted a ' free ' hand for getting easy access to large, cheap supplies of labour, for free and expanding foreign markets in which to sell British manufactures and buy abundant food and raw materials to feed their works and workers. ' Free ' land, in the sense of a removal of hampering covenants and other extortionate conditions, ' free ' money, in the sense of cheap capital and credit, even ' free ' education, so far as it conduced to efficiency of labour, were secondary implications of the doctrine.

So far as politics were involved, it can hardly be contended that the philosophic principle of Natural Liberty was necessary. The new business classes were quite capable of finding their own politicians to look after their interests in Parliament and in the country. But thinkers were required for the more solid intellectual work of establishing moral confidence in the Capitalist régime. In England it has never been necessary to employ crude methods of purchase, or other material inducement, in order to obtain them. When so useful a service is needed, there are plenty of volunteers. Strong-brained men from the business world, like Ricardo or Babbage, will theorise out of the material of their own experience. Philanthropists, or publicists, like Malthus, drawn to the support of some advanced position, lend a useful hand. Academic economists, Civil servants and other social students help to piece together these positions into an authoritative system at once consistent and serviceable to the powers that be.

In accepting this account of the pressures upon economic theory it is quite unnecessary to impeach the intellectual integrity of any of these different classes of supporter. It may well be admitted that business champions and controversial publicists are more or less consciously 'out to make a case', and the former, at any rate, must know tolerably well what they are doing. But it is quite easy to admit that strong practical men always believe genuinely in the rectitude of reasoning that justifies their own conduct, while public controversialists, as we have seen, soon come to identify their personality emotionally with any position, especially a weak one, into the advocacy of which they have once entered.

" Malthus ", we are told, " discovered his Principle of Population in the course of an attempt to damp his father's hopes of progress." . . . . " In bringing out the first edition he was inspired, not so much by the desire to publish the existence of the Principle, whatever it may have been, as by the desire to disprove the possibility of any great improvement in the material condition of mankind, and thus to produce acquiescence, if not contentment, with the existing order of things."[1]

It is fair to add that Malthus himself claimed that " he had not acquired that command over his understanding, which would enable him to believe what he wished, without evidence, or to refuse his assent to what might be unpleasing, when unaccompanied by evidence." [2]

§ But though the ordinary public will pay respect to the arguments of successful business men and talented publicists, they cannot escape a sense of *parti pris* attaching to such reasoning. For ' disinterested ' science they will look to students who have no personal axe to grind, and who will formulate laws and principles in a really ' scientific ' system. What they fail, however, to understand is that a science of economics so disinterested is impossible. The secret makers of Political Economy, those whose economic interests it is designed to serve, need not instruct, induce, or otherwise directly or consciously influence, the academic scientists to produce the desired theory. Such pressure would, indeed, defeat its end. The economic scientist must produce the ' good ' theories of his own accord, along lines of thinking congenial to his own nature. Why should he not ? Is he not consciously imbued by early education and associations with a sympathetic interest in the success of the successful classes ? Must he not value the sort of success which is valued by the society in which he has grown up ? As a student of business systems, can he fail to concentrate his interest upon the salient acts and personalities, those of entrepreneurs ? They are the successful practitioners of arts in which he is a mere spectator and

---

[1] Cannan, p. 384.   [2] Wright, *Population*, p. 21

investigator. If, as commonly in England, strong personal ties of family or friendship unite him to ' property ' or ' rule ', these connections cannot fail to tell upon his thinking. Finally, if he is a whole-hearted lover of his subject, he cannot but be aware that some lines of thinking will be favourable, others unfavourable, to the support his ' science ' will obtain from the propertied and influential classes. The accumulated bias of these various considerations cannot be ignored. They are plainly discernible in the processes of the selection and rejection of competing facts and theories which in the mid-nineteenth century moulded and gave survival value to the Classical Political Economy.

§ Let there be complete liberty of contract, movement, occupation, trade, throughout the economic world, the greatest body of wealth will be produced and will be distributed in the most serviceable way, everyone getting his proper share, and that too a larger share than he would get in any other way. This is conceived as the true Economic Art, based on the Natural Harmony of individual interests in Society, and Economic Science is devoted to expounding the laws of wealth in a society so ordered, and incidentally in exposing the follies and fallacies of all existing or proposed obstacles to this system of Natural Liberty.

The most revealing comment upon this ' simple ' system is that it is not so ' simple ' as it sounds, in that it is based upon a denial of ' real ' economic liberty to the vast majority of the population of every country. For the major premiss of the system should require that there be equal access for all to the natural resources of the earth, the past accumulation of tools and other ' capital ', and the heritage of knowledge. Without these equal opportunities the so-called economic liberty of man is unreal.

The ignoring of this premiss is, indeed, an eye-opener

into the psychology of the making of Economic Science. For these defects in liberty were exposed to a steady fire of criticism from social-economic reformers during the very time when the structure of the Classical Economics was being hammered into shape. A number of able and trenchant critics of the new capitalism, and the established landlordism, used material from the Smithian and Ricardian quarries, not only for weapons against the monopoly of land and capital, but for corner-stones in some hastily improvised system of constructive socialism. Labour being the admitted source of wealth, real liberty for labour was the one essential for a healthy economic society. They, therefore, set themselves to define and demand the substance of this liberty, and to build upon it an edifice of co-operation for the Commonwealth. Some of these economists accepted the system of natural liberty, with the psychology of individual self-interest as its operative force, and merely demanded that liberty should be realised in equality of opportunity. Others held, with Owen and his followers, that a New Moral and Economic World needed a conscious human co-operation, based upon a reasonable plan and a common purpose. But for our discussion it is not the respective merits of these divergent schools of thought that count, but the fact that in the conflict of ideas and theories drawn from a common stock, one school survived, triumphed, and became the accepted intellectual authoritative science, while the other perished so quickly, so silently, and so completely, that the very names of its chief representatives were unknown to economic students of the next generation.[1]

No fair-minded reader to-day could fail to find in Thompson, Gray, Bray, Hodgskin, and others of these

[1] It is safe to say that Foxwell's Preface to a Translation of Menger's *Right to the Whole Produce of Labour* came as a revelation to economic students of the 'eighties.

radical reformers, powerful arraignments alike of the economic system and of the orthodox political economy of their time. No student of to-day, reading the rigorous analysis of Dr. Cannan, can fail to discern the hopeless illogic of the accepted doctrines of the Classicists. What other conclusion can be drawn than that the suppression of the former and the survival of the latter were due to the complexion of the Committee of Selection, that is to say, the academic, journalistic, and other intellectual advisers of the general reading public ? And this Committee of Selection made its choice because it ' sensed ' correctly the intellectual needs and desires of the ruling and owning classes. This sense on the part of the committee of their solidarity of interests with the rich and powerful classes need not, indeed must not, ascend to the level of clear consciousness. For such clear consciousness might evoke in ordinarily honest teachers, writers, and reviewers, a hampering sense of intellectual dishonesty. The professor, or director of studies, the publisher, the editorial writer, the professional critic, librarian, or lecturer, must not believe or feel himself to be servile to outside authorities. And these authorities must take care that the pressures or other inducements they bring to bear in the selection and rejection of economic theories and opinions, are so unobtrusive that the subjects of this influence can easily be ' unaware ' of its exercise. Certain cruder forms of influence, no doubt, are always operative in particular cases. But the subtler, more indirect, and less conscious forces, making for the selection of safe, conservative, or otherwise convenient theories, and the rejection of disturbing and inconvenient theories, are the most formidable enemies which the ' disinterested ' Science of Economics has to meet.

Much has been written about the economic interpretation of History in general which can only be made plausible by

an illicit stretching of the term ' economic ' to cover other,
biological and psychological, activities. But for reasons
which are sufficiently obvious the economic interpretation
of economic theory has a far higher degree of validity. So
plain, immediate, and powerful, are the reactions upon
economic practice of thought and feeling embodied in economic theory, that business practitioners must constantly
desire that certain economic theories shall prevail, and
must be disposed to use their influence upon the organs of
public information and opinion to make them prevail.

It is equally manifest that the working classes, either as
a whole or in sections, e.g. town *versus* rural labourers,
skilled *versus* unskilled, manual *versus* mental, productive
versus distributive, should tend to formulate an economics,
each in accordance with its own outlook and interests.
Racial and national proclivities and situations also plainly
find their reflections in the varying economics of the social
revolution. How vigorously all these working-class interests
assert themselves in the welter of the current economics of
Communism, Socialism, Syndicalism, Guild Socialism, Co-
operation, and other working-class policies, only needs a
passing recognition here. For our immediate purpose is to
interpret the evolution of authoritative economic theory,
under the conditions of a growth in which ' disinterested '
science is subject to the disturbing influence of external
interests.

§ It was inevitable that the theory of Political Economy
emerging from this conflict of interests, desires, and beliefs,
should be one that was conducive to a free hand for the
new capitalist-entrepreneurs of the factories and mines,
shipping, railways and banks, who were transforming
the economic system, expanding production, extending
markets, and increasing their share of the increasing real
income of the nation. This theory must be at once con-

servative and liberative, in order to utilise the full
advantages of the 'obvious and simple system of natural
liberty '.   Its liberalism will take shape in laws and policies
designed to remove all obstructions to free profitable enterprise for the new capitalism, in a demand for free control
of large, cheap, submissive supplies of labour, a free access
to overseas markets alike for import and for export trade,
the removal of hampering conditions in the tenure and use
of land, the easy and mobile provision of the capital and
credit needed by the new capitalism, the reduction of
State interference, either by public ownership, legal restrictions, or taxation, to a minimum.   Its conservatism will
consist in the recognition and support of all existing legal
and economic inequalities in ownership of, and access to,
land, capital, and the social heritage of knowledge, except
so far as any of these inequalities may obstruct the free
profitable activity of the entrepreneur.

The loose web of economic theory, thus picked up at the
place occupied by the new capitalist-entrepreneur, fell into
convenient shape.   To furnish these masters of production
with the requisite supplies of the factors of production at
a cheap rate, and to find expanding markets for their
products were of primary importance.   Free Trade for raw
materials entering their factories, and for cheap foods to
feed their workers, was desirable, not only upon its own
account, but in order to save them from the extortions of
English landlordism.   The sound doctrine that, in order to
sell freely and profitably abroad, they must buy freely and
profitably abroad, has done the best of services, not only in
giving a reasonable meaning to " *laissez faire, laissez aller* ",
but in securing for the Classical Theorists credit for the
humanitarianism of the cheap loaf and the political
enlightenment of a pacific internationalism.

But the main concern of a theory subservient to the new
capitalism was to furnish 'laws' conducive to abundant

and reliable supplies of capital and labour at 'reasonable' prices. The 'Natural System' demanded for its operation 'the economic man'. As wage-earner, this man would reproduce himself more rapidly if real wages rose above, less rapidly when they fell towards, a bare subsistence. If they fell below that level, working population would decline, and then rising wages would stimulate more reproduction. Whether this 'natural' wage lay at the bare subsistence level (an 'iron law'), or somewhere above, so as to leave a margin of comfort or improvement, was not a strictly relevant consideration. For the desired corollaries of this principle or law of natural wages were two ; first, that wages, thus determined by natural law, cannot be raised by combination of the workers ; second, that poverty of the working classes is attributable mainly to reckless pro-creation, not to greedy and oppressive action of employers. The economic man, as wage-earner, will 'tend' to move from any locality or occupation where wages are low to where they are higher, a movement making for a single wage-level.

Custom, ignorance, personal attachments, inequality of contract, other interferences with quite accurate movement towards the highest rate of wages, were either ignored or treated as 'friction' in the working of this natural law.

§ This important doctrine that wages cannot be raised by combination of workers, or by State intervention, or by any other outside interference, was further fortified by the 'laws' relating to supply of capital. The human will came into the economic system as a control, by the exercise of thrift and saving. For the maintenance, enlargement, and improvement of production were due to the sacrifice of the classes who had some surplus income beyond their require-ments for subsistence and chose to save that surplus.· The amount of such saving was determined by the operation of a natural incentive, interest or profit (the two not clearly distinguished then or ever), but the moral respectability of the origin of capital, taken in conjunction with the beneficent part it played in providing employment and wages for the workers, must receive close attention in any psychological interpretation of the classical doctrine. For the voluntary thrift of the propertied classes (who else could do much saving ?) not only provided the factory, mining, and marketing equipment, together with the other tools and materials for production, but expressed its abstinence in the provision of large stocks of food, clothing, and other consumables, that formed a wages fund to maintain the workers during the next period of their labour output. These two beneficial results came from saving and investing money income instead of spending it on personal enjoyment. So the thrift of the saving classes was at once the source of economic and of moral energy in the operation of the economic system. For modern testimony to this doctrine we have Mr. J. M. Keynes writing : " The immense accumulations of fixed capital which, to the great benefit of mankind, were built up during the half-century before the war, could never have come about in a society where wealth was divided equitably. The railways of the world, which that age built as a monument to posterity, were, not less than the Pyramids of Egypt, the work of labour which was not free to consume in immediate enjoyment the full equivalent of its efforts ".[1]

Professor Gustav Cassel thus endorses this agreeable doctrine : " A more democratic distribution would materially lower the degree of saving of the community. Particularly would this be the case if the increase of income were predominantly on the side of the working class ".[2]

The more people were induced to save, and the larger pro-

---

[1] *Economic Consequences of the Peace*, p. 19.
[2] *The Theory of Social Economy*, vol. i. p. 229.

portion of their income they saved, the greater the improvement in economic equipment, the larger the volume of employment, the higher the wage rate, and the greater the output of wealth to be consumed, or saved. The theory that capital puts industry into motion and supports labour was a nutritious intellectual food to the self-approval of the new industrial magnates who had snuffed in with their hard puritan traditions that reconcilement, nay co-partnership, of God and Mammon which has furnished to British capitalism so much spiritual energy for successful money-making. Industry, thrift, enterprise, initiative, honesty, responsibility—here are the moral keys of a successful business career for an individual as for a nation ! Any member of society by his character can constitute himself an economic man, making and seizing opportunities for business success, as workman, capitalist, or entrepreneur.

The unreality of this clear-sighted, calculating hedonism and of the access to all economic opportunities which its mobile operation involves, will be easily detected by social students of to-day. But the prevalence of these doctrines, not only among the rising business classes, who stood to benefit by them, but among the professional and educated classes as a whole (with here and there a paradoxical dissenter) well illustrates our thesis of the power of the dominant economic class to deflect a social science from its straightly rational course into supplying intellectual and moral supports for special group interests.

§ How to get business on to a big and profitable footing was the practical problem which underlay the whole structure of this classical economics, with its clumsy aspirations towards ' disinterested science '. This practical problem demanded the settlement along ' favourable ' business lines of a number of current troublesome controversies, relating to the wastes of the old Poor Law, with its doctrine of

Settlement and its encouragement to laziness and large families, to the Corn Laws and the hostility of the landlord class to free exploitation of the mineral and other natural resources of the country, to the Combination Laws, and to the attempts of Government to hamper profitable enterprise by Factory Acts and other restrictions, or even to substitute public for private business in some municipal and national undertakings.[1]

§ The entire devotion of this science to Capitalist Production is, however, most strikingly displayed in the absence of anything that can be called a theory of distribution or of consumption.   The assumption underlying all this economics, that the consumers' interests and welfare (the formally admitted end of all productive activities) are so adequately conserved by the play of self-interested hedonism under ' the simple system of natural liberty ' as to need no place in economic policy, and therefore in economic theory—this assumption is a curious record in intellectual obliquity. The obvious truth that there are arts and standards of consumption as delicate, as complex, and as capable of improvement, as the arts and standards of production, and that the human value or utility of a given quantity of objective wealth vary with the conditions of its consumption, equally as with those of its production, never seems to have found entry into the mind of any of these economists. Indeed, when it was propounded with skill and eloquence by Ruskin, it was rejected by them as an absurd irrelevance.

---

[1] Cannan, p. 391 : " Now for the settlement of the controversies under the influence of which it was created, the system of economics which prevailed after Malthus and Ricardo had written was admirably adapted. Where it was clear and correct, its points against what was practically evil were well and precisely made ; where it was confused and erroneous, its confusions and errors were such as to assist rather than hinder its work ; where it was deficient its deficiencies were not of much practical importance ".   For a concrete presentation of this policy, see Hammonds' *Town Labourer* and *Skilled Labourer*.

The consumer only came in, as it were, for politeness' sake, when he happened to be wanted. In this rôle he made an occasional visit into the discussion of Free Trade, the incidence of Taxation, and the *modus operandi* of the retail market. By the doctrine that " a demand for commodities is not a demand for labour ", since saving, or non-consumption, was the true source of employment, the obvious and direct dependence of production on consumption was excluded.

The quantitative aspect of Consumption was excluded by the assumption that, since everything that was or could be produced must be consumed, there could be no general over-production. The qualitative aspect was only recognised by one exceedingly illuminating distinction, that between productive and unproductive consumption. This distinction, so far as it has meaning, rests on the audacious claim that consumption, for economic policy, is only a means and instrument to further production. Consumption that is ' unproductive ' i.e. not directly conducive to economic efficiency, is matter for reprobation.

Now, since in any true science of economic welfare, a prime test of a successful system will lie in the amount and variety of the surplus wealth which, overflowing the needs of purely productive efficiency, is available for disinterested enjoyment, this treatment of unproductive consumption is a startling instance of the mutilation of economic theory in the hands of a combination of cotton-spinners, railway promoters, bankers, and their intellectual confederates.

It must not, however, be supposed that these early makers of Political Economy were heartless or inhuman men because they were propounders of a doctrine designed to support and defend capitalist production. Not all of them would even have assented to the distinction of Nassau Senior : " The subject of Political Economy is wealth, while the subject of legislation is not wealth but human welfare ". From the writings of many, if not most, of them can be culled passages expressing a benevolent attitude to the claims of labour. " The wages of labour ", wrote Adam Smith, " are the encouragement of industry, which, like every other human quality, improves in proportion to the encouragement it receives. . . . It is but equity, besides, that they who feed, clothe, and lodge the whole body of the people, should have such a share of the produce of their own labour as to be themselves tolerably well-fed, clothed, and housed ". Ricardo, in his firm adhesion to the Benthamite principle of " the greatest happiness of the greatest number ", writes that : " The friends of humanity cannot but wish that in all countries the labouring classes should have a taste for comforts and enjoyments, and that they should be stimulated by all legal means in their exertions to procure them ". McCulloch, one of the hardest theorists, has melting moments, when he declares that " The best interests of society require that the rate of wages be elevated as high as possible, and that a taste for the comforts, luxuries, and enjoyments of human life, should be widely diffused, and, if possible, interwoven with the national habits and prejudices ".

But such amiable *obiter dicta* have no place in and no support from the ' laws ' and ' principles ' of the economic doctrines that were claiming the authority of science.

§ The absence of attempts to formulate any law of Distribution of the product, as between the owners of the several factors of production, has been a subject of frequent comment among readers of the Classical Economics. Among these economists the problem of Distribution, as it is now understood, not merely was not solved, it was not set. No serious endeavour was made to find any law governing the proportions in which the annual product, or real income, was distributed, either between the owners of the several factors of production, land, labour, capital, or between the possessors of property on the one hand and the active producers on the other.

The accepted division of incomes into wages per head, interest per cent., and rent per acre, each following a separate law of its own, afforded no common measure or method for comparing the claims of the several factors of production upon the product. An occasional *obiter dictum*, such as Ricardo's opinion that rent and wages were destined to take a larger, profits a smaller, proportion of the product "in the progress of society", cannot be regarded as a serious recognition of the central problem of economics.

This curious neglect, however, does not involve either wilful culpability or lack of intelligence. It follows, naturally enough, from the two ruling conceptions of the science to which attention has been drawn, viz. the ' system of natural liberty ' and the adoption of Production as the end or aim of an economic system. The two conceptions work together to make the discussion of Distribution seem unnecessary. For in a society of economic men with Natural Liberty, the product will flow out of the productive system into the hands of the various classes of consumers with the same accuracy of adjustment towards economic needs as governed the supply of the various sorts of productive resources going into the making of the product. Once accept the point of view of efficient production as the economic goal, for the purpose of the science, Distribution is only relevant, so far as it concerns the purchase of labour per head, capital per £100, and land per acre, i.e. the customary way of providing for the continued supply of the resources of Production. Therefore, though the real problem of Distribution was sometimes approached by the Classical Economists, it was never properly presented, nor was an attempt made at its solution.

This was an inevitable consequence of conceiving wealth in terms of concrete product instead of human welfare. It was, however, also, an instructive testimony to the reluctance of economists to construct a science which might have disturbing reactions upon the complacency of the pioneers of economic progress and the contentment of the working classes.

A curious little commentary upon this pragmatic interpretation of the Classical Political Economy is furnished by its attitude towards landlords. As we see, in various ways, not merely economic, both political and social rivalry existed between the rent-receivers and the new industrialists. In an atmosphere heated by these controversies the economists thoughtfully supplied the Law of Rent and other weapons to their patrons, enabling them to draw attention away from their own profiteering and sweating practices and to fix it on the landlords, envisaged as obstructionists of economic liberty and the sole recipients of an increasing toll on honest industry. To represent land rents as the only unearned values, the only income that can bear taxation without damaging reactions upon trade and employment, was a curious and interesting cunning of capitalist defence, so plausible that it continues to-day to deceive many honest persons of reforming proclivities. But the Classical Economists were careful not to carry too far their exposure of the ' idle landlord ' and his loot. They were no friends of confiscation or of revolutionary violence. They felt in their bones that the trouble, once begun, might spread, and that the ignorant workers might not treat landlords as their only enemies. Moreover, as their factories, mines, and railways grew apace, they found themselves possessing just those ground values which were appreciating fastest. Rent was fusing more and more with Profits. While, then, the Law of Rent still served some useful purpose as a lightning conductor, it became more and more convenient to stress one aspect of that law, viz. that rent was not an element in cost of production and therefore was no cause of rising prices. In other words, the erstwhile ' villain ' of the economic drama was not really to blame; he was the innocent receiver of an inevitable surplus, a bounty of Nature, to which he had a legal claim and of which he could not rightly be dispossessed. The superior taxability of landowners, however, still remains as the main contribution of this economic theory to the movement of practical reform.

This convenient intellectual stockade for the defence and furtherance of the interests of the new economic potentates was, as we have seen, a very naïve piece of improvisation, claiming the name of Science with far poorer credentials than those of Adam Smith. I desire once more, before dismissing it and passing on, to guard against misunderstanding. Most of the builders of this system were men of intellectual integrity, hardly, if at all, conscious of the biases, personal or class, that were continually operative in their choice of intellectual starting-points, terminology, and formulas, the adoption of working hypotheses, and above all in the valuation of evidence. The utmost that can be said in moral blame of them is that, as controversialists on heated topics of current interest and passion, they ought to have been aware, when professing to enter the cooler atmosphere of scientific exposition, that they were liable to carry with them passions, interests, and prejudices likely to distort their reasoning, and to make them, what in effect they became, the intellectual defenders of the new economic power.

The recognition of the services of the new science as a corrective of working-class discontent is well illustrated in the proceedings of the Royal Commission on Education, of which the Duke of Newcastle was chairman, and Mr. Goldwin Smith, Mr. Nassau Senior, and other eminent educationalists were members. Their report, issued in 1858, contains the following passage :

" Next to religion, the knowledge most important to a labouring man is that of the causes which regulate the amount of his wages, the hours of his work, the regularity of his employment, and the prices of what he consumes. The want of such knowledge leads him constantly into error and violence, destructive to himself and to his family, oppressive to his fellow-workmen, ruinous to his employers and mischievous to Society." [1]

§ A really dramatic catastrophe was the collapse of this structure in the hands of J. S. Mill soon after he had brought it to completion. Those who have felt surprise that Mill should have ever committed himself to a system of thought so ill-constructed and so repellent to the finer feelings of mankind are justly reminded that the younger Mill had taken on in childhood a heavy legacy of mixed wisdom and error from the utilitarians and economists who were his early pastors and masters. Endowed by Nature with a larger measure of disinterestedness, a keener feeling for humanity, and more rigorous standards of intellectual honesty than other thinkers of his day, he came in fuller manhood to question and dismiss one after another the cruder foundations of the philosophic radicalism in which he had been bred.

Just as in ethics, by asserting the doctrine of qualities in pleasure, he broke the keystone of the Benthamite utilitarianism, so in economics, his abandonment of the individualism that was the *vis motrix* of the Classical Political Economy brought the whole structure to the ground. It is no wonder that he did not fully realise the extent of the havoc he had wrought. But his frank recognition of the failure of the ' simple system of natural liberty ' to produce any guaranty for a tolerable economic condition of society, together with the abandonment of the central

[1] Quoted *Life of William Ellis*, p. 208.

operative principle of capitalism, the wage-fund theory, heralded the downfall of the science whose completion he had been recently celebrating.

But the formal register of this collapse lay neither in Mill's abandonment of individualism, nor in his jettisoning of the wage-fund theory, but in a series of attacks upon the theory of value, or ratio of exchange for goods and services of different kinds, which had asserted a supreme authority in Economic Science. The law, expressing value purely in terms of comparative ' costs ' and taking ' utility ' for granted, was a serviceable asset in a Political Economy which took Production for its actual goal. The slight and quite subordinate place given to Consumption made it seem reasonable to compare units of different sorts of wealth purely in terms of ' cost ' of production, and when other efforts than that of common labour had been incorporated in costs, and a determinant part accorded to the cost of the most expensive portion of a supply, Mill's triumphant assurance that nothing further remained to be added to the theory of value seemed justified. But ' final cost ' did not long hold the field. The logic of a more humane Political Economy assailed the fundamental positions of the cost theory, and insisted on the supremacy of human satisfaction, or utility, in testing and measuring economic values.

CHAPTER II

NEO-CLASSICAL ECONOMICS IN BRITAIN

§ NEO-CLASSICAL economics in Britain is most conveniently dated from the work of Stanley Jevons. For it was he who first tilted the balance in value theory from cost to utility, applied mathematics to the supply and demand curves, and conceived the project of building with elaborate statistical material an exact science. This science he defined as 'the mechanics of human interest'. There are not a few passages, especially in the opening chapters of his *Theory*, which show how near his mind came to a broader and more balanced statement of the utilitarian calculus than that which he actually took.

"Political Economy must be founded upon a full and accurate investigation of the conditions of utility; and as we understand this element, we must necessarily examine the character of the wants and desires of men." Now 'utility' taken broadly in any utilitarian system should include disutility, or cost, since these clearly enter into the wants and desires of man. The elementary psychology by which Jevons explains the utility of consumption with its grades of variety and intensity is equally applicable to production. In this very book, indeed, Jevons made an elementary excursion into the intensity of labour, relating it to hours of labour, etc., and in his Preface he definitely states, "In this Work I have attempted to treat Economy as a calculus of Pleasures and Pains". Yet nowhere did he link up into a single calculus the pleasures and pains of the processes of production and consumption. No, " The whole theory of Economy " as he saw it, " depends upon a correct theory of consumption " (p. 47). In the last chapter of his *Theory* he says, " The great problem of Economy, may, as it seems to me, be stated thus : Given, a certain population, with various needs and powers of production, in possession of certain lands and other sources of materials ; required, the mode of employing their labour so as to maximise the utility of the produce " (p. 255). It seems curious that he should have failed to add the words " and so as to minimise the disutility of producing it ". Here was a real turning-point in economic theory. Had Jevons worked out his prefatory promise, the study might have been put upon a sound basis of utility conceived as human welfare ; the utilities as well as the disutilities of production might have been put into the account, together with the disutilities which attend certain forms and portions of consumption.

How far the definitely hedonistic turn of the utilitarianism, which Jevons had taken on from the Mills and Bentham, would have served him for a satisfactory art of human welfare, may be open to discussion. But such an application of the utilitarian method would have been a great advance along the road to a science for the interpretation of economic processes in terms of human well-being.

§ It might, however, have been expected that followers of the Jevonian method would have repaired the defects of their master. Had they done so, the Jevonian theory of value, resolving wealth into the various degrees of utility or enjoyment it furnishes to consumers, might have been the harbinger of a human political economy in Britain. Disinterested Science had only to take two tolerably obvious steps in order to construct a valid basis of a Science or Art of Economic Welfare. The first was to apply to the Production or Supply side of the equation of value the same subjective analysis as was applied to the Consumption or Demand side. If you are to evaluate a given quantity of concrete wealth, you must ask two related questions: how much utility it furnishes in its consumption, and how much disutility it involves in its production. For only by this double analysis can you realise what this wealth is really worth in human terms of net satisfaction or enjoyment. For, if each consumer, in purchasing a quantity of any article for consumption, gets for the last shilling of his expenditure a utility or satisfaction that is " just worth while ", it follows that for every prior shilling of that expenditure he gets a positive gain increasing in magnitude as it approaches the first shilling the utility of which may, if the article in question be a necessary of life, be infinite. This concept of a surplus or fund of positive gain for consumers is, of course, equally applicable to the cost or supply side of the problem of purchase. If it is just worth while for the producer to put forth the last and costliest unit of productive effort incorporated in a supply which fetches a price of one shilling per unit, then on every earlier unit of productive effort he gets, in the shilling he receives, something more than an equivalent for that effort, i.e. a producer's surplus, measuring the diminishing subjective cost of the earlier units. In theory, at any rate, the first unit of this output of productive energy may be considered to have a vital cost that is immeasurably small.[1]

Such might seem to be an obvious first step towards a scientific hedonist calculus. The second step would have been an orderly correlation of the results of this double analysis, a setting of the human costs of production represented by a stock of concrete goods against the human

---

[1] This producer's surplus must be distinguished from that which arises from the possession by a producer of some specially favourable position enabling him to produce his whole output, including its last unit, at a lower subjective cost than his competitors.

utilities of their consumption—a profit and loss account. In the process of both analyses it would have become evident that, though costs predominated in production, and utilities in consumption, some elements of costs found a place in consumption, some elements of utility, or satisfaction, in production. Wide inequalities of distribution would signify that some goods passed the barrier which separated utility from satiety, while certain kinds and amounts of productive energy are pleasurable in their output. In the analysis of any given stock of goods, therefore, it would be the net utility of consumption that would be set against the net disutility of production.

This analysis would inevitably have led to a new reorientation of the problem of Distribution. For it would have become evident that the total amount of satisfaction, enjoyment, welfare, attaching to any given quantity of wealth would vary with the ways in which the efforts of making it and the enjoyments of consuming it were apportioned among the members of the community. Such an apportionment, or distribution, of productive efforts as would involve the smallest aggregate of disutility in making it, and such apportionment, or distribution, of consumptive opportunities as would yield the largest aggregate of enjoyment, would evidently maximise the 'welfare' which attaches to any given quantity of goods.

§ Here a third step in the new subjective science might have been expected, involving a literally vital change in the method of the hedonist calculus. It might have been recognised that the costs and utilities attaching to the production or consumption of any set or class of goods cannot be discovered by a separate analysis of the processes of producing and consuming these goods. For these particular costs and utilities are associated with others derived from other sets of goods in a standard of production and a standard of consumption. The latter standard is self-evident in its bearing on the hedonist calculus. The utility of any single article of consumption depends on, and in some measure varies with, the utility of other articles incorporated in the personal standard of consumption. The division of labour has, however, gone so far in modern industry as to obscure what should be the equal significance of a human standard of production ; a varied day's work should by its organic composition reduce the total disutility and incorporate elements of positive utility. To some extent this variety of work can be made to subserve efficiency and total productivity within the factory system : in other cases it requires a sufficient quantity of leisure to enable workers, earning their main livelihood in some single craft or routine process, to choose subsidiary occupations that provide relief elements and give play to otherwise thwarted instincts of workmanship in body or mind. This conception of an interrelation between standards of work and of consumption, based upon a comprehension of the harmonious needs and satisfactions of man as an organism, might have been evolved from the crude beginning of the Jevonian theory of value.

An advance along these lines might have been expected to produce a subjective Science and Art of Economic Welfare which would have realised Ruskin's assertion " All Wealth is Life ", and pointed the way to a general social economic movement of reform.

This did not happen. It was not for want of intellectual leads. As early as 1854 Giessen published a book [1] containing an outline of this utilitarian calculus of utility and disutility. But nowhere in Britain did the method receive much attention. This was partly due to the concentration of most economists upon the conflict between ' cost ' and ' utility ' theories of value as the central problem of

[1] *Gesetze des menschlichen Verkehrs.*

Economics. Not until Marshall had achieved a peace treaty between these combatants by showing how the 'final cost' principle and the 'final utility' principle are undoubtedly component parts of the one all-ruling law of supply and demand, each compared to 'one blade of a pair of scissors', did English orthodox economics attain the equilibrium needed for resolving wealth into the sum of its utilities and disutilities.

But even then this subjective or human interpretation of wealth was sedulously avoided. Though Marshall opened his *Principles of Economics* with the comprehensive statement, "Political Economy or Economics is a study of mankind in the ordinary business of life; it examines that part of individual and social action which is most closely connected with the attainment and with the use of the material requisites of well-being", he nowhere proceeds to correlate the two processes of 'attainment' and 'use' from the standpoint of well-being. The elaborate studies of supply and demand curves in the determination of prices and the measurement of values in the various acts of purchase which constitute economic book-keeping, so thoroughly absorbed most of those who accepted the 'scissors' metaphor [1] as to keep them upon a mechanical plane of inquiry precluding any close psychological analysis into the human values affecting the constitution of these curves.

Though Marshall recognised more clearly than any of his academic predecessors the delicacy and intricacy of the choices and adjustments that went into the operations of the economic system through acts of production and consumption, he made no serious and continuous attempt to

[1] "The 'cost of production' principle and the 'final utility' principle are undoubtedly component parts of the all-ruling law of supply and demand: each may be compared to one blade of a pair of scissors. When one blade is held still, and the 'cutting' is effected by moving the other, we may say with careless brevity that the cutting is done by the second; but the statement is not one to be made formally, and defended deliberately."—Marshall, *Principles*, 4th edition, p. 569.

go behind these choices in order to convert them into terms of the human satisfaction which underlay them. Nowhere do we find in his work any attempt to express economic income in human welfare. Doubtless the sense that human well-being is the end of economic activities may be said to pervade his work. But it is never formulated.

§ It seemed as if this reconcilement of Economic Science with humanity was the definite task to be undertaken by Marshall's pupil and successor, Professor Pigou. The title of his work, *The Economics of Welfare*,[1] suggests that a full and formal examination of the contribution of economic art to human well-being will be made. In his opening chapter this purpose from time to time flickers before our eyes. Dr. Pigou clearly recognises that the subject matter of Economics (whether as a science or an art) is a part of welfare. Wealth, in other words, he regards not as a mere aggregate of concrete products, but as a body of satisfactions. He carried his subjectivity so far as to insist that " welfare includes states of consciousness only and not material things " (p. 10).

There are passages which might suggest that ' the states of consciousness ' are to be submitted to some objective test of ' the desirable ', in the sense of a contribution to ' the real good ' of a man or a society, and not in the sense that they are actually desired. But these are evidently unintended departures from his explicit declaration that his Economic Science is " a positive science of what is and tends to be, not a normative science of what ought to be " (p. 5). In a word, we are to deal with current satisfactions.

The subject matter of Economics being thus a part of welfare, we ask what part, and are told " that part of social welfare that can be brought directly or indirectly into relation with the measuring rod of money " (p. 11)—an

[1] Edition 1920.

ominous suggestion of a return to the position that money is the measure, not merely of value, taken in its market meaning, but of that part of human values contained in welfare. With Professor Cannan, who also shows coy hankerings after the humanisation of economics, he recognises that no sharp demarcation is possible between economic and non-economic satisfactions. " Nevertheless, though no precise boundary exists, yet the test of accessibility to a money measure serves well enough to set up a rough distinction. Economic welfare, as loosely defined by this test, is the subject matter of economic science" (p. 5). ' Rough distinctions ' and ' loose ' definitions are perhaps no very strong foundation for a scientific study which in its detailed superstructure aims at nicety of measurements. But it is undoubtedly true that the only possible demarcation for economic phenomena is to confine them to things that are bought and sold, and we may presume that it is the welfare related to such marketable things that Dr. Pigou proposes to investigate.

But, though we may seem to be able at any given time and place thus to distinguish concrete economic goods from non-economic goods, when we turn to examine them, as they meet and even join in the consciousness of which they are ' states of mind ', new difficulties crop up. If we are to correlate the part, economic welfare, with the whole, human welfare, we must at any rate keep the same meaning for the term ' welfare '. We had supposed that, as the ' ought ', or normative law, was to be excluded from economic welfare, it must also be excluded from human welfare, reduced *pro hac vice* to the currently desired.

But hardly is this established than we come (p. 12) to a discussion of the objection that " an economic cause may affect non-economic welfare in ways that conceal its effect on economic welfare ", illustrated by the damaging reactions which excessive industrialism may exercise upon the appreciation and cultivation of " the beautiful in Nature or in art " forming " an important element in the ethical value of the world ". Surely any such assessment of ethical value would seem to involve an introduction of the normative element just expressly excluded from the province of Economic Science.

In further discussion of the relations between economic and non-economic welfare, Dr. Pigou adduces two considerations, which, had he followed out their implications, would have led him far upon the road to a complete utilitarian calculus. That calculus requires, as we see, first, the recognition of satisfactions and dissatisfactions of production in their bearing upon economic and non-economic welfare ; secondly, the interaction between this set of satisfactions and dissatisfactions and the set on the consumption side of the equation. Economists had hitherto failed in two ways, first, by looking exclusively to the yield of satisfactions from the consumption (or further application to production) of the real income of the community ; secondly, by omitting to take account of the satisfactions of production (when they made their tentative analysis of human costs) or of the dissatisfactions of certain sorts and quantities of consumption.

Now Dr. Pigou seems in his opening analysis to recognise that the ways in which income is earned and spent have important reactions upon ' non-economic welfare '. On the production side " the surroundings of work react upon the quality of life. Ethical quality is affected by the occupations—menial service, agricultural labour, artistic creation, independent as against subordinate economic positions, monotonous repetition of the same operation, and so on—into which the desires of consumers impel the people who work to satisfy them " (p. 15).

" In the Indian village collaboration of the family members not only economises expenses but sweetens labour. Culture and refinement come early to the artisan through his work amidst his kith and kin."

Now while these indirect results of conditions of labour may be classed as 'non-economic', why should those conditions be so regarded which directly raise or lower the dissatisfaction, or human cost of production ?

Then again, Dr. Pigou affirms that " non-economic welfare is liable to be modified by the manner in which income is spent. Of different acts of consumption that yield equal satisfactions, one may exercise a debasing and another an elevating influence " (p. 17). Here once more he brings to bear upon non-economic welfare a normative standard, which really puts his whole calculus out of gear. Either one must accept provisionally current standards of ' the desired ', alike for economic and non-economic welfare, or frankly apply to both fields some normative science of human values. Dr. Pigou recognises formally a part of his difficulty, though he does not appreciate its magnitude. For he argues (p. 18), " These very real elements in welfare [i.e. ' ethically superior ' interests in literature and art, etc.] will, indeed, enter into relation with the measuring-rod of money and so be counted in economic welfare, in so far as one group of people devote income to purchasing things *for* other people. When they do this, they are likely to take account of the total effect, and not merely of the effect on the satisfactions of those people—especially if the said people are their own children ". In other words, here the ideally desirable is substituted for the actually desired. The importance of this distinction, fatal to Dr. Pigou's economic calculus, is seen when we remember that quite twenty-five per cent. of the current income of the country is spent by public authorities in this way. The State's attitude both to production and consumption it is impossible to correlate with the estimate of economic welfare on the basis of " a positive science of what is and tends to be, not a normative science of what ought to be ". The parent in spending money on his children, the philanthropist in doing good to others, and the State in its public expenditures, are manifestly concerned with ' what ought to be '.

It seems impossible to deal with a national income by excluding a normative science and sticking to the current standard of the desired. The cleavage between economic welfare estimated on the latter standard, and non-economic, or total, welfare estimated on the former, is wholly inadmissible. Either we must take actual current satisfactions and dissatisfactions for our standard, apply them to both sides of the economic question, and extend the same standard to non-economic welfare, or we must apply to the entire area of consideration some normative method based on ethics or biology. The attempt to reconcile these two standards must land us in intellectual chaos.

Dr. Pigou seems to have some inkling of his difficulty, for he admits that " any rigid inference from effects on economic welfare to effects on total welfare is out of the question ". He falls back, however, upon a presumption, " an unverified probability " that total welfare will probably vary with economic welfare in direction, though not in magnitude. This means that more wealth per head is presumed to carry more total satisfaction, irrespective of the methods of production or the distribution of its toil, upon the one hand, the nature of the wealth, its distribution and the uses or abuses of its consumption on the other hand. The presumption is, I think, open to grave doubt, at any rate until it is shown that with growing wealth there is some normal tendency towards lightening the day's work for the average worker, and towards more, not less equalisation, in the distribution of incomes.

§ I have laid stress upon the failure of English economists to interpret economic welfare with equal regard to the production and consumption processes. This oversight is, however, formally corrected by Dr. Pigou in his Chapter IV stating " The relation of economic welfare to the National Dividend ". There he lays down the doctrine that : " The quantity of economic welfare associated with any volume of the dividend depends, not only on the satisfaction yielded by consumption, but also on the dissatisfaction involved in production " (p. 43). One may complain of the assumption that no positive form of satisfaction involved in production is recognised, but the passage does appear to furnish a consistent standard for measuring economic welfare as he defines it. You would assess in economic welfare any stock of goods according to the total satisfaction it afforded in its consumption over the net dissatisfaction attending its production.

But having given this formal recognition to the part which disutility plays in economic welfare, Dr. Pigou proceeds to deal with the national dividend, as a concrete annual product, *exclusively with regard to the effects of its distribution, in the shape of income,* upon economic welfare. The differences in amount of economic welfare, attendant on various shifts in distribution of income, and the special problems of State or business machinery by which changes in distribution may be brought about, occupy almost the whole of his long treatise.

Nowhere is there any further recognition of the truth that the economic welfare of a man, or a class, or a nation, is dependent on, consists in and varies with, the conditions of the production of the national dividend, as much as upon its consumption.

Economic welfare is thus in fact confined to utilities or satisfactions of consumption. And these utilities are to be assessed in terms of current desirability. Dr. Pigou does not seek to go behind existing standards. For purposes of economic welfare a dollar's worth of dope equals a dollar's worth of food or other necessary of life, for " of different acts of consumption that yield equal satisfactions, one may exercise a debasing, and another an elevating influence ". Such bad consumption reacts apparently upon the quantity of welfare but not of economic welfare ! This is made abundantly clear on page 28 : "The first asserts that additions to work-people's wages do not really lead to economic welfare, but are merely dissipated in worthless forms of exciting pleasure. This objection is, indeed, obviously irrelevant, when economic welfare is defined as we have defined it ".

§ The strongest and most serviceable part of Dr. Pigou's analysis consists in showing with precision how economic welfare, connected with the consumption of any given body of resources, increases the more evenly this body of resources is distributed between them. It would seem to be an obvious corollary that economic welfare, connected with producing these same resources, increased the more evenly the human costs of producing them were distributed between the producers. But though, several times, in elaborating his argument, Dr. Pigou introduces parenthetically some consideration bearing upon economic welfare from the production side,[1] some tough barrier in his thinking prevents him from giving it its proper place as a factor in economic welfare. What this barrier is remains a mystery. Perhaps, however, light is thrown upon it by the curious treatment of ' costs ' which has crept into the Cambridge doctrine, formerly confined to the theory of foreign trade. The most naïve statement of this doctrine is thus presented by one of the ablest of the young Cambridge economists, Mr. H. D. Henderson.

[1] E.g. p. 343. In discussing the further operation of utilities he notes that as regards " the position of a public servant as it owns attraction in itself and also makes appeal to altruistic motives " there is created a new value " in the extra satisfaction which the said engineer or manufacturer derives from the fact of serving the public".

" The real costs which the prices of a commodity measure are not absolute but comparative.   Marginal money costs reduce themselves in the last analysis to the payments which must be made to secure the use of the requisite agents of production.   These payments *tend* to equal the payments which the same agents could have commanded in alternative employments.   The payments which they could have commanded in alternative employments tend in their turn to equal the derived marginal utilities of their services in those employments. It is thus the loss of *utility*, which arises from the fact that these agents of production are not available for alternative employments, that is measured by the money costs of a commodity at the margin of production." [1]

Ignoring the difficulty of understanding in what possible sense ' payments ' can tend to ' equal ' utilities, one wonders why it should seem even plausible that it is easier to compare respective ' losses of utility ' in other goods than costs or disutilities involved in producing the actual goods that are the objects of exchange.   The doctrine that the real cost of anything is the foregone utility of other things [2] perversely rules out all human considerations related to the supply side of exchange, by substituting an indirect and strictly irrelevant test for a direct and relevant one.   It reminds one of the famous definition of sugar as " the stuff which makes tea nasty when you don't put any in ".

§ This change-over in post-Jevonian theory from the producer point of view of the older classical political economy (where consumption had no valid place and no utility save as it was ' productive ', i.e. contributory to the end of promoting more production) to this modern stress upon the utility of consumption, as not only the practical end of the economic costs, but the first principle of economic theory, is often claimed as a great advance in humanism. Utility, as issuing from wealth, real income, is now in the

[1] *Supply and Demand*, pp. 164–5.
[2] " The real cost of *anything* is the curtailment of the supply of other useful things which the production of that particular thing involves."— *Supply and Demand*, p. 166.

saddle. Economists concern themselves more and more with the problems of increasing the output of concrete goods, and of enlarging their utility by better distribution. But the twist of mind which leads so many of them to hold that it is easier and more relevant to welfare to evaluate goods for purposes of exchange, or for inherent satisfactions, by confining attention to the utilities of consumption they embody, is the more amazing since their professed master, Dr. Marshall, performed his greatest single service to economic theory in his balanced interrelation of supply and demand prices and the equality of their importance in the determination of value.

Nor is this disparagement of the human interpretation of costs, and the disposition to transmute them into utilities, confined to British economists. Here is Professor Taussig declaring that, " In the last analysis, the income of an individual, or of a community, consists of a sum of utilities steadily accruing from its store of economic goods. It consists, that is, of the total utility of all its goods ".[1] So Professor Taussig, like Professor Pigou, appears to envisage economic welfare entirely in terms of concrete goods shedding utility in processes of consumption.

It is particularly strange that this one-sided theory should have attained such vogue, at a time when practical reformers in every industrial country devote so much attention to problems of lessening the human costs of production : by shortening hours of labour ; restricting the employment of younger and weaker workers and imposing intervals of rest or of alternative work ; lightening the muscular and nervous strains ; improving factory hygiene ; and otherwise trying to reduce the net human costs of production by what is significantly called ' welfare work '.

§ The failure of the post-Jevonian, or neo-classical econo-

[1] *Principles of Economics*, vol. i, p. 134.

mists of Britain and of the United States to humanise economic theory, in the sense of finding methods of expressing concrete economic goods and processes in terms of human welfare, is contained in four chief defects :

First, their failure to interpret the human welfare attaching to a concrete body of wealth (a real dividend) so as to include equally the utilities and disutilities of producing them and of consuming them, with due regard to the actual conditions of the producing and consuming processes.

Secondly, their failure to realise adequately the difficulties attending the processes of applying ' the measuring-rod of money ' to : (a) the varying satisfactions or dissatisfactions of different persons at the same time and the same persons at different times ; (b) the separate measurement of different kinds of satisfactions or dissatisfactions in a standard working day or a standard of consumption.

Thirdly, their failure to keep consistently to the professed assessment of economic welfare and the total welfare into which it enters, in terms of present desiredness.

Fourthly, their hesitant attitude in assessing, as elements of the National Dividend, Personal Incomes and Economic Welfare, the products of public services, such as health, education, insurance, art, recreation.

Some of these defects I have here sought briefly to expose. Others are best reserved for discussion in a more formal criticism of Marginalism.

§ Our immediate problem is to try to understand how it came about that the neo-classical school of British economists failed to develop the subjective treatment introduced by Jevons, so as to produce a consistently human theory of wealth. It was doubtless partly due to the force and vividness with which the objective structure and processes of the industrial system imposed themselves upon observers. This objective system of the business world with its productive processes and its markets absorbed so much attention that little was left for considering the consumptive processes, though the utility associated with them figured as the formal goal of economic activities. Consumption only figured indirectly through demand curves. More and more the neo-classical economics concerned itself with the determination and movement of prices within the limits of the business world. How strong the influence of this school has been is well illustrated in the recent work of the Swedish economist, Gustav Cassel, whose *Social Economy* resolves all economic problems into questions of *price* based on scarcity.

This concentration upon price movements and their causes and effects in terms of the business system has been due partly to the discovery of a fascinating field for abstract reasoning. It is not without significance that so many of the younger school of economists in England and America received their academic training in mathematics. For, as will presently appear, the notion that all qualitative differences can be resolved into quantitative may be regarded as the modern substitute for that economic man moving in the " simple system of natural liberty " by which vested interests defended themselves against dangerous assaults in the earlier era of modern capitalism. The mathematical mind, set to work upon supply and demand curves and the conditions which regulated them, rapidly constructed an abstract economic system operated by the movement of identical and infinitesimal units whose accurate adjustment produced a new ' economic harmony '. It was not necessary to assume a society composed of ' economic men ' with completely informed selfishness as their single motive. A series of minute adjustments at the margin of each supply and demand will do all that is required. This is provided chiefly by the intelligent application of new units of capital, labour, and other factors at the several points of vantage in the system, and by the gradual letting down of productive power at points where less is wanted. This unceasing movement of insensible increments on the producing and consuming sides tends both to put the technically right amount of the factors of production in each employment for the maximisation of the product, and to distribute that product in accordance with the separate productivity or economic worth of each factor of production. It is not contended that there are no obstacles to the accurate operation of this ' tendency '. But science, which can only deal with tendencies, may legitimately ignore such friction as is itself immeasurable !

§ The acceptance of this new method and instrument for economic service is due, however, not merely to the craving of scientific men for exactitude. Its immanent conservatism recommends it, not only to timid academic minds, but to the general body of the possessing classes who, though they may be quite incapable of following its subtleties of reasoning, have sufficient intelligence to value its general conclusions as popularised by the press.

Disconcerted by social and political ' attacks on property ' and by socialist propaganda, sometimes also by social compunctions relating to the unfair apportionment of this world's goods, they not unnaturally look with favour upon the line of defences which this new political economy provides.

Now for their purpose the main use of this new doctrine is that it serves to dispose of the charge against capitalists of exploiting labour. In England the best example of this treatment is given by Mr. Wicksteed, in a work which is at once the most complete and the most naïve exposition of Marginalism.

If the final unit of capital, labour, or any other factor in a business or an industry, gets just as much in value as it produces (and it cannot get more or less, for otherwise a larger and a smaller number of units would be employed), then there is no surplus over and above these necessary marginal payments. For since the marginal units are neither more nor less productive than other units, but only marginal in the sense that they represent the limit to the total number employed, all units are equally productive and equally remunerative. As Mr. Wicksteed puts it :

" We now see once for all that the Marginal distribution in our sense (that is to say, the distribution of the product amongst the claimants in proportion to the significance of the addition or withdrawal of a small increment at the margin determined by the present supply) exhausts the whole product."

Again :

" It is not open to anyone who understands the facts to argue that when, by a marginal distribution, every factor, reduced to the common term, has been satisfied, there remains any residue or surplus to be divided or appropriated. The vague and fervid visions of this unappropriated reserve, ruling upward as we recede from this marginal distribution, must be banished for ever to the limbo of ghostly fancies." [1]

Not only is there no unearned surplus to fight over among the owners of several factors of production, but substantial justice is done to every separate producer by paying him ' what he is worth '—that is, his market value on a fair and equal computation under existing economic conditions.

" If it is a fact that the most miserable earners of starvation wages are getting *all their work is worth*, the lamentable fact of the existence of a vast population worth so little must, when once recognised, force us to face the question how we can make them worth more." [2]

There are two main ways of ' making people worth more '.

" One is breeding, rearing, training and educating them from the beginning, so that they shall possess the vision, the habits, and the particular skill which are likely to make them worth most. . . . The other is to shift them to places and conditions in which they will be worth more than where they are."

[1] *The Commonsense of Political Economy*, pp. 572–3.
[2] *Idem*, p. 345. (Italics mine.—J. A. H.)

In a word, the only way of enabling the workers, collectively or individually, to get more is by increased productivity. Dr. J. B. Clark expounds in America the same simple doctrine of natural equity, showing how, along the lines of this marginal analysis, " the market rate of wages (or interest) gives to labour (or capital) the full product of labour (or capital) ". And not only to collective labour, but to the individual worker, for—" Each man accordingly is paid an amount which equals the total product that he personally creates ".[1] In what sense a man's product can equal his pay, and how a man's product can be measured, are questions rightly relegated to a closer study of the curious logic of Marginalism. Here we are mainly concerned to show how the emergence of this doctrine in Economic Science is accommodated to the requirements of the influential classes for the defence of their economic interests.

It supplies a complete substitute for the wage-fund-cum-Malthusianism of the older Classical Economics. For, if everybody gets for his labour, or any other factor of production, just what it is worth, and can only get more by making it more productive, since the payment to each of ' what he is worth ' exhausts the entire product, leaving no surplus over which to quarrel—why, we are living in the best of all possible economic worlds, and anyone who, by agitation and wilful misrepresentation, tries to incite envy or stir up discontent is as foolish as he is wicked. The charge of profiteering is meaningless, and combination can get nothing solid for the workers.

Leaving aside for the moment the question of the truth or falsity of this doctrine, consider how beautifully it fills the requirements of conservatism ! What a rebuke alike to the envy and class hatred of the workers, and what an exposure of the folly and futility of ca' canny ! What a sedative to the foolish compunction astir in the minds of many men of

[1] *Essentials*, p. 92.

great possessions when they survey the condition of the poorer classes! And all this got out of a refined application of Butler's famous tautology that

> " . . . . the value of a thing
> Is just as much as it will bring ",

equity being imported into the convincing proposition: " Every man gets what he can get ".

The earlier uses of margins, as we see, made for the disclosure of rents and quasi-rents, not only in the case of land, but in other factors of production, yielding a large composite body of surplus, unearned, unnecessary payments, capable of being diverted by appropriate action either into higher wages or public revenue, while the Jevonian calculus of subjective utilities visibly led towards a still more dangerous revelation of the inequality of apportionment of satisfaction in the processes of production and distribution. The effect of the later Marginalism has been to side-track both these inconvenient applications of theory, and to substitute one admirably adapted for the re-establishment of confidence in the natural equity and efficiency of the economic system as it stands.

This statement I propose to support by a closer account of the logic of the use of Margins.

CHAPTER III

MARGINALISM IN NEO-CLASSICAL ECONOMICS

§ In discussing the progress of Neo-Classical Economics in Britain, I have laid stress upon the increasing tendency to endeavour to convert Economics into a purely quantitative science. For the attainment of this object there are two chief prerequisites. The first is that the material measured shall be minutely divisible, its quantity growing or dwindling by infinitesimal units. This is the essential for the use of curves. The second is that all apparently qualitative differences shall be treated as capable of resolution into differences of quantity, by reference to some common standard. These two assumptions will be found to underlie that marginal calculus by which it is sought to secure for economics something of the authority of an exact science, as well as to render it a serviceable instrument for the defence of the existing economic system by displaying the economy and harmony of its normal working.

The marginal concept, as first employed by an extension of the Ricardian application in grading the productive qualities of the several factors of production, has a definite use. Just as in the utilisation of the available supply of land for wheat or any other agricultural purpose, there is some land which, at the price of the product ruling in the market, it is just worth while to employ (marginal land), so with the existing supply of concrete plant or other capital available in a given industry, where it varies in efficiency, some of it will be only just worth while employing at a given price level for the product. If that price level should fall, the marginal capital (like the marginal land) will pass out of use. Similarly with labour, where the available supply exceeds the normal demand, there will at any time be a marginal grade of workers just worth employing.

It is sometimes alleged that, regarded from the standpoint of payment, there is a difference between the marginal concept as applied to the several factors. Marginal land may yield no rent, marginal capital may yield no profit, but marginal labour must have a subsistence wage. But this distinction is invalid. If marginal land is to remain in cultivation, what is taken out of it in fertility must be replaced by rest, recuperation, and fertilizers : concrete capital, if it is to be kept in use, must have its wear-and-tear provision. These costs correspond strictly to the subsistence wage of labour.

There is nothing mysterious in this use of margins of occupation or employment to designate the portion of the supply of any factor of production which, by reason of its quality, position, or some expense of utilisation, is just worth using. This grading is a simple deduction from the fact that there can be only one price for the same article in the same market. It furnishes a convenient rule of thumb or observation-post for reckoning the rises and falls of prices, rents, profits, wages, in particular industries.

§ But when economists began to apply the concept of a margin intensively, as well as extensively, they began to get into difficulties. James Mill first popularised the conception of a farmer applying to a given piece of land ' dose ' after ' dose ' of capital and labour (either or both) until he reached a ' dose ' which added so little to the previous net product that it was only just worth while, i.e. the additional product, thus got, only just paid for the unit of capital and labour, leaving nothing over to remunerate the landowner. Now since no part of the produce of this marginal or most intensive cultivation can be regarded as rent, while the expense of raising this marginal product measures the price of the whole supply, it seems to follow that rent does not enter into, or form part of, the supply price. Dr. Marshall, showing that this argument is applicable not to agricultural produce only, required us to hold that " ground rent does not enter into the expense of manufacture ".[1]

The fallaciousness of this conclusion from the intensive use of the margin appears at once if we apply to *a fixed quantity* of capital or labour the same dosing method. Take a given factory, or store, and apply to it successive doses of labour in the shape of operatives or shop clerks, you will come in time to a marginal employee whose productive work adds to the previous total product no more than just suffices to pay his wages (or strictly speaking a ' minimum ' more). The goods which this marginal worker may be conceived as making, pay wages only, with only a nominal provision for profit to the employer. Since the conditions of this marginal unit of supply must be regarded as regulating the conditions of price for the whole supply, it would appear that profit cannot enter into the price of the manufactured product or the retail goods. The same result will evidently issue, if we take a farmer, or a business manager, representing a definite amount of organising and executive capacity, and apply to him increasing quantities of capital and labour, so that his energy is spread over a larger and larger area of productive activity. There will be a limit to the size and complexity of the operations he can best undertake. So there will be a marginal product which only just remunerates the last dose of the capital and labour and leaves him no appreciably larger reward for his ability than he would have got by refusing the last extension of his business. His wages of management appear by this reasoning to play no

[1] *Principles*, second edition, p. 462.

part in the price of the product of his business, for the marginal product can pay no more than the ' cost ' of the marginal capital and labour involved.

§ The palpable absurdity of this line of reasoning is due to a false application of the Law of Diminishing Returns, and arises from an improper treatment of one factor of production as fixed, while another is variable. But though some recent adherents of Marginalism admit this application to be illicit, they still cling to one of its implications, viz. the attribution of a separate productivity and a separate value to the marginal increment of a simple or a composite factor of production. Some of them also persist in attributing, if not a causally determinant, at any rate a regulative part to the marginal increment in the theory of prices.[1]

The whole trouble is due to a misunderstanding of, and an exaggerated appreciation of, the Law of Diminishing Returns. The Law of Diminishing Returns is not peculiar to agriculture, and does not depend upon the ' niggardliness of Nature '. It applies to every sort of business and industry. It simply means that in any line of industry there are efficient types of business which cannot be increased in size without damage. As regards the structure of whole industries, it implies that there is a tendency to throw all the business contributing to a market, e.g. the market in steel rails or cotton cloth or shoes, into forms best adapted to financial

[1] " There is a commercial principle which causes the first or marginal part of the supply to be strategic in its action on the value of the whole group. The value of the whole crop . . . *conforms* to that of the marginal bushel. If there are marginal labourers, in the sense in which there are marginal quantities of wheat, cotton, iron, etc., then the final or marginal men are likewise in a strategic position ; *for their products set the standards* of everyone's wages. . . . The last increment in the supply of any commodity *fixes* the general price of it."—Clark, *Distribution of Wealth* (1899) p. 90. " The specific productivity of labour fixes wages—that is the thesis to be supported in this volume " (*ibid.*, p. 47). " There is before us the picture of social labour co-operating with social capital. Both are governed by the law of diminishing returns and their earnings are *fixed* by the productivity of their final units " (*ibid.*, p. 373). Cf. Davenport, *Values and Distribution*, p. 470.

success. At any given time, having regard to selling prices, there will only be room for a particular number of such businesses (or plants) and they will all tend to be on a level of productivity and profit. If any more of these representative businesses pressed in (unless invited by some increase of demand in relation to available supply, raising prices) there would an oversupply at previous profitable prices and a diminishing return of profit to the trade.

The Law of Diminishing Returns simply means that in every business there is a type or types of maximum efficiency and productivity and profit, and that in any industry or market there is at any given time a limit to the number of such contributing businesses. So far as this law has meaning and validity it is equally applicable to all departments of industry. It is, indeed, an obvious deduction from the very concept ' Economy '.

Every department of production alike is subject to this economy. The so-called Law of Increasing Returns, supposed to be applicable to most departments other than agriculture, is based on a misapprehension of the economies of large-scale production. The power of a growing business to reduce its costs of production is only operative up to a certain limit. That limit reached, any further extension would bring an increased cost from diminishing efficiency of management. There may be businesses whose total available market is not yet large enough to evoke their full economy of large-scale production, and which, in consequence, appear to be conformable to a law of increasing returns. Some modern trusts or combines may achieve such continuous economies in production that, even after establishing a virtual monopoly, they have not fully exhausted the net economy of large-scale production, and still continue to be able to produce more cheaply as their monopolised market expands. But this only means that the limit which would launch such a big business on to an economy of diminishing returns has not yet been reached. It does not mean that there exist either businesses or industries free from this limit.

§ This explanation of the so-called Law of Diminishing Returns should suffice to gain admission for my central thesis, that the existence in every branch of production of a type or types of business with maximum efficiency negatives the conception of marginal factors of production less productive than non-marginal factors determining, or even regulating, by their separate productivity, the supply-price for a market. Supply prices are directly regulated by, and measure, the normal average cost of production for a unit of supply in a representative business. Reduced supply prices are due to some improved technique or organisation, or access to cheaper materials or labour, for such representative businesses operating in free competition through enlargement of supply.

How have economists been led to regard this separatist treatment of the marginal factor and product as intellectually satisfactory ? They appear to visualise an entrepreneur who plans a business balancing the advantages of putting in labour-saving machines, or employing more hand-workers, and hesitating whether to employ so many male workers in a department or so many more female workers. They see an employer deciding after some experience that it is worth while increasing his staff in some department by so many men or reducing the staff in another, though the size of his market remains the same. But this only means that an entrepreneur has not firm knowledge of all relevant facts and so feels liable to error, or that he actually commits errors and corrects them. But neither Marginalism or any other principle can rest upon the assumption either that an entrepreneur doesn't know the proper plan of the business he is laying out, in his own mind, or that his correction of a miscalculation he has made by adding another machine or another worker can play any determinant part in the regulation of output or supply price.

Given an entrepreneur with complete understanding of his problem, he will apportion his available resources in the purchase of so many plots of land, so many workshops or office buildings, so much equipment of various sorts, so much money for purchase of materials and for wages and salaries. All these quantities will be definite and involve an accurate apportionment of his total capital resources to different purposes. Taking all together, he may consider that a capital of £150,000 is just what he requires. But this way of looking at it gives no significance or serviceable determination to the last £1,000, or to the last, or any other, unit of productive power in the different departments.

§ The recent extension of Marginalism treats 'doses' as infinitesimal quantities, applies them to the demand as well as to the supply side of the economic equation represented in a market or a normal price, and to all economic activities and saleable articles. Economic life is thus reduced on its objective side to a number of infinitesimal activities and transfers of matter, on its subjective side to a number of infinitesimal acts of choice, both registered in the monetary medium.

Money being a single absolute standard of values and infinitely divisible and fluid, the concrete economic objects that it handles, measures and moves have a similar character imputed to them. This is the great bluff which the mathematical economists have put up. They have transferred to the organised industrial system the qualities of identical nature, infinite divisibility and absolute fluidity that belong to money. In other words, they have taken the abstract or book-keeping aspect of economics and applied it to concrete economics. Now concrete economics deals on its objective side with matter and physical activities, on its subjective side with feelings and valuations that are different in quality or kind. To neither side is it rightly applicable. For these objective and subjective factors are finitely, not infinitely, divisible, and of slow and difficult mobility. In a word, the treatment of economics by the calculus of the infinitesimal is a wholly unjustifiable abstraction from the material of the study. Science, of course, must always proceed by abstraction, i.e. by ignoring not merely individual characters but such general characters also as are not relevant to the nature of its generalisations. So mathematics applied to astronomy ignores the chemical composition and all other characters of heavenly bodies other than the movements with which it is concerned. Mathematics applied to economic phenomena may similarly ignore the special characters of particular industries or standards of consumption in stating laws of supply and demand. But it cannot properly abstract from, or ignore, characters which belong to that very economic nature which is professedly the object of study. Yet this is what it does when it treats economic facts and forces as infinitely divisible, absolutely mobile and capable of being reduced to a single kind by resolving qualitative differences into quantitative. It is not the abnormal or the irrelevant which it thus abstracts from, but the normal and the relevant.

Ruskin was right in charging the economists of his day in their treatment of the economic man with a folly analogous to that of a physiologist who should treat the human body as if it had no skeleton. Our modern Marginalists commit a similar mistake in affecting to treat economic material in general as being quite other than it actually is.

Let us take first the infinite divisibility of economic quantities, whether goods or factors of production, involved in the application of marginal increments to industrial movements. Continuous supply curves are based on the accumulation of such infinitesimal increments, effected by minute rises or falls of price operating on the agents of production. Now no concrete goods are infinitesimal in size. Even water is for purposes of supply composed of sizable drops. The earlier ' doses ' employed by economists were of appreciable size. Even the ' marginal ' shepherd of Marshall's theory, just worth his keep in the extra sheep he saved, was a whole human unit of labour.

But in dealing with supply-curves representing the units of supply, the true unit is the representative business. Differing in form and size in each industry, there always exist one or more types of up-to-date, properly planned and equipped plants, whether they be factories, workshops, stores, mines, or farms, which, because of their efficiency, tend to survive and to occupy the whole industry and market for the goods they produce. If increased demand for any of these classes of goods by raising prices stimulates increased supply, that increase proceeds, not by insensible and infinitesimal increments, but by whole representative plants. If an addition to supply is made in the cotton industry, it takes shape in a new up-to-date mill. That is the minimum unit. If more steel rails are wanted, a whole expensive plant must be installed. In any highly organised industry this happens. The limit of supply, or ' dose ', if the term be preferred, is a whole new business involving a considerable amount of capital and labour. An infinitesimal, or very minute, rise of supply prices will have no effect in bringing about this enlargement of supply. The rise of supply price must attain a certain size and security before it can bring in a new representative plant. Merely momentary or casual movements of prices may, of course, be met by speeding-up, or overtime, or other fuller use of existing factors of production. But even these increments in an organised industry are not ' infinitesimals ', but of considerable sizes. All increments or decrements of hours, or wages, or other conditions affecting costs of production, output supply prices, are of sensible size. When the Millers' Association decides that too much flour is being produced in this country, it decides to close down so many mills, recognising the mill as the unit of supply.

The representative mill is the unit of production, its full output is the unit of supply, its cost of production the regulator of supply price. The whole trade tends to be concentrated in mills of this type, though at any moment there may survive a few obsolescent or ill-managed mills carrying on a precarious existence and doomed to early extinction, just as there may be one or two super-mills with some special advantage of a secret process or some other pull.

§ The actual material of economics on its supply or productive side is thus seen to consist not of infinitesimal but of definitely sized quantities, organised units of production. But the same is true of the demand, or consumptive, side. At first sight this is not obvious. Consumption consists, it may be urged, of innumerable little single acts of purchase for use by individuals. Infinitesimal or minute changes in market price might seem to exert similar minute changes in quantity purchased by consumers. Though elasticity of demand will be different in different markets, curves can, it is urged, legitimately be drawn expressing by infinitesimal changes the effect of price-changes upon volume of demand.

But, just as on the supply side this theory ignores (or abstracts from) the organic structure of a business, the unit of production, so, on the demand side, it ignores (or abstracts from) the standard of consumption. For, just as it is the composite structure of the representative plant that determines how many machines or workers in the different processes shall be employed, so it is the standard of living in a representative family, or group, that determines how many units of this or that article of consumption shall be demanded. Though there will be wider variations in families and their standards than in businesses, the procedure of ignoring the complex nature of these standards of consumption is equally invalid. Infinitesimal rises and falls of market price are not reflected in demand and consumption until they have accumulated into sensible magnitudes. Otherwise expressed, changes in demand take place by increments of considerable size, according as some effect is produced by a price change upon the standard of a class.

A class standard of living is an organic complex, involving the purchase for consumption of a large variety of articles of kinds and quantities determined in part by real or supposed physiological needs or satisfactions, in part by habit, or tradition, or fashion. Everywhere some slight element of individual taste or need will be superimposed upon, or will vary, the standard. But the proportion of expenditure expressing the class-standard in most family incomes is very large.

But even the variations from a class-standard consist of sensible increments, not affected by insensible price changes. Most changes in personal consumption are not continuous and minute but sudden and considerable. When taxation on tobacco and liquors causes individual consumers to give up cigars and take to pipes, to substitute beer for whisky, or to give up the consumption of one or both, these are changes of considerable magnitude, affecting, by imitation or common consent, whole groups of consumers and exercising a large mutation of demand.

I use the term 'mutation' deliberately because of its connection with the theory of development in organisms. For one of the main charges against the application of the infinitesimal calculus to economics is that it treats organic material as if it were inorganic. Or, if the term 'organic' be questioned, in its applicability to a business or a standard of living, the term organised, expressing the active will of organic beings, supports the same charge. Changes in organisation are not accomplished by insensible but by sensible increments.

Moreover, alike in business and standards of living, the changes that take place are determined, not at the margins of production or consumption, but at the centres, and affect the whole composition of the bodies. When a business changes by taking in some new machine or process, this mutation is sudden, and reacts in countless ways upon the various other material and human agents. Similarly with a standard of consumption, when any new article of consumption enters or is removed, the change involves a new composition of the standard. Prohibition in America, so far as effectual, has changed the whole distribution of the family income, involving, not merely an expanded use of sugar, but an increased demand for Ford cars, with innumerable other economic and vital alterations.

§ It is the neglect of the organic nature of business and standards of living that leads some economists to think that not only definite size can be abstracted from, but qualitative differences. Money, as the measure of all economic things, can substitute quantitative for qualitative value. Different kinds of costs and utilities can be brought to a common measure at their margins !

The treatment runs as follows: Whenever you buy anything, you may either set your mind on the utility or satisfaction attaching to the thing you buy, or on the cost of doing without the other thing you would have bought if you hadn't bought this instead. Since what everyone is really after is some sort of satisfaction, it is best provisionally to take the view that every purchase expresses a preference for a particular kind of utility over other kinds. This is evidently true both of a producer buying factors of production in his business or of a consumer buying consumable goods for his family's livelihood.

Now if a business man's accounts show that in any given year or week he spends a number of different sums of money upon the purchase of raw materials for his works, coal, rent for his premises, wages for manual and clerical labour, it must be admitted that the last pound he pays for any one of these things purchases the same amount of productive service or utility as the last pound spent on any other. If he is found spending £60 a week on manual wages, £8 on clerical wages, the sixtieth pound in the former must be considered to buy the same amount of utility as the eighth pound in the latter. This follows from the warranted assumption that our business man is an economist and knows what he is doing. The fact that he has apportioned his expenditure in this way seems to carry an implication that he has carefully and separately balanced the services of the office boy he has included in his clerical expenses with the services of another young machine tender he might otherwise have got for the same money or with the extra ton of coal he might have laid in, in anticipation of an early rise of coal prices.

Now these several productive utilities, though quite different in kind, are supposed to be referred to some common standard of utility in the mind of our business man. The earlier units in each set of expenditures are taken for granted as belonging to the accepted routine. But the final units are matters of delicate balance and selection between different advantages. It may not be easy to envisage psychologically how the relative advantages of smoother office work, increased output, and provision against a future coal-shortage can be brought to a common denominator in the mind of our business man. But the action taken seems to imply that this miracle has been performed, differences in kind being reduced to differences in quantity of some common good.

Still more interesting is the application of this principle to the consumer. The housewife who spends three-and-sixpence in buying seven pounds of sugar, instead of spending three shillings for six pounds and putting the odd sixpence into a fund she is accumulating to buy a pair of boots, has compared two marginal uses of this sixpence and decided in favour of the seventh pound of sugar. The whole of her expenditure of the family income involves, it is urged, a number of these delicate marginal choices of alternatives which appear to differ in the kinds of utilities they procure. Or, if these utilities seem not widely different in kind, take the case, cited by Mr. Wicksteed, where a man decides to spend a loose pound, in six shillings on a dinner, four shillings on a concert ticket, ten shillings on a contribution to a missionary society, when he might have distributed the same on these same objects in some different proportion. Has he not succeeded in performing the feat of comparing the various sorts of satisfaction which good feeding, music, and moral satisfaction would procure by reducing these diverse goods to some common subjective standard ? Has he not decided that the tenth shilling given to missionary enterprise just yields more satisfaction than another course at dinner or a slightly better place in the theatre ?

§ Now it would be foolish to deny that there are circumstances under which these delicate adjustments at margins of expenditure, apparently involving comparisons of different sorts of units of satisfaction or utility, take place. What are these circumstances ? They arise when some alteration in a standard of production, or of life, is required.

Taking the case of a representative business, I have shown that, since the quantity of each factor of production is pre-determined by the unity of the business plan, no significance can be attached to the final units of each factor. The mind of the entrepreneur does not concern itself with comparing the final units of expenditure upon each factor to see that they yield the same productive utility.

Now the same holds of a consumer laying out a regular family income on an accepted standard of living. The housewife, with her £4 to spend upon the maintenance of her family, proceeds on the lines of an accepted budget, which expresses, not a number of separately measured items, but a certain unity or harmony of needs or requirements. Each of the items has a definite quantity or limit, but that quantity is determined by the general plan of family well-being conceived by the housewife with sufficient clearness of consciousness to guide her actions.

She lays out the regular family income on the same principle as the entrepreneur lays out his capital in running a representative business, so much on this item, so much on that, the ' so much ' in each case derived from the consideration of the composite standard.

Now if standards of business and of living were absolutely static, in respect to goods, services, and prices, this explanation would suffice. But, of course, they are not. Neither for the business man nor for the housewife is this week an exact replica of last. Some change, however small, in the income available for expenditure may take place, some changes in the prices of goods and services are always happening, and some changes in the nature of the family needs. Now when such changes are reasonably predictable, they can be provided for in the plan or standard of a business or a family maintenance, and can thus be incorporated in the standard. A reserve or insurance fund will often provide for such changes. But when they are not, when some unforeseen business incident, or change in income, requires some deviation from the accepted standard of expenditure, the procedure inevitably concentrates upon marginal alterations. The standard remaining substantially the same, no attention need be paid to most of the units in

its several factors.   But when the required reform involves
a number of small but disproportionate reductions in the
size of several factors, in order perhaps to incorporate some
new factor, the paring process must be closely watched and
the shifting carefully measured.

If our business man is called upon to add some new
process, involving an economy of current expenses or of
factory space, the detailed adjustments he makes will
involve taking just so much from this and from that in
order to find just so much of the new accommodation.   If
he is not quite certain of his ground, he may proceed by
trial and error, making a series of little adjustments ' at the
margin ' until he settles down to the new economy.   But,
all the same, this new economy, the exact ' how much ' for
each item of expenditure, is regulated by the organic character of the business as a whole, not by the changes at the
margin.   These changes are consequential in their nature
and size upon the new economy of the business as a whole.

Just the same with the housewife who is called upon to
economise in other items of her budget in order to make
special provision for a sick member of the family.   This
sudden obligation to extemporise a new standard of living
compels her to examine closely the parts played by her
former purchases in the old standard, so as to see how much
she can transfer from each of the old factors to make provision for the new.   Now, that she must pare off just so
much from this, just so much more or less from other factors,
perhaps leaving some untouched, is obvious.   But how far
must we visualise her making marginal comparisons of
different kinds of utility or satisfaction, in order to get the
new standard ?   Her new standard will involve buying a
pound less butter, suspending the weekly shilling towards
new boots, knocking off a joint of meat, and reducing by
ninepence the family expenditure on ' the pictures '.   She
has thought out, or more properly she has felt, what the new

standard involves and this is what it comes to. But in what sense has she made the set of separate comparisons of marginal utilities which this scientific analysis of her conduct implies ?

Is there any way in which she can be conceived as balancing the utility of another half-pound of butter against ninepence of ' the pictures ' and just deciding against the latter ? I think it is a psychological error to represent her as doing this. The error consists in reading a psychological act which does not take place into an objective act that does. Undoubtedly she thinks, " How much does the new emergency require me to knock off this item, and how off that, in order to provide for an estimated new expense ? " But she doesn't perform the impossible task of comparing marginal values of two different kinds of satisfactions. The emergency has put into her mind a new standard of living with changed valuations for the old items, regarded *en bloc*. These changes of valuations *carry with them* reductions of purchases of different sizes and properties. The mathematical treatment, imputing a number of separate acts of measurement and a reduction of different kinds of feeling to some common term, misrepresents the nature of a personal act of judgment and a personal economy.

§ A person adjusting the use of his resources to the demands of a new situation makes a number of delicate adjustments at the margins. But the determinate judgments, of which these delicate adjustments are expressions, are made, not at the margins, but at the centre. They are the quantitative implications of the new organic plan he has applied. If we regard him as a creative artist working out a new ideal with the materials at his disposal, we shall get nearer to the true psychological interpretation. A painter in mixing colours to get some particular effect must exercise care to obtain the exactly right proportions. This care will be greatest when in mixing he comes near the limit, and is in danger of putting too much or too little of the several colours into his mixture. A marginal economist, observing him, might pronounce the judgment that he kept adding increments of the different colours until he stopped, and that therefore an exactly equal art value must be attached to the last increment of each colour. For if the last brushful of turkey red had been found to have less value than the last brushful of green, another would be added, so as to even out the values of the different colours at the margin.

Now this, of course, simply means that in every sort of composite plan, economy or harmony, involving the use of different materials, some exact amount of each material, is required. In forming such a plan no special thought is directed to the marginal unit of each factor. But in carrying out a change of an existing plan, the process of shifting pieces from the old plan to the new involves a series of operations at the margins. The size of these operations is, however, determined and laid down in the conception of the scheme as a unity. The painter, not knowing exactly how much of each colour is required to produce his effect, may try a little too much of this or too little of that, rub out, and begin again until he has it just right.

But the idea of imputing any special value to the marginal units, or of regarding the artist as comparing the colours at each margin by some common standard of art value, is alien from the psychology of art. As soon as it is clearly compre-hended that the business man, the consumer, and every man pursuing a line of policy or conduct, is acting as an artist, the invalidity of Marginalism will be equally apparent in their cases.

In any line of conduct where quantities of different factors are involved, the plan of conduct involves in its execution exact manipulation of these quantities. But there is no meaning in assigning to the final units of the different factors

9

the same value, or, indeed, any separate value. Such separatism or atomism is the repudiation of creative action and the organic unity which it expresses.

Summarising, we may say that when a statical condition of a business or an industry, a family or a class standard of living, is the subject of inquiry, the separate cost or utility of the marginal unit, were it ascertainable, would have no significance. The exact quantity (and therefore the margin) in each case is determined, in the causal sense, by the organic make-up of the business industry, or standard of living, as a whole.

Where a new standard is in course of formation, the operation involves a number of quantitative changes in the factors of the old standard which occasion a rise or fall of the margins. There may be a practical utility in watching and measuring these marginal changes which register the differences between the old standard and the new. The acts of composition and substitution, of which economic conduct so largely consists, demand many of these marginal adjustments.

CHAPTER IV

THE ECONOMICS OF HUMAN WELFARE

§ So far we have been dealing with objective standards of production and consumption and their monetary indices. But any treatment of economics, as an art, or science, of human welfare, involves the translation of the fund of objective wealth, its factors of production and of consumption, into terms of human or subjective utility and cost.

The product of a business, or an industry, will, it appears, vary in the amount of economic welfare it contains, according as the total cost or disutility of producing and the utility of consuming it are high or low. The amounts on both sides of the equation will evidently vary with the distribution of the productive cost and the consumptive utility. The maximum wealth, or welfare, attaching to a stock of goods will involve such a distribution of the productive energy as will yield the minimum of painful or injurious effort on the one hand, and such a distribution of the consumptive utility as will yield the maximum of pleasurable or serviceable consumption. The true principle of ' economy ' is thus expressed in the maxim " From each according to his powers, to each according to his needs," for this would assign the lowest aggregate cost and the highest aggregate utility to any product. The art of political economy should evidently be directed to the contrivance of methods for the fullest possible application of this principle. But when we come to subjective costs and utilities, satisfactions, and dissatisfactions, how far is it possible to aggregate them by additions, or by setting off one against another ? And in such a process, so far as it is possible, what part is played by margins or surpluses ?

In this problem of envisaging a body of objective wealth in terms of subjective wealth, or welfare, it is impossible to give a separate treatment to the cost of production and utility of consumption. For the amount of ' satisfaction ' which such a body of wealth represents must take both into simultaneous consideration. Both the individual and the group, or society, must be treated from a producer-consumer standpoint. You cannot, even theoretically, consider the amount of disutility, or painful cost, which goes into producing a body of goods, separately from the consideration of the amount of utility, or satisfaction, it yields in its consumption. For these two considerations evidently interact. Conditions of production, in respect of hours of labour, nature of work, etc., must react upon conditions of consumption, i.e. capacity for utilising or enjoying objective wealth. Conversely, conditions of consumption, e.g. amount of leisure, skill in utilisation of commodities, will, by reacting on efficiency, make a given working day easier or more difficult. This will be true even as regards the translation of a given concrete body of goods into human welfare. It will, however, be much more important if the concrete body of goods is not given, but depends for its composition upon the needs and desires of the producer-consumer group.

Here we come to the proper setting of the problem of economic welfare. How to utilise the human and material resources of the group for the best satisfaction of their wants ? That satisfaction must have equal regard to the most serviceable and least injurious employment of human activities in production and in consumption. It must not take activities of production as mere means to consumption, even if there be a general presumption in favour of diminishing the total activities of production and increasing those of consumption.

Welfare may be taken to reside as much in the instinctive and trained activities of a man for constructive work as in the application of the product or concrete result of these activities to some human use or consumption after its production is ended. In the realm of economic goods the kind of production termed ' art ' is the chief example of the close relation between the producing and consuming sides. It also serves to disabuse our minds of the assumption that a stock of goods must represent some net cost, or disutility, in its production. This is evidently untrue of work which is, upon the whole, interesting, pleasurable, and not too exacting in the terms of its performance. The central problem of economics may thus be conceived as " How to get as much work as possible to yield a net balance of utility or satisfaction in its performance, consistently with an equal regard to the utility or satisfaction obtainable from the products after they are produced ". The trouble is that a large proportion of the work required to satisfy primary physical needs appears to be such as must involve some net cost of disutility or disagreeability to the producers, only to be made up to them in their consumer capacity.

§ We are, however, concerned here not with proposals for the establishment of an ideal economic society, but with the narrower question how far a mathematical calculus is applicable to the problem. And here, I think, psychology must have a decisive word to say.

We have already seen that an individual possesses, in some general unified conception of his personal good, a power of valuing the rival claims of different sorts of satisfaction or dissatisfaction. Crusoe's economy would clearly be directed by some such general conception of his producer-consumer personality. His distribution of his time and energy among various activities of production would follow the lines of his thought, or feeling, in relation to the interest, arduousness, disagreeability, or risk, of the different sorts of work, with due and simultaneous regard to the importance or satisfaction of the uses of the product of each sort of work. He would give just so much time and effort to producing just so much utility of consumption of different sorts. It is thus possible to conceive the last minute Crusoe gives to cutting down a tree as having the same cost as the last minute given to roofing a shed, or digging a bit of land. But this marginal equivalence has no real significance. It simply follows from Crusoe's total conception of his plan of life, including the utility of consuming the product of his last unit of labour together with the irksomeness of producing it. Nor would this quantitative analysis yield a separate producer's surplus for one particular kind of work, or even for his work-day as a whole. It is true that if he decided to dig his field for just two hours, by breaking up this time into a series of five-minute units we can discover a curving surplus of producer's gain, growing in size towards the first unit.[1] But since in the subjective valuation of his digging he included the utility of the various units of consumption with the disutility of the various units of production, his margin of digging and the producer's surplus would be affected by the marginal consumption of the food produced and the consumer's surplus. In other words, he is after the largest producer-consumer's surplus, and the margins on each side of the equation are determined by this whole plan of work and living.

§ Now this economy of his is dependent on and derives from his organic unity or harmony. Can we impute a similar economy to a society or group of producer-consumers? Were it possible for a completely socialist society to operate successfully, such an economy might seem attainable. It

[1] Not, however, an even curve, as industrial psychologists now show, for the first five minutes is more disagreeable than the second.

would, however, involve an abandonment of the strictly subjective or personal valuation in a Crusoe economy and the substitution of a social valuation which would be more abstract in the sense of disregarding the closely individual feelings that enter into work and enjoyment. Having to decide how much productive energy of different sorts, and operating under various conditions, should be put into producing variously sized stocks of goods for the immediate and postponed satisfaction of many different wants, it would have begun with substantially the same problem as Crusoe. But not having the same closely unified personality to test the various claims and choices, it could not solve it as effectively. It could not add together the subjective values of its different members, for such a psychological performance is impossible. There is, strictly speaking, no standard for comparing A's pain or pleasure, in his first hour of work, or his day's work, with that of B, and the same applies to their respective satisfactions in consuming any given good.

All that the socialist society could do would be to erect standard economic men and women, by arranging the indications of the subjective valuations as objectively expressed in measured curves of supply and demand. They would have to ignore all deviations from these standards, or at least to make certain allowances which would, in their turn, be standardised averages. This criticism is no reflection upon socialist experiments, which are based upon assumptions about common needs and common human nature.

But such a socialist society would have to ignore certain important qualitative facts which should rightly play an important part in determining any aggregate of economic welfare. For instance, the obligation it would impose on all alike to perform a certain minimum of routine service for society would involve very little, if any, subjective cost on persons who enjoy, or do not mind, such work, while it would involve a heavy, sometimes almost intolerable, cost on others. Equality of sacrifice, in other words, involving impossible subjective estimates, could not be even approximately secured. Nor could a socialist society, apportioning the product according to some objective standards of need, allow for the wide differences in capacity of enjoyment or utilisation in persons possessing different tastes or trainings.

Nor could these defects in the subjective producer-consumer economy be remedied adequately by the statistics of a price-system. For though it might be held desirable for a socialist state to regulate the rates of production and consumption of different goods by adjustments of wages for labour and of commodity prices,[1] this would by no means secure the ideal distribution favourable to the maximisation of welfare. For the inequalities of income it would involve would have no determinate relations to consumers' needs or utilities. Or conversely, changes in consumption, thus occasioned, which involved some large increase of heavy routine labour in production, might involve a net loss of producer-consumer welfare, the total real income representing a rise in subjective costs that exceeded the rise in subjective utility or satisfaction from the alteration in the standard of consumption.

§ In other words, a socialist state, not having the organic sense or consciousness of a Crusoe, cannot be capable of making those delicate references to a standard of personal values which are possible for the individual producer-consumer.

Can a competitive society of producer-consumers fare better ? By delicate discrimination and choice, free owners

---

[1] An exceedingly able account of a collectivist community conducted on these lines is presented in *Collectivist Economics* (Routledge), by Mr. J. Haldane Smith.

of labour and capital may apply their factor to such productive activities as will yield them the largest net advantage. The owner of labour will weigh producer costs against consumer utilities ; the owner of capital will weigh present consumers' goods against future. Such is the hypothetical procedure. But is there anything in it to guarantee, even approximately, a maximisation of economic welfare as expressed indifferently in productive and consumptive costs and utilities ? Professor Pigou, as we have seen, confining his analysis of economic welfare to the consumer side, does not furnish any answer to this question. His elaborate application of Marginalism gives a general endorsement of the view that under free competition the product will be maximised, and that the natural distribution of it cannot, even in the interests of the poorer classes, be advantageously interfered with. 'Artificial' interference with distribution may, indeed, be effective in increasing the ' welfare ' attached to the product, so far as ' monopoly ' conditions attach to an industry, or where an increase in the workers shows results in increased working efficiency, and in one or two other exceptional cases. But

" generally speaking, a transference of resources from the relatively rich to the relatively poor, brought about by interference with the natural course of wages at any point, is unlikely to do otherwise than injure the national dividend, and therewith, in the end, the real income of the relatively poor ".[1]

The relevant and important fact, that in most normal processes of bargaining, the inequality of power between the relatively rich and the relatively poor (apart from any definite monopoly) gives to the former a share of the product which is excessive, in the sense that it furnishes no necessary incentive to productive activity, is excluded from Dr. Pigou's analysis. This exclusion, which follows inevitably from the application of Marginalism, precludes economic

[1] *Wealth and Welfare*, Part III, ch. viii, s. 2.

policy from all effective steps to a better distribution of the product. For, though Dr. Pigou admits at the outset of his analysis that there are sound grounds for holding that "other things being equal" an approximate equalisation of increase would enlarge the 'welfare' attaching to the national dividend,[1] his method of procedure rules out all possibility of accomplishing such equalisation, except by steps which, in his opinion, so reduce the dividend that even the poorer classes will be worse off than before. Although this depressing judgment is qualified by an admission that some artificial interference with natural laws of distribution, so as to secure the poor against 'extreme want', is justified, that very qualification contains an implicit recognition of the futility of the whole procedure regarded as a mode for correlating economic wealth with economic welfare. For here the collapse of the quantitative analysis appears in the admission that "the good of abolishing extreme want is *not commeasurable* with any evils that may follow from the diminution of the dividend".[2] When Dr. Pigou goes somewhat farther, as he does, in endorsing the economic feasibility of a higher minimum in a relatively rich country,[3] one feels that he is imperilling the delicate and fragile structure of his calculus in favour of some humanitarianism that is grit in the mathematical machine.

§ But, reverting to our main topic, this able application of Marginalism to the correlation of wealth and welfare fails altogether to deal with the subjective problem.

It fails in the first place, as I have already noted, because it takes no direct account of the 'welfare' represented in the different modes and distributions of the utilities and costs of producing the national dividend. This is an error of primary importance. For, by a separatist treatment of the distribution of the dividend, Dr. Pigou fails to present the

[1] *Wealth and Welfare*, p. 66.   [2] *Ibid.*, p. 395.   [3] *Ibid.*, p. 397.

problem of economic welfare in its true organic unity as the collective efforts of the human instincts and desires to obtain satisfaction in an economic system. All the changes in the distribution of the dividend, which he discusses, must have reactions, through changes in the nature of consumption and demand, upon the productive activities, and so upon the net human ' costs ' involved in the dividend. Consideration of the interactions between the distribution and qualities of production of the dividend and the distribution and qualities of its consumption is essential to any fruitful correlation of wealth and welfare.

But, apart from this central flaw, Pigou's application of Marginalism to distribution of the product suffers from the general defects we have already noted. Marginalism by its *modus operandi* negates surplus income by assuming perfect terms of divisibility, mobility, and opportunity for all new factors of production. Though Pigou and some other Marginalists introduce qualifications afterwards, by admission of monopoly powers or imperfection of mobility, these admissions go no farther than allowances for frictions in an otherwise perfectly working mechanism.

For furnishing a calculus of economic welfare, comparable to the process by which a Crusoe regulates his economic life, Marginalism, representing a large number of separate acts of choice made by separate persons, is inherently incapacitated. The predetermined harmony by which these seemingly unrelated acts are wrought into a unity of social well-being does not exist. It is simply assumed by excluding every element of economic truth that conflicts with it. This is not a legitimate process of abstraction rightly employed by science for its generalising work It is an illegitimate attempt to rule out the qualitative differences related to different human personalities, by pretending to resolve them into quantitative differences.

The admission, frequently made, that there are some parts

of consumption, i.e. those of vital necessaries, which are infinite or immeasurable in utility, accompanied, as should be the case, by a similar admission that some ' costs ' are likewise infinite and immeasurable, should have put economists upon their guard. For just as there is no way of measuring necessaries against unnecessaries (for " all that a man hath will he give for his life "), so there is no legitimate way of measuring in subjective terms of human good higher kinds of work and higher kinds of satisfaction against lower. The methods by which they *appear* to be measured, i.e. market prices, do not really measure them. What they do is to extract an average economic man and measure them in him, treating him as a Crusoe for this purpose. Now this process of abstraction or generalisation seems to enable them to give a social human value to a national dividend, according to its quantitative distribution. But it ultimately rests on an assumption that, when two persons give the same sum of money for the same amount of a commodity, they are getting the same subjective utility, or human gain, out of the bargain. Now this assumption will not bear scrutiny. The equal price does not warrant this identity of gain. A rich man pays sixpence for a loaf of bread. So does a poor man. But by admission there is no commensurability between the utility or welfare conveyed in the one case and in the other. The false assumption is a double one. It assumes first equality of income or purchasing power ; secondly, identity of personal needs and valuations. It is the latter false assumption that invalidates all purely quantitative valuations of subjective welfare. You cannot average these differences of kind, or refer them to a social standard analogous to the personal standard Crusoe brings to bear.

§ But though no social standard exists for the direct measurement and valuation of subjective utilities and costs, it by no means follows that science is helpless in the matter. The problem is familiar to psychologists. No direct measurement of psychical phenomena is possible. But when these are accompanied by physical phenomena, the latter are often susceptible of accurate measurement. So far as economic welfare consists in subjective good, it cannot come within the mathematical calculus. But where reliable physical indices of welfare are found, a social standard may be erected out of them, sufficiently reliable for practical purposes.

The correlation between statistics of wages and employment and certain accepted hygienic standards is one among many examples of this method. Low mortality and disease rates are legitimate indices of subjective welfare. Statistics indicating the increased demand for higher education, the diminishing expenditure per head on alcohol, unsanitary housing, and many other measurements of the objective standard of life, are rightly taken by statesmen, social reformers and others as sound evidence of an advance or decline in social economic welfare. Statistics of the reduction of hours of labour in industries, the advantages of rest intervals, as shown in reduced accidents or better output, may similarly be taken as sound evidence of reduced human costs of production. Not only the science but the art of economics is largely based on assumptions that human welfare is affected favourably by a more equal distribution of material goods, and a more equal call upon productive energy. But though, alike for statesmen and reformers, these are warrantable assumptions, enabling them to erect social standards, it cannot be held that such standards are endowed with the qualities of exactitude that belong to the statistics utilised in their making. Nor is it true that any two statesmen or reformers, translating the measured evidences of improvement into their welfare content, will apply the same standard. For, in the last resort, it will be his own personal appreciation of what is good for others that will form each statesman's subjective standard of reference for the various objective economic gains or losses.

These considerations, however, do not invalidate social standards as much as might appear. So much stress is commonly laid upon human differences as to conceal the size and importance of ' common humanity '. In asserting the valuation of various ingredients in a standard of living, any two values are likely to be in close agreement as regards nine-tenths of the substance of the standard, as is shown by comparisons of the actual expenditure of different members of the same economic class. While, therefore, a social standard of economic welfare will be less exact for a society than for an individual, it will be conceived in the same way. Instead of a Crusoe referring each claim of production and consumption to the organic standard of his personality, the policy of a society, so far as directed by some general regard for public good, will operate by setting up a standard, or several standards, which express the agreed elements among the different valuations of those who are effectively responsible for these standards. The adoption of a ' common rule ' for conditions of labour, and in general for various standards of living, is thus to be regarded, not as the addition of a number of separately measured desirables, but as based on an organic conception of social economic good, involving and imposing certain proportions in the expenditure of time, money, objective energy, and other measurable things.

The use of index figures and other modes of measuring exact movements of wages, employment, prices and volumes of trade, money and other economic objective facts and forces, is the assistance they render by enabling us to see where and how some existing standard of work or living is being weakened or undermined, and where and what steps can best be taken to safeguard it or to improve it. In progressive economic communities such measurements are serviceable chiefly in helping the application of new and higher standards rendered possible by increasing wealth.

§ But the belief that economics can become even a moderately exact science rests upon fundamental misconceptions of the limits of science in dealing with economic conduct. The chief misconception, as above indicated, lies in the claim that somehow qualitative differences can be converted into quantitative. This has always been the crux of mathematical hedonism in all its applications. The utilitarian calculus is inapplicable to differences of kind. The mathematical hedonist economics, as Veblen shows, is unable to deal with development of the economic system as distinguished by mere growth. " Like other taxonomic sciences, hedonistic economics does not, and cannot, deal with phenomena of growth, except so far as growth is taken in the quantitative sense of a variation in magnitude, bulk, mass, number, frequency." [1] An improvement in the quality of work or of consumption, in its reactions upon worker or consumer, cannot be quantitatively assessed. You cannot say ' how much ' better is the ' higher standard ' of work, or consumption, than the ' lower ' whose place it has taken, any more than you can say that a noble character is fifty per cent. better than an ignoble, or a great work of art worth twice as much as an inferior work. Money, the measure of all things economic, is inapplicable to measure qualities, even as reflected in current desirability. All art is a denial of the validity of this quantitative valuation. For though it involves exact quantitative measurements, these are always subordinated to considerations of organic unity or harmony of parts, qualitative considerations.

One point remains to complete our statement of the limits of a quantitative calculus in economics. In the

[1] *The Place of Science in Modern Civilisation*, p. 192.

main we have followed the usual course of science in dealing
with things as they are, not as we conceive they ought to be
or might be.   We have shown that, taking current standards
of valuation for economic welfare, the methods of mathematical calculus can yield no results corresponding to their
formal exactitude.   For their assumptions of infinite divisibility and absolute fluidity of the material involved are not
legitimate assumptions, while the method by which differences of kind appear resolvable into differences of degree
involves a *petitio principii*.

So far, however, current desirability, as reflected in the
appraisals of all who take part in the economic operations,
has figured as the underlying, though intrinsically immeasurable standard.   But we cannot in the art of Economics
exclude the other sense of the desirable, viz. what ought to
be desired.   This exclusion could only be possible if the
attitude of the organised society, as State, merely kept a
ring, and let the competing or combining interests in the
economic sphere fight it out among themselves, each actuated by his own sense of the desirable.   But the increasing
part played by every modern State, in the control or regulation of economic matters, makes it no longer possible to
identify the desirable with that which is currently desired.
The State imposes standards of desirability based avowedly
on hygienic, moral, and economic politics, not representing
the currently accepted conscious desires of those concerned,
but some ideal of health, education, or other element of
social welfare incorporated in a standard of life higher than,
or different from, that expressed by any average or representative valuations along current lines of desire.

Though seldom departing very far from the current
standard of values, it gives a ' lead ' in certain directions,
guided by some half-conscious ideal.   If, therefore, we are
to take all relevant considerations into our view, we must
envisage economic welfare as a mixed or compromise

concept, in which average current desires are qualified by social ideals. From the standpoint of a science aiming at exactitude this is, of course, very unsatisfactory. But we find the same compromise between current satisfaction and more distant aspirations in every art of conduct. Everywhere it limits the ability of man to make clear, precise, and certain plans for his immediate and future conduct.

CHAPTER V

PROLETARIAN ECONOMICS

So far we have traced in brief outline the distortions to which a disinterested science of political economy has been subjected by the intellectual volunteer forces of the propertied classes enlisted for the defence of ' vested interests '.[1] But the difficulties which beset this branch of ' social science ' would be realised very imperfectly if we failed to recognise the similar process of distortion from the hands of the intellectuals of the proletariat, engaged in the assertion of the claims of labour, and the assault upon ' vested interests '. Labour movements, in the form of trade-union policy and tactics, co-operation, or political action for raising the standard of working conditions, are doubtless conducted with a very fragmentary minimum of ' conscious ' theory on the part of the rank and file, or even of their leaders. But little groups of theorists have always marched along with the organised workers, furnishing such intellectual comfort as seemed serviceable. For though simple, uneducated folk manifest suspicion, often coupled with contempt, for all forms of ' higher learning ', these feelings conceal a strongly superstitious respect for the mysterious virtue of high-sounding formulas, and an eagerness to conciliate and attach them to their cause. There is a pathetic *naïveté* in the fact that ' scientific socialism ' pretended to draw its first spiritual sustenance from the barren ground of Hegelian dialectics. The sheer delight in

---

[1] Veblen defines a ' vested interest ' as " the legitimate right to get something for nothing."

abstract terminology, and the enunciation of 'highfalutin' laws and principles, irrespective of the attribution of any clear meaning, right or wrong, has nowhere been better illustrated than in the hold of 'scientific socialism' upon its adherents. Historians may perforate the principles of economic determinism, the phases of social evolution, and the law of 'increasing misery': class-economists may expose the fallacies of the Marxian theory of value and surplus-value: psychologists may disclose the unworkability of an economic society by the single incentive of Social Service. But many thoughtful workers, who seek a larger meaning for their movement than is furnished by the fragmentary opportunism of their trade union, are drawn irresistibly to the intellectual 'myths' that exhibit present capitalist robbery and future triumphant proletarianism in the aspect of a great spiritual drama where the instincts of self-assertion and hard feeling are enlisted in the service of reason and justice. In part it is a habit of hasty generalisation, in part that admiration of large showy formulas which comes with the attainment of a low level of literary education, the hypnotism of 'good words'. But the main impelling motive to the acceptance of this 'science' is an emotional blend of combativeness and humanity. By this latter I mean the natural craving for a fuller life with more security, comfort, interest, and enjoyment; by the former I mean the appeal of the collective struggle for the attainment of these 'rights'. The sharp antitheses of bourgeoisie and proletariat, capitalist-exploitation and wage-slavery, the class-war and the establishment of the dictatorship of the proletariat, in a society where the instruments of production would be socially owned and operated for the service of all, instead of for the profit of a few—such a social picture cannot fail to appeal to the dawning intelligence of 'the masses', newly exposed to the rich possibilities of life in a world of newspapers, cinemas, motor-cars, telephones, aeroplanes, wars, sporting events, and other sensational apparatus. What wonder they should gulp in doctrines, theories, formulas, and plans of campaign, designed to give intellectual and moral confidence to a policy of quick transformation of the social-economic order! If an economic science can help to establish this 'confidence', and so evoke energy for action, it must win wide acceptance. Quite irrespective of its truth? Certainly not. Just as in our investigation of the 'classical' political economy we found a genuinely disinterested study struggling to preserve its virtue against the inroads of the interests and passions, so with this proletarian 'science'. As the former has been perverted and distorted for the purposes of defence, so the latter for purposes of attack. The positive tactics of assault demand bolder, simpler, and more inflammatory myths than the more passive tactics of defence. But in each case the 'science' must desert its proper rôle of disinterestedness, in order to furnish ammunition to the combatants. In each case it will conceal, both from itself and others, this act of desertion by some specious intellectual covering. In the case of capitalist economics, the earlier cover was a genuine faith in the determinant part played by the capitalist in the economic system. His virtuous saving 'produced' the means by which labour could be employed, and so increased the reward of labour. His self-sacrifice was the driving and directive force of the system. Among the capitalist class and their educated supporters this doctrine was able to win easy real acceptance. More recently, however, the defence has shifted on to another centre. With no formal or clear abandonment of the creative rôle attached to capital, the more mechanical structure of modern joint stock capitalism ascribes less importance to those who furnish the capital, more to those who furnish business ability. Modern psychology has helped to win recognition for the attributes of the business man, his inventiveness, initiative, audacity, responsibility, foresight, organising power, as the creative energy of the economic system. Socialism, and in general the labour movement, by interference with this intellectual and moral control, and by encroachment upon the ' profits ' which evoke this personal productivity, would slow down the wheels of industry and retard the process of material advance ! The business man is dramatised as the sole and rare repository of these creative gifts, and profit as the key that winds him up and makes him function. The nucleus of truth in this capitalist myth is sufficiently substantial to establish the required confidence in those whose interests inspire them with the ' will to believe '.

§ The extreme character of the opposing proletarian myth is very helpful to the defence. For the socialist and other class-conscious workers are imbued with the doctrine that labour is the sole source of wealth, and that rent, profits, and interest, are forcible deductions from the product of labour taken by predatory oligarchies, the ' monopolistic ' owners of land and other instruments and opportunities of industry. Now how much support would ' disinterested ' science give to this position ? Any answer to such a question must be dogmatic, and any dogmatist runs the risk involved in his own personal equation, of importing his individual interests and class bias into his judgment. But to run this risk is essential to my present purpose. Assuming, therefore, the rôle of disinterested scientist, I hold that the true labour case lies, not in an insistence that labour is the sole source of wealth, still less in the narrow meaning of labour which excludes or disparages brain work, but in a clear, informed insistence upon the wasteful application of the incentives applied to evoke all the best physical and intellectual powers of production in their right proportions and combinations. This wasteful application of incentives arises from the unsatisfactory conditions of the ' markets ' in which the various requisites of production are bought and sold, that is to say, in the bad conditions for the distribution of the economic product in the form of income. This, in its turn, is due to inequality of bargaining power, which gives an unfair advantage at each stage to the buyer or the seller, resulting in a trebly wasteful apportionment of income. Those who get more than suffices to evoke the best use of the ability, labour, land, or other productive instrument they sell, tend to employ that ' surplus ' wastefully, either in setting productive power to make luxuries for their consumption, or in enabling themselves to consume their share of necessaries without contributing their share of work to the common stock, or else in setting productive power to make increased instruments of production in excess of the possible demand. Those who get less than is required to support and evoke their best use of their labour, or other productive instrument, are thereby rendered less efficient producers. These two wastes of overpayment and underpayment are evidently the convex and the concave of the same fact. But this realisation of the true origin and nature of ' waste ' in our economic system involves a complicated analysis of many different sorts of bargain, and is not easily accommodated to the needs of an inspiring ' myth '. It fails to establish a dramatic hero and villain, and so to evoke the emotional excitement of a sporting conflict, with a knock-out blow and spoils of victory. It is quite true that the theorists of socialism commonly disclaim the ' personal ' nature of the conflict. It is not the capitalist or employer they seek to destroy, but the ' system '! But it is quite evident that a system makes a bad villain and a bad hero, and that when the energy of conflict has to be evoked, the principles of good and evil must be personified.

§ The same difficulty may be illustrated from the sphere

of taxation. There is one defect of the first magnitude common to the analysis of the conservative and the revolutionary economists, the failure to distinguish the part played in inheritance and bequest in the problem of distribution. The ever-increasing importance of capital in modern industry, trade, and finance, signifies a correspondingly increasing proportion of claims upon the annual product, real income, of the nation, continually passing by the decease of the previous owner into the hands of those who have contributed nothing, even in the way of cunning, extortionate bargaining, or parsimonious living, to the formation of this wealth. This claim, of men who have made money, to endow their descendants with the power to consume a large share of the annual product without contributing to its production has been very slow to come under question either upon moral or economic grounds. The sacredness of property was long held to carry a right of absolute disposal. Interference with, or limitation of, this right was an invasion of the liberty to do what we like ' with our own '. The absolute right of disposal after death was a mere implication of ownership. Conservative economists showed little disposition to question this right. Any limitation of inheritance or bequest they were disposed to regard as interfering with the serviceable motives to thrift and accumulation. Reforming or revolutionary economists, again, were so deeply absorbed in condemnation of the sweating and exploiting processes by which landowners, capitalists, and employers accumulated wealth, as to ignore the smooth and inconspicuous facts of its transmission.[1] Though Bentham and J. S. Mill put in powerful pleas for a qualification of the right of inheritance and some right of reversion to the State, the recent tendency of modern States to draw even more largely from inheritance

[1] Dr. Hugh Dalton in his important work, *Inequality of Incomes*, gives a full and most convincing treatment of this failure of economists.

taxes as a source of public revenue must be attributed to the wisdom and expediency of State financiers rather than to general considerations of ethics and economics. In every country, owing to the growing requirements of public revenue, there is a disposition to test the extreme limits of ' ability to bear ' in this source of taxation. It is recognised as the line of least resistance to the increased demands of the tax gatherer. The possessing classes, confronted by alternative methods of ' confiscatory ' taxation, usually regard as lighter and less reprehensible that which diminishes the income of their heirs and assignees, than that which assails their own. The difficulty of tracing and measuring the surplus as it passes into income limits the effective yield of income taxes and makes it seem the more desirable to tap great wealth when it changes hands. Though reformers and revolutionists are willing to avail themselves of this method of securing ' surplus ' wealth for society, they have devoted little thought to it. They are apt to regard it as a concession intended to buy off cheaply the wider cause of economic justice. The fact of the concessive attitude arouses the suspicions of ardent reformers eager for the fight as much as for the fruits of victory. Subconsciously they are unwilling to attack the dead hand. They require a living personal foe, a wicked exploiter who is alive. They do not wish to get economic justice by a number of intricate readjustments of property rights within the system. They want to see the system dramatised in the personal devil of a sweating, exploiting capitalist, the sight of whom shall rouse their fighting spirit.

This brings out the double nature of the ' myth ', the false abstraction by which it furnishes intellectual comfort to the ' faithful ' and the dramatisation that provides the fighting force. The pseudo-exactitude of the mathematical ' marginalism ' which wins for the ' Cambridge School ' the title of defenders of the capitalist faith, is confronted by a similar feat of 'abstraction' performed by the Marxian theorists in anchoring their faith upon a principle of value based on "abstract necessary social human labour", measured in time units so as to determine the exchange-ability of the various sorts of concrete goods, or services involved. Confronted with the same difficulty as met the 'marginalist', namely, the reduction of qualitative to quantitative differences, Marx and his adherents resort to an extraordinary device best described in Marx's own language:

> " Skilled labour counts only as simple labour intensified, or rather as multiplied simple labour, a given quantity of skilled being considered equal to a greater quantity of simple labour."

But how is this done, how is the standard applied? He replies:

> "The different proportions in which different sorts of labour are reduced to unskilled labour as their standard, are established by *a social process that goes on behind the backs of the producers*, and, consequently, appear to be established by custom. For simplicity's sake we shall henceforth account every kind of labour to be unskilled, simple labour; by this we do no more than save ourselves the trouble of making the reduction." [1]

For simplicity's sake! *O Sancta Simplicitas!* But this " social process which goes on behind the backs of the producers" is the operation of the very capitalist system that Marx sets out to overthrow. To accept the respective valuations this 'social process' assigns to the different sorts of human effort is nothing less than a complete acquiescence in the existing system of distributing wealth. For, if we include, as we must, the most highly skilled work, say, of the expert lawyer or surgeon, we shall account the half-hour's work he gives to considering a case or performing an operation, as the equivalent of a month's work of a

---

[1] *Capital*, vol. i, p. 12.

common labourer. Needless to add that this method of 'weighting' the time unit entirely disposes of the theory of surplus-value and the capitalist exploitation which rests upon this basis. There is no 'simple' labour to be measured in time units, and no way of translating 'specialised' labour into simple. This abstraction of quality and intensity of labour, in order to secure a simple single measure for all economic factors, is closely analogous to the method of abstraction employed by the 'marginalists'. The Marxian labour ranks for simplicity, mobility, and divisibility, with the post-Jevonian cost and utility as registered in standard money.

§ The glorification of labour as the single source of value is dearly purchased by this false abstraction. For the exploitation myth built on this foundation, with its repudiation of the claims of property and profit, though designed to whet the fighting appetite of organised labour, has two injurious reactions. On the one hand, its frankly predatory and levelling policy serves to bind in a common bond of instinctive self-defence all owners of property or 'unearned' incomes, irrespective of size, origin, or use. On the other, the excesses of its pseudo-intellectualism offend the 'common sense' which everywhere, especially in Britain, tempers the respect for intellectual authority, and is recalcitrant to 'extreme' measures. It is largely the sense of these defects that has hindered the acceptance of Marxian 'scientific socialism', both among the leaders and the rank and file of labour in this country. For, though energetic and inspiring 'myths' with intellectual pretensions have their vogue here as elsewhere, they are of more various origin, more concrete character and less inflammatory appeal. Land values yield a 'gospel' through the lips of Henry George; co-operation and co-partnership aspire in other quarters to become prime instruments of social salvation ; syndicalism and guild-socialism offer attractive visions of economic government ; while the recent part played by money in the calamities of nations has made many envisage the New Jerusalem in schemes of cheap expansive credit. It is perhaps in the study of these more naïve schemes of salvation that we can perceive most clearly how interests and passions play with ideas and fit facts to preconceptions.

For each of these schemes, however illusory, has at its root some genuine appeal to reason, some specious hypothesis. The single owner of an isolated island could legally maintain in economic servitude the whole population, compelling them to work for a bare subsistence and to yield to him the entire surplus. There seems no reason why an intelligent society of co-operators should not obtain land and capital on lowest market terms, and organise the whole of industry under their own government and for their own profit. Or by a bold policy of ca' canny, the organised ' workers ' in each industry might freeze out the capitalists, obtain the possession and control of the industry, and operate it by a representative body of workers, regulating the exchange of the product against the products of other syndicated trades by some federal body of representatives. Or ' socialisation ' of credit might secure for the workers a speedy and full release from the trammels of class-capitalism, by destruction of the money-power. Or restriction of the birth-rate, exercised by the workers, might enable them, by limiting the supply of labour, so to increase their share of the product as to reduce rent, interest, and profit to a negligible minimum, and to take in a rising standard of comfort virtually the entire gain of each industrial improvement. Eugenics, devoted to the qualitative aspect of this population question, would, by breeding for better brains, furnish a progressive economy so efficient as to complete the conquest of man over Nature for all material requirements. As an incidental consequence of this quantitative and qualitative control of population, the secular causes of war would be eliminated, and the establishment of lasting peace and close international co-operation would liberate all the powers of man for social progress.

§ In some of these Utopias or panaceas there is a contradiction or fallacy in the primary concept, or the reasoning built upon it. This is the case with Profit-sharing and Douglasite credit [1] as instruments of economic revolution. But in most cases it is false abstraction, or the ignoring of conflicting or qualifying factors that enables the ‘ myth ’ to exercise its sway. We have observed how among intellectuals, and in general the ‘ educated classes ’, there is a blend of intellectual and æsthetic satisfaction in the acceptance and consideration of some simple, large generalisation, claiming to bring harmony into a world of apparent conflict or disorder. Nor can it be doubted that in circles of humbler education this same disposition prevails, to accept and approve large generalisations stamped with authority by accredited thinkers. This may be regarded as a natural co-operation of curiosity with an æsthetic instinct. But not every sort of ‘ myth ’ can thus win acceptance. It must be plausible, and the standard of plausibility will vary with the intelligence and knowledge of the individual. To pass a sophism upon a person of trained powers of criticism is necessarily a more delicate process than to pass it on a simple-minded person. But, if it be a very attractive sophism, with a strong, closely personal appeal of interest, it may rush the fence of criticism and win an immediate emotional acceptance. It is wonderful how slight a protection the keenest intellect offers to this rush of a belief or theory which enlists for its acceptance one or more of the

[1] Cf. Chapter viii in my *The Economics of Unemployment* (George Allen and Unwin, Ltd.).

primitive passions. War experience shows that the standard of credulity for the inherently improbable does not differ much among different grades of education. Professors, and other intellectuals in every belligerent country, swallowed with the same uncritical avidity the patriotic ' myths ' hastily fabricated by their Press or Government to support the ' moral ' of the nation and the will to victory. It may be said, however, that when scientific theories are offered for acceptance, education is a safeguard. And this is doubtless true. It would be more difficult to foist upon a body of trained economists fallacies so crude as those which lurk in scientific socialism. Their ' disinterested science ' would have a higher protective power. This does not prejudge the issue between the capitalist and the labour economics from the standpoint of objective truth. For on the assumption that our actual economic system is the expression of capitalist thinking and policy, a truly disinterested science of economic welfare may be expected to support many of the critical and constructive positions of the labour economists. But this reasonable belief, involving the scrapping of many of the laws, principles, and policies in our academic textbooks, does not warrant us in ' ignoring ' the distorting influence which class and personal interests and passions will exercise in moulding labour and socialist economics.

Perhaps the greatest temptation besetting the radical reformer is the adoption of a ' soft ' psychology. Workers, for instance, we are told, are no longer willing to work for the profit of the employer, but they will work for the community. Public service is to furnish a better economic incentive. Now what is working *for* the community ? In one sense all economic activity is and has been *for* the community, as expressed in the social structure of a market. This is the doctrine of ' the invisible hand '. But this, it is said, is an incidental and unconscious process. What is

needed is that the economic structure should be so trans-
formed as to enable workers to realise that they are working
for the community. Now, if this means that the process-
worker in a factory is consciously to be sustained in the
performance of his tedious task, by desiring the service
which the goods, to which he contributes some fractional
aid, will render to some unknown consumer in India, Brazil,
or even in his own country, it is a preposterous pretence.
A person working, in order that he, or some member of his
family, or some community close to his heart, such as his
tribal group, or in extreme emergencies his nation, may
benefit therefrom, may be said to have the common good as
an actual incentive. A professional man may realise the
good of his patient, or his client, as a definite conscious
object of desire. But it would be idle to pretend that the
ordinary routine work, even of a skilled labourer, can be to
any appreciable degree consciously affected by his desire to
put some useful object into the hands of some unknown
member of the community. When Mr. Hodges claims that
the coal-miner " wants to know the social purpose of his
work ",[1] I feel sure he is alluding to a few class-conscious
theorists in South Wales rather than to the mind of the
normal miner. There are many motives which may enter
into the consciousness of a worker, such as personal gain,
regard for his family, loyalty to group feeling, constructive
ingenuity, exercise of skill or personal prowess, the impetus
of habit, fear of losing his job. It may be added that,
other things equal, he would rather do something the
utility of which he realised than something which conveyed
to his mind no sense of utility. This may be said to carry
by implication some feeling for the community. Except in
cases of rare emergency this is as far as the common good
enters the worker's mind as a contributory to his effort. It
may be said that some general feeling for the community is

[1] *Nationalisation of the Mines*, p. 111.

present in the shape of a desire to be a worker rather than a shirker, or a sponger on society, and that it assumes some measure of consciousness in the recognition that he ought to do his bit. But to pretend that ' social service ' or ' the good of the community ' can be a leading incentive to the performance of our daily task in ordinary industry will not bear investigation.

§ It is easier for uneducated people to accept Utopias, panaceas and sudden revolutions, than for persons with some training in history. Moreover, the aggressive ' myth ' has, in its very appeal for strong immediate action, a potency greater than that contained in the defensive ' myth '. Bolshevism or Fascism is even more inspiring as a faith than as a fear. While, therefore, it may well be true that a disinterested science and art of economic welfare would lean more to socialism than to capitalism, the fact that socialism is the aggressor, alike in the intellectual and the practical fields of conflict, will lead us to expect in it larger elements of fallacy and fiction. I have used the term ' myth ' to describe the false ideas and beliefs which interest and passion engender in the body of a social science. These myths are partly fallacy and partly fiction. Now scientists often admit a use of fiction, in the sense of concepts based on no known facts but serviceable in the description or explanation of natural phenomena. Aether, atoms, electrons, hormones, the force of gravitation, are familiar instances. Here is an admitted element of art in science. Poets and artists, of course, make a fuller and more constant use of fiction. Its value for them, as for the scientist, is pragmatic. It helps them in getting results or ' effects ' which could not otherwise be got, and which are ' true '. But if this be so, the fiction itself must contain something of the nature of truth. It is not a blind or casual invention. The ' alloy ' that must be mixed with gold to make the perfect ' ring ' can only *work* with gold by virtue of some common nature.

> " Well, now : there's nothing in nor out o' the world
> Good except truth : yet this the Something else,
> What's this then, which proves good yet seems untrue ?
> This that I mixed with truth, motions of mine
> That quickened, made the inertness malleable,
> Oh ! the gold was not mine—what's your name for this ?
> Are means to the end themselves in part the end ?
> Is fiction which makes fact alive, fact too ? "

Sorel's defence of the revolutionary myth is just this, that it ' quickens ' matter otherwise inert. A bright vision of a swift perfect achievement will evoke the maximum of human effort ! But is this the real equivalent of the scientific fiction ? The latter is employed in winning consistency for some presentation of facts. It involves no deceit, appeals to no interest other than that of truth. It is otherwise with the social myth. Its motive and effect are the evocation of passionate desire by misrepresentation of facts. The picture of a sudden general strike, paralysing the whole existing economic order and leading to a seizure of the reins of economic and political government by the organised workers of the world, is an example of the revolutionary myth. Such a myth might, under otherwise favouring circumstances, evoke an intense and widespread ' will to power ' among the proletariat. In this sense it would be effective. But its ' fiction ' would not be scientific. It would not give marching orders to events. It would not enable those accepting it to ' make good ', either intellectually or in the world of facts. It would fail, not because it was fiction, but because it was false, i.e. containing misrepresentations of the order of Nature. In other words, ' the will to power ' which it set out to evoke, would not possess that force and consistency of purpose adequate to realise the myth, and this inadequacy would be partly due to the inherent incompatibility of the ' myth ' with the facts of human nature.

§ In this discussion of the revolutionary 'myth' we may seem to have strayed far from our main path, viz. the biases of proletarian economic science. But, in fact, the syndicalism, of which Sorel was prophet and professor, by claiming scientific value for its psychology of revolution, furnishes an extreme instance of a revolutionary complex which distorts economic science and policy in more moderate labour circles. I use the term ' complex ' in the sense given by modern psychology to a gathering of various instincts and their emotions around some central sentiment or ' idea ' which acts as nucleus. Now, though the complex is usually associated with morbidity, a single centre of emotion arrogating to itself full possession of the personality, this need not be the case. We can, for example, conceive a type of social reformer with so passionate a sentiment of social justice and humanity that his social science and art are not sensibly disturbed or deflected by the instincts of self-assertion, combativeness, or other egoistic force, which might be pressed into the central service. But it would be idle to deny that in many socialists and labour men disinterested humanitarianism is warped or overlaid by other sentiments and the beliefs which they inspire. The naïve conservative psychology which explains the agitator as motived by envy, malice, and a love of mischief, working on an inert suggestible mass-mind, has enough truth to make it plausible to those who have the wish to believe. Envy and snobbishness are prone to drape themselves in the flag of equalitarianism, as licentiousness may pose as liberty, and personal pride as patriotism. In nations like the British, where class status and its economic preserves are not so rigorously marked out as to keep out vigorous aspirants, the instinct of self-assertion is richly nourished by possibilities

of social-economic success. Every sentiment and belief
that stimulates the self-assertive instinct, and justifies it as
right and reasonable, will be pressed eagerly into the service
of the aspirant. Resentment against 'betters', 'masters',
the ruling or possessing classes, is easily aroused and
inflamed by theories, myths, or formulas, which represent
class power and wealth as based on sheer robbery and
oppression. Take the statement which makes a grievance
of treating labour as a commodity. "Even when the
wage-earner is getting what he calls 'good money' and
'steady work', he resents the fact that he, like the machine
with which he works, is bought as an instrument of production", write Mr. and Mrs. Webb.[1] But does he resent,
except when listening to an orator denouncing the capitalist
system and its slave-labour? Does he normally, or indeed
ever, feel that he is a machine, or hold that there is any
resemblance between labour and machinery?

Where working-class resentment is formally directed, not
against persons but against a system, this is little else than
a 'rationalisation' serving to justify hatred of particular
employers, capitalists, or landowners. For hate is needed,
and very few men are capable of hating a system. Revolutionary 'science' must then, from the nature of the case, be
poisoned by the "envy, hatred, malice, and all uncharitable-
ness" of its passionate expositors. For here, as in the
capitalist science, there is no sufficient body of 'disinterestedness' in the sense of love of knowledge for its own
sake : economic science is quite consciously intended for
directing the art of business, though each side pretends
that this is best accomplished by keeping clean the intellectual instrument, i.e. by keeping 'interest' out of the
descriptive and analytic processes out of which emerge
economic laws. The term 'pretends' is, perhaps, too
suggestive of hypocrisy. The humour of the case consists

[1] *Decay of Capitalist Civilisation*, p. 48.

in the fact that both conservative and revolutionary theory is built up by thinkers who genuinely believe themselves working in the ' dry ' light of disinterested science, being incapable of seeing the personal and class biases which at every stage of their work, observation, classification, analysis, generalisation, formulation, interfere with the rigour of their reasoning. In one way the proletarian science suffers more than the capitalist. For, addressed to a less ' educated ' public, its laws, or principles, must be simpler, more all-embracing and more striking in their appeal. Its doctrine of labour as the sole source of wealth (with some sleight-of-brain for reducing capital, and specialised skill to common labour), its indiscriminate lumping of rent, profit, and interest in a single predatory category, its application of a single formula of ownership and control for all the diverse forms of industry in all the different countries that contribute to the international economic system, suffice to illustrate this tendency. This drive towards false simplicity is immanent in the appeal of revolutionary policy, " Workers of the world unite ! " The unity, not the diversity of their needs and interests, must be the subject of appeal, and a ' science ' must emerge that shall give intellectual authority to this appeal !

A further stroke of humour in this analysis is the accuracy with which each party detects the pragmatic or interested reasoning of the other, while it seems compelled by the very nature of this mental process to ignore the corresponding bias in itself. This intellectual Pharisaism extends to the various sects into which conservative and proletarian science and art may be divided. The Marxian socialist, the philosophic anarchist, the Syndicalist, the single-taxer, the crediteer, is as self-confident in his intellectual integrity as is the individualist-libertarian, the marginalist, the co-partnership peacemaker, or the theorist of benevolent autocracy. Each is convinced that human nature and the facts of the situation are on his side, and that he is their dispassionate exponent.

Here, then, it might seem that psychology is capable of performing an inestimable service, first, by getting these schools of ' economists ' to recognise the inherent probability of injurious biases entering their ' science ', second, by helping them to detect and correct such biases as they can recognise, and so to purify their science and enable it better to serve the art of economic welfare. While, as we have seen, there are many warping influences due to the nature of the subject matter and the instruments, the most injurious of the poisons and distortions proceed from the intrusion of personal and group interests and passions. Here is the real test for the disinterested scientist, his ability and willingness to put his own disinterested character to the question. " Conscious as we are of one another's shortcomings ", is it inevitable that we should remain unconscious of our own ?

§ The issue, though it relates to intellectual process, is primarily a moral one. It opens up a deep-seated problem of the nature of intellectual honesty. We have recognised that the makers and followers of this partisan science are unconscious of their partisanship. But ought they to be, and must they be, unconscious ? Is not their unconsciousness, the very integrity they plead, due in part to their refusal to explore the field of motivation, for fear they should discover some motives that would injure their intellectual self-esteem, and impair their confidence in the sort of science they produce ? This suggestion pushes back one stage the question of integrity or honesty. A worker in any field of social science, with any acquaintance with psychology, ought to think it his duty to hold a constant watch upon himself, for fear lest interested motives may insinuate themselves into the several processes of his reasoning. For he should recognise that these attempts on the part of his instincts and their intellectual servants are certain to be made, and with a cunning adapted to the defences that would repel them. When the social scientist is a man of great intellectual keenness and a high standard of sincerity, the ' rationalisation ' practised by his instincts of self-assertion, intellectual pride, group-sentiment, will be correspondingly subtle. Nothing but a highly cultivated self-scrutiny can, therefore, avail to enable him to keep clean his intellectual instruments. The real moral struggle arises in the temptation to shirk or scamp this scrutiny, i.e. to push ahead into some inquiry into facts or process of induction, or the framing of some hypothesis, under the secret drive of some interested motive.

In all the social sciences, and not least in economics, the ' polemic ' motive is perhaps the most direct source of trouble, i.e. the instinct for self-assertion through successful fighting. The particular danger here is the facility with which this fighting instinct ' rationalises ' itself by assuming the garb of duty. To see your intellectual opponent as an enemy, not of yourself but of the truth, to realise the public danger of his conduct, and the obligation imposed on you to expose and castigate him, is an easy ' stunt ' for the combative instinct in the scientific controversialist. And in a field of social science where truth is so difficult of attainment, and theory is in such close contact with interested practice, opportunities for the intrusion of the polemic spirit are frequent.[1]

I shall rightly be reminded, however, that the fighting or polemic spirit does not function in the void, but that some-

[1] An exceedingly interesting example of an avowal of the polemic motive in a scientific work is furnished by Professor McDougall in the Introduction to his *Outline of Psychology*. He recommends the science of his treatment on the ground that it is polemic directed to kill the false and poisonous doctrines which have claimed to capture the study of psychology. He seems quite unconscious that his polemic purpose carries any danger of its own.

thing valuable to be 'fought for' is requisite. It is precisely for this reason that economic science furnishes the best field for observation of the secular struggle between disinterested science and the interests. For the interests which mould conservative and proletarian economics alike are primarily economic interests. The rival interests of profiteering and of labour 'put up' the fight and exploit, each in his own cause, the 'will to victory'. Only, therefore, by a sedulous psycho-analysis can the science and art of economic welfare steer a clear course in the world of thought and conduct.

APPENDIX

ECONOMIC UTILITARIANISM

§ THE rejection of Utilitarian concepts and standards of value by many modern schools of thought is chiefly due to a mixture of two lines of attack, neither, I think, wholly sound. One relates to the motives, or urges, to conduct, the other to the standard of values for conduct. So far as Utilitarianism in economic, or in general conduct, was associated with and made dependent on a pleasure and pain calculus, modern psychology may seem to have disposed of it. The hard-shell rationalism of a century ago, when men were supposed to be determined in their voluntary actions by separate calculations of the pleasures and pains attendant thereon, is no longer tenable, in view of the part which instinctive urges and activities are known to play in every sphere of behaviour. Even in the simplest animal activities, pleasures are seen rather as added incentives than as original urges ; and, when we come to higher levels of animal conduct, pains are incurred for the sake of some good which cannot, and does not, figure consciously as a greater pleasure. Even if we substitute for the sensations Pleasure and Pain what are called the feeling-tones of Pleasantness and Unpleasantness, we do not escape from the thicket of psychological criticism. Records of personal sacrifice in martyrdom, or otherwise, suffice to indicate that man does not always prefer the more pleasant, any more than the more pleasurable, of two courses. Any contention to the contrary merely begs the question by identifying ' the pleasant ' with ' the preferable.' Pleasure, or the pleasant, is not to be taken as his necessary motive, still less as his accepted standard of conduct. Pleasure is no fitting term either for his urge, the object he is after, or the criticism of human values. If we substitute the larger, looser term Happiness, do we fare better? The gulf which separates pleasure from happiness in our language falls a good deal short of that which separates in Aristotle's language Hedone from Eudæmonia. The Happiness defined by the Greek as ψυχῆς ἐνεργεῖα κατ' ἀρετὴν ἐν βίῳ τελείῳ is far less associated with ' the feelings ' than our use of the term. It vests Happiness far more in the region of contemplation, and makes far less provision, if any, for the due satisfaction of our animal desires. Though our use carries perhaps too much immediate reference to 'the feelings' for an accurate account either of the motive in conduct or the standard, it comes a good deal nearer to meeting our requirements than the Greek Eudæmonia. Indeed, it may well be urged that to find a single term to express both the current urge, or motive, and the standard is an impossible task. For the standard of conduct must be set in terms of the intrinsically good or desirable, while the current urge is either incapable of being represented in desire at all, or, if it is, it relates to the actual desire which may not accord with the ' desirable.'

§ But, though the dilemma cannot completely be escaped, judicious use of terms may reduce its pressure. We need some single word to express both what a man is ' after ' and what he ' ought ' to be after. Especially do economists need this term, if they are to reconcile themselves with recent psychology. With this object in view I have chosen ' Welfare' as the least defective. To straddle the gulf it must be kept large and elastic. It is the business of the Arts of Conduct to put concrete meaning into it. Its advantage is that it covers, on the one hand, the vital services, or utilities, of the instincts, or innate dispositions, without offending the modern psychology of motivation, while, on the other, it gathers into a single whole all spheres of human activity that rank as ' good.' Though by usage it has come overmuch to emphasize a State rather than an activity (ἐνεργεῖα), that can be remedied by developing the part well-doing plays in well-being.

The accepted economic language regarding costs and utilities can, I think, be readily accommodated to this envisaging of human values in terms of welfare. A cost will rank as a negative, a utility as a positive, contribution to welfare. We should thus be enabled to adjust the science and art of economics to the requirements of psychology, taking due account of the satisfactions of the crude or sublimated instincts, in which psychology finds the urge of life, and the material out of which special activities are found. The harmony of activities under the growing conscious direction and control of intelligence for the achievement of an ever higher and larger Welfare, in society as in its members, furnishes to us a picture of Progress, consistent with the teaching of science. A society, thus regarded, would be progressing in proportion as its arrangements contributed to providing free, full, varied, and harmonious play to the human instincts or dispositions, by sublimation, combination, repression, and suppression, directed by the growing consciousness of a human *esprit de corps*.

§ Though the utilitarian standard of ' the greatest happiness of the greatest number ' has quailed before the logical onslaughts to which it has been exposed alike from psychologists and philosophers, it may stand as a rough serviceable expression of what social progress consists in, or is ' after.'

Welfare, however, conceived as a harmony, forbids the separate quantitative calculus which was a leading defect of the older Utilitarians, and obliges us to consider each factor, or event, in its bearing on the structure and working of the harmonious organic whole.

This consideration is of primary importance in the application of our revised Utilitarianism to Economics. Regarding Economics as a tributary to the larger art of Human Welfare, we are continually brought up against the interaction of the different factors in the welfare of an individual or a social group. An analytic study, for example, of any social economic group, in a rural village or a factory town, might seem to break up into inquiries into conditions of work, upon the one side, and conditions of living, or standards of comfort, on the other. But it would soon become evident that standards of living, as expressed in the customary family budget in certain working groups were strongly affected by the character of the work they did. Even the proportions of different sorts of food will vary widely with the work of the male wage-earner, while cost and character of housing will largely depend on place and conditions of employment. Marriage and size of family, and therefore the whole habit of expenditure on standardised and free consumption both of money and of time, will vary with trades. It is needless to labour the fact that ways of living, employment of wages and of time, will react upon efficiency of work, which, again, in turn will affect wages. These are commonplaces of economics, though still neglected sorely by the apostles of supply and demand curves.

Modern psychology, in other words, by regarding human life as consisting in the activities of a number of organically related instincts, or dispositions, is bound to interpret the desirable life, or human welfare, alike for individual and group, in terms of the due satisfaction of these instincts.

It will thus establish Utilitarianism upon a new and defensive footing, regarding as useful anything contributory to welfare.

§ If social development be treated as the process of achieving, or expressing, this welfare, the progress alike of the individual and the group will imply some measure of natural harmony between the actually desired, here and now, and the desirable, between what people want and what they ' ought ' to want, if they knew their true interests. This harmony is based upon a conception of the organic unity of man and of society, and involves the assumption of some central urge, or control, expression of this unity. Whether this central control be called Reason, or Immanent Will, or something else, is immaterial to our present purpose. What is important is to recognise what this conception of organic harmony in social development signifies for Economics. The harmony between the actually desired and the desirable is, of course, very incomplete, and social progress may be regarded as engaged in working towards its completion, an ideal never attainable, since the desirable is itself a moving object. But, taking Welfare to express the humanly desirable, Economics, as an art, is concerned with the contribution made to Welfare for the side of those activities concerned with the making and spending of Income. These activities will fall primarily under the two heads of production and consumption, though, as we have seen, directly we translate these two terms into this psycho-physical costs and utilities, they are recognised as intimately interacting and jointly contributory to economic welfare. When the light of psychology is turned upon the economic processes, it exposes these as aiding and thwarting in intricately interwoven ways the various instincts whose harmonious operation constitutes welfare.

A rational evaluation of the existing economic system from this psychological standpoint will take the current concrete income of goods and services, and reduce them into terms of instinctive satisfaction, as contained in the work that has gone into making them and the use made of them by consuming them. This evaluation will involve a close assessment of all methods of production, with a view to discovering what provision the productive activities make for the creative and constructive instincts, for the display of skill, initiative and adventure, and other factors in a sound personality, how far the conditions of labour favour a sense of comradeship and *esprit de corps*, or, *per contra*, how far they starve, repress, or damage otherwise such instincts by the conditions of dull, mechanical, degrading and exhausting toil which they impose. Similarly, an evaluation of the use of this real income by consumers will assess its value in terms of instinctive satisfaction, having regard, not only to its strictly vital services, but to the contribution which it makes to the higher standards of life as interpreted in finer harmonies of living. It will assess also the *per contra*, or cost account, in terms of bad luxuries and wastes, recognising here, as in the productive analysis, that gains or losses of welfare will widely vary with the distribution of the labours of production and the articles of consumption. Though no exact comparison and measurement of pleasures or pains, or of satisfaction treated in terms of personality, is possible in dealing with different persons, the admittedly common character of mankind will suffer to furnish some very serviceable rules for the betterment of economic life, i.e. for the enlargement of economic welfare.

This distinctively organic treatment of welfare dismisses as unsound the separatist analysis of costs and utilities, and of the pains and pleasures which they carry, and demands a fourfold study of organic interactions. First, it must be recognised that the worker has a number of his instincts affected, for good or evil, by the work he does, and that all of these should be considered as factors in his organic life. Secondly, the consumer should be subjected to a similar analysis based upon the organic nature of his standard of living. Thirdly, the identity of producer and consumer, as an economic organism, should be studied and the interactions of the two factors taken into due account. Fourthly, the part played by group life, or society, in its bearing upon economic welfare and the general life of the community, should be carefully treated, with special reference to the reactions of economic processes upon the group feelings which promote or hinder willing intelligent co-operation in the service of a widening common good.

An analysis of economic welfare along these lines in the arts of industry will, of course, involve a corresponding reform in economic science, the prime desideratum being a substitution of an organic treatment for the separatist hedonist calculus hitherto employed.

PART III

FREE-THOUGHT IN POLITICS AND ETHICS

CHAPTER I

POWER-POLITICS

§ WE have endeavoured to trace in Economics the chief ways in which narrower 'interested' motives openly or secretly interfere with this work of a 'disinterested science'. We chose that branch of social science, partly, because it is in some true sense the most advanced, and, partly, because the play of particular interests and passions in moulding its doctrines are more easily discernible.

If now we turn to Politics, or the art of government, in order to consider how far it can secure the disinterested service of a science, we are confronted with greater difficulties. The science and the art are there so intricately bound together that it is difficult to distinguish theories and principles which claim to be generalisations from history from those which claim to be guides to good government. Though statistics and laws of averages are put to large use in real politics, incommensurables and imponderables are so prevalent that no student claims for his study the same measure of exactitude which many economists claim for theirs. When history was held to repeat itself or to move in cycles, some fairly accurate estimates of current tendencies and forecasts of the future for a nation, or a civilisation, seemed possible. But when the rule of an external Providence or a rigid internal destiny yielded to the idea of an unlimited development of human affairs, in which the 'free will' of man seemed to play a determinant part, the baffling nature of that factor interposed new obstacles to any 'science' of history. Nevertheless there appeared to be enough regularity in human nature and its environment to enable us to trace their general interactions as they went to the moulding and working of large-scale human institutions. The earliest students of political forms and theories in the rich laboratory of the Eastern Mediterranean found sufficient material for generalisations, some of which have stood the test of time. But the writings of even the ablest and most ' disinterested ' of these thinkers show how deeply affected were their investigations into fact, their generalisations and their speculative judgments, by prevalent ideas rooted in emotion. If such great minds as those of Plato and Aristotle could not disentangle themselves from current Greek sentiment towards barbarians, slaves, mechanics, women, how could it be expected that modern political thinkers, from Machiavelli, Hobbes, and Locke, to Rousseau and Hegel, Mill, Spencer, Bryce, should escape the emotional entanglements of their time and country in the pursuance of their ' science ' ?

§ If we put the issue of disinterested politics in a shape analogous to that to which we have subjected economics, we might state it thus : " In what forms of government can the intelligent will of peoples be best evoked for the attainment of political welfare ? " This, of course, implies that we believe that ' political welfare ' is capable of some fairly reliable description, at any rate for certain political groups at a given time. The general modern acceptance of the idea of Progress precludes any finality in the conception of ' political welfare '. But, for any given nation, or other grouping, at any given time, it will form an operative ideal, a best attainable condition. Now, as in our economic analysis, so here we are not concerned to find the answer to this question, for the world at large or for our own nation. Our proper concern is to discover in what sense, and within what limits, the thinking which goes to this science and art of politics can be disinterested, and to indicate the several ways in which interested pressures interfere with scientific and popular thinking.

To endeavour to trace fully the development of political theory, even in modern times, in pursuance of this object, would not here be possible. I shall, therefore, confine myself, first, to a brief citation of some leading questions to which political science and art profess to furnish answers, and shall thus pass to consider how far these answers and the methods of thought employed in their attainment are disinterested.

Scrutiny into historic origins will first ask : How does the art of government or group control, for general purposes of security and common enterprise, as distinct from co-operation for other specific purposes, arise in different types of primitive society ? What are the forms of this group-control in the appointment and powers of leaders in war and peace, the creation of councils or assemblies, the origin, declaration, and enforcement of laws and decrees ? What are the relations of neighbouring groups and by what stages and under what stimuli do groups grow in size towards the typical political group of the present time, the nation-state ? How does the federal principle operate at various stages of political development, in the two directions of decentralisation or local self-government on the one hand, and the cession by smaller groups of circumscribed powers to a single central government on the other hand ? And how are these two federal processes related to one another ?

The development of forms and powers of popular self-government by various devices, elective and other, for obtaining the ' consent of the governed ', or for giving expression to some general ' will ', is a study of profound interest at the present time, alike for those who accept some form of ' democracy ' as necessary to achieve political welfare, and for those who believe it to be either undesirable or impossible. In this study emerge various controversial issues, partly of objective fact, partly of psychological import.

This comparative study of constitutions, written or unwritten, with particular regard to the parts assigned, respectively, to the electorate, the elected persons, as legislators, judiciary, or executive, and the various orders of non-elected officials, the distribution of power between the several governmental bodies, the enlargement or other alterations of these powers in accordance with new views of the functions of government and new needs of modern society, in particular the growing tendency everywhere to increase State functions in two directions, constructive work of social security and progress, and regulative work for the control of economic operations liable to injure life, liberty, or property, if left to unfettered private enterprise—such are some of the chief matters upon which politics, as science and art, is concentrated.

§ Some departments of this study are evidently capable of being more ' disinterested ' than others. The difficulties for politics begin with the study of raw facts. Out of the floating mass of political phenomena what shall we observe ? In economics large orders of obviously relevant facts are ' hard ', in the sense that they abide our questions and present the same face to all. In politics fewer facts are ' hard '. An event is too often a matter of combined observation and interpretation, and into its description enter the personal prepossessions and valuations of the individual recorder. Even more important is the constant selection of some facts as relevant, the rejection of others as irrelevant. Relevant and irrelevant to what ? Evidently to some question containing a preconception, or a point of view. Next comes the difficulty of keeping the definite interest involved in the preconception and point of view from biasing the various processes of reasoning from evidence towards some judgment in the shape of a law or principle, or the verification or rejection of an accepted hypothesis. To keep the instrument clean in so delicate an operation requires unusual integrity and watchfulness.

§ I have named 'power' as the most prevalent among the interfering interests. Self-assertion, the craving for power, to be a cause, to see things and men move in the fulfilment of our will, is everywhere an operative, often the dominant, motive in politics. In its more innocent or useful moods this craving of the personal group self calls itself 'the legitimate need for self-expression or self-realisation'. The desire to exercise power in moulding the material environment to our purposes is evidently the main source of economic progress. But the sense of power which enters politics is primarily power over persons, not things. The main defect of the economic interpretation of history lies here. Property, beyond the means of subsistence, evidently serves less as an instrument of direct material enjoyment than as a means of prestige and power over other persons. When, as we shall see, the economic motive enters, and often governs, politics, it is, as a rule, none the less the servant of this instinct of self-assertion. Everywhere, what may be termed the legitimate aim of politics, the development and working of socially serviceable forms of government, is deflected by these selfish thrusts of the will-to-power finding satisfaction in the forcible subjection of the will of others. Not only property or the acquisitive instinct, but leadership, herd feeling, the combative instinct, are enlisted in its service. The desire for power thus becomes the nucleus of a 'complex' round which gather various other instinctive drives with their emotional and ideological contributions. These various arrangements of the power-complex employ intricate subterfuges and decorative trappings to conceal the naked egoism at their core.

This we can best study in the several 'isms' of political science and art. But it is worth while observing at the outset the testimony which etymology undesignedly contributes to the importance of the Power 'concept'.

The description of nation-states as Powers, great or small, the Powers of Europe, the corresponding use of 'Cracy' (the Greek for Power), in the relations of classes towards the national Government, the familiar expression 'the Party in Power', are naïve records of what politics actually means. The 'spoils of office' is but a slightly cruder revelation of what politics are 'for' in the mind of 'politicians'. It is no use pretending that a science of politics can grow up in such a world and keep itself unspotted from this world. The most disinterested devotees cannot wholly escape the contamination.

The intrusion of this love of power into the theory and practice of conduct is, however, not necessarily an assertion of control. Its pressure is a matter of degree and its influence proportionate to that. Often it may be a mere adjunct, affording a spice of personal satisfaction to a substantially disinterested piece of conduct, as in much philanthropy. The element of personal ambition which seems essential to the labours of the finest political career, may even be regarded as a useful alloy, helping, not hindering, the play of a genuinely public spirit.

§ The part played by Power in the amalgam of social motives will vary much with the size, composition, and human significance of the social grouping. The earliest nursery and practice-ground of Power is the family. Though there are those who deny to the family the name of a 'political' entity, Power should first be studied there. For nowhere else can despotism be so absolute and intimate, nowhere can the egoistic lust for bending the will of others to your own be practised with such impunity. Nowhere else can the rationalisation of this lust, namely, the identification of your pleasure with 'their good', be so complete. The power of the 'Old Man' in the family group of primitive society must have long preceded and surpassed all other tyrannies. Resting, partly, on the possession of superior brute force and the love of its exercise, partly upon prestige and 'rightful' authority, its utility, biological and social, has consisted in strengthening the group for common action in the struggle for life. But the incidental cruelty and misery of its abuses have probably been throughout the ages the heaviest item in the tale of human suffering. For all wider forms of government are light, casual, and remote, as compared with the government of the home. The father who realises his instincts of cruelty and power in beating his wife and children, 'for their good' and because he has a right to do as he likes with his own, stands as the prototype of all 'interested rulers'. His rationalisation of his motives is identical with that presented by 'the autocrat of all the Russias' or the dictator of the proletariat.

The exploitation of the family as a means of personal prestige has been so fully described by Mr. Veblen in his *Theory of a Leisure Class* [1] as to call for no extended notice here. The ostentatious leisure and conspicuous waste by which the family of the successful business man is made the expression of his business power, is hardly a more tolerable abuse than the physical brutality it has superseded. Yet this man is regarded by the members of the society in which he lives, and commonly regards himself, as a 'good family man', sacrificing his own pleasures for the benefit of his wife and children. The desire to see his family 'have a good time' is itself a protective covering for his craving to realise his personal power in his close personal environment,

[1] London : George Allen and Unwin, Ltd.

and his prestige in the wider social world in which he moves. The genuine family affection which enters in is 'drugged' by this craving, so as to prevent all realisation of the injuries he inflicts upon his repressed and parasitic family.

Another interesting example of the secret play of power in this narrow circle is Nepotism. Here family affections and his 'duty to look after those nearest to him' are real incentives to put a member of his family into a lucrative or influential post in preference to a more competent outsider. This glow of emotion dispenses him from any obligation to appraise the claimants on their separate merits. It also serves to hide the pride of personal influence exercised in favour of a kinsman. This feeling is evidently stronger where the kinsman is recognised not to be the better man, and so could not have hoped to secure the place by his own unaided efforts. 'I did it' is essential to the glory.[1]

But the family itself, as distinct from its head or ruler, may have a personality which exercises prestige and realises power, either in collective domination over other families, or in furthering the influence and interest of any of its members. This is commonly dignified as *esprit de corps*. How far this is a fiction under which particular individuals give respectability to their personal aims, or how far it is a genuinely collective sentiment, modifying the narrower in favour of the broader egoism, will be matter of controversy in particular cases. But this family sentiment, as the most limited *esprit de corps*, serves well to introduce a sentiment which figures so prominently in all wider arts of politics. For the individual member of a family to which he gives value or importance by his presence, is also a member of many other wider circles of diverse character, in which he plays a similar though usually a weaker part. So far as his interests and activities are

[1] As Lord Palmerston put it : " There is no damned merit ." in appoint-ments to Knighthoods of the Garter.

commingled with those of other members of these circles, town, club, church, party, nation, etc., there springs up a belief, with an accompanying sentiment, that his co-operation with the other members in pursuit of a common object is public-spirited and disinterested. His part in the co-operation may be purely and even consciously selfish : he may simply be using the collective activity as a means to get his private end, his share in the common gain. But this clear-conscious egoism is rare. For the habit of cultivating sympathy with members of our circle is so manifestly useful in binding them to us for activities which are necessarily social, that we learn early to give rein to the tender emotion derived from parenthood and the gregarious instinct which coalesces with it, to evoke a wider emotion of comradeship.

§ So valuable does the belief in the pure disinterestedness of public spirit and patriotism appear that any close attempt to scrutinize such sentiments as to origin and contents seems impious or cynical. If, for instance, anybody ventures to point out that the rush of young men to arms in 1914 was not motived solely by love of country, but that various other motives entered in and often predominated, such as the combative instinct, fear of public opinion, love of adventure, coercion of employers, he is reproved as belittling the sacrifice of those who fought and died for their country, i.e. the other motives are ruled out as irrelevant ! In point of fact, patriotism, in the sense of an appeal for ' King and Country ', did not actuate the more sensitive nature of the early recruits so powerfully as the more disinterested sympathy with outraged Belgium and the resentment against her violation. Patriotism came later. Patriotism as an actual operative force is always a composite sentiment. It is not simply ' egoism writ large '. But when one reflects that the best British patriot would have been the best German patriot, had the accident of birth given him that nationality, the ego nucleus cannot be belittled.   In the patriotic precept ' My country, right or wrong ' the emphasis rests on the ' my '.   But though this country of mine is ' sacred ' to me because it is mine, it does not follow that patriotism is merely a camouflage of selfishness.   The identification of my good with that of my fellow-countrymen, the common affection for ' our country ', the thoughts, feelings, and activities, directed in common towards its defence, the conscious community of single concentrated purpose permeating this national co-operation—this patriotism involves a surrender as well as an extension of the narrower ego.   The smaller is sucked into, and partially absorbed by, the larger ego of the nation.   In ordinary times the subordination of the narrower to the wider egoism is slight.   It is, indeed, significant that patriotism should thrive most in war.   For that seems to indicate that ' the disinterested love of country ' must be impregnated by the combative instinct to give it life.   In times of peace professions of patriotism are usually suspect.   Nobody believes that anyone is deeply concerned about the good of his country. The flag-waving and other patriotic ritual evoke and express brief waves of superficial sentiment among the rank and file of loyal citizens, nothing more.   Plenty of persons are genuinely interested in public causes, some of them nation-wide, but the express cultivation of ' our country's good ', as a distinctively inclusive patriotism, has little bite.   Just as I keenly realise my personality over against yours, so my country, or my nation, realises its collective selfhood by sharp distinction from other countries or nations.   As my conflict with you braces and tightens my sense of personality, so conflict with another nation generates patriotism. It is idle to seek to gloss the fact that the opposition of a selfish struggle is an indispensable condition for the production of a strong, compact, conscious self in individual or group. There are those who regard both selfish products, the hard-shell, competent individual and the proud self-sufficient nation, as the best results and carriers of civilisation. Others maintain that the finer character of personality and of nationality is inhibited by this preponderance of the combative instinct, and that upon the abolition of war and competitive industry the progress, perhaps the survival, of civilisation depends. It is not, however, with the settlement of this contention that I am here concerned, but with securing a sober, clear-sighted understanding of the concept patriotism. The Italian 'sacro egoismo' perhaps tells the most essential truth. It sanctifies, or claims moral authority for any action of national self-assertion, regardless of its effect on other nations or upon individuals or groups within the sacred circle of the national ego. In this latter claim it overrides and tramples down the individual will to power, subjecting the claims of the person to those of the State, as representing the nation. This is the state-absolutism with its unlimited will-to-power, which we have agreed to reprobate as Prussianism. But, put to the test, every modern State has claimed and exercised this power by virtue of the same 'sacro egoismo', with such slight qualifications as a rickety internationalism, a faint humanitarianism, or a fear-inspired discretion may bring into play.

§ Sovereignty is the reputable formula for this collective sentiment of power. For the power-concept finds its political embodiment in a sovereign state. This State strictly regarded is an absolute will-to-power. It is absolute in relation to individuals, groups, and institutions within the area of its government, and also in relation to other sovereign states and the territories and populations which they claim to govern. This internal absolutism has itself emerged as the result of conflicts of power between rival groupings of inhabitants in political, economic, religious, or other organisations. Of such struggles, that between Church and State in many countries has been the most intense and prolonged, embodying the keenest rivalries of authority and allegiance, i.e. of leadership and submission. Over a large proportion of the world to-day the nation-state nominally wields an absolute supremacy over its members and all their other institutions. In accordance with the laws or rules it has laid down for its normal behaviour, or, in cases of emergency, in violation of such laws (for which it grants to itself an indemnity by a special exercise of sovereignty) it can take the life, liberty, or property of any of its members. This absolute power wielded by a State may be vested in a Monarch, or divided between him and some limited body of non-elected potentates, or it may devolve wholly, or in part, upon some assembly purporting to express the will of a narrow or a wide electorate. This, however, is only a description of the forms of government, which gives often a misleading account of the actual origin and exercise of the power. The naïve theory of democracy well illustrates the tendency of the executants of naked power to clothe this nakedness under more reputable forms. For there are three manifest defects in the application of the principle of popular self-government. The first is the necessary inability of ' the people ' to check or control in any adequate way the large and increasing share of governmental power vested in permanent officials, who, in the last resort, are persons with interests and propensities not wholly accordant with the public interests or the popular will. The second is the secret or open influence exercised for their particular ends by special interests, chiefly economic, upon legislatures and the administrative machinery of State. The third and gravest defect is the ignorance and apathy of the vast majority of the people, which disable them from exercising real power through choice of representatives, referendum, or any other act of judgment or consent. To some psychologists this may seem an inevitable and a salutary operation of the instincts of leadership and submission, by which the most virile and aggressive members of the herd assert and exercise rule over the submissive majority, representative institutions only serving as a sifting or selective process for the self-assertion of naturally dominant members.

Indeed, if we start by accepting a sharp distinction in every group between a few natural leaders and many willing followers as desirable for the protective and aggressive activities of the group, in dealing with its internal and external relations, we appear to have ruled out the possibility of democracy in the accepted or any intelligible meaning of the term. For the sort of ' consent ' given by the submissive many, confronted by the forceful rule of a self-assertive few, can hardly be held to possess even the rudiments of democracy.[1] There have been political philosophers bold enough to claim that the failure of successful rebellion under an autocratic Tsar attested a true ' consent of the governed '. And in many so-called democracies there is a disposition to gloss over the three damaging defects above described, and to impute to the machinery of popular self-government a reality it does not possess. Lip-service to public opinion, by those conscious of the power to manufacture it, and to electoral machinery, by those conscious of the power to manipulate it, is an instructive barometer of popular self-government. It signifies a recognition by the real rulers that the exercise of the power of the State must be consistent with the maintenance of a measure of popular contentment, and a reliable material

---

[1] For a most penetrating criticism of the inadequacy of passive ' consent ' to the working of a ' real ' democracy, see Miss Follett's *Creative Experience*, chs. xi. and xii.

basis for the same, and that cunning must be substituted for crude force in working the instruments of popular consent. Hence the growing importance of the control of the press, the school, the church, the cinema, and other machinery for procuring 'the consent of the governed' to the exercise of power by the ruling classes. The hard figure of the State, with its arbitrary will and its executant bureaucracy and soldiery, must for such purposes be encircled in a nimbus of patriotic sentiment. This sentiment it has always been difficult to maintain by a purely self-regarding internal policy. The failures of the State, real or imagined, are too visible and too annoying in times of peace. Discontents thus arise which embarrass statesmen, and dispose them to 'stay giddy minds with foreign quarrels'. No lesson of political psychology has been more thoroughly taught. But it is not learned.

It is the supreme peril of our own and of all times that the groups that wield State-power, chiefly as the expression of their personal will-to-power, are constantly driven to external policies which have the double use of healing internal discontents that otherwise threaten their political and economic rule, and of exercising that will-to-power upon an imposing and prestige-creating scale in the external activities of their State.

§ It is common knowledge how easily and naturally Patriotism, as policy and sentiment, spills over into Imperialism. Strictly considered, both policy and sentiment supervene upon activity. Empire precedes Imperialism. This is what Sir John Seely so aptly explained when he said Britain acquired her Empire in 'a fit of absence of mind'. No conscious policy was needed: planning would have interfered with performance. Empire came to us by separate bits of local improvisation. This does not imply sheer drift. Behind each bit of the acquisition and combative activity which went towards Empire some more or less similar personal impulses are operative. But in its earlier formation there was very little of what may be called a public policy of imperial expansion. Public policy was no doubt involved in each act: kings, statesmen, pro-consuls, moved partly by public, more keenly by private considerations of prestige and power, played their necessary part in directing diplomacy and armed force at the several points of advance. But, save in rare instances and for brief periods, there was nothing of an imperialist policy in these casual incidental acts by which State pressure co-operated with private ambition or gain. Only when gathered by the historian into some general survey does any pattern of general purpose emerge. The fragmentary improvisation, indeed, appears in the very texture of the government of our empire, its varied adaptation to particular circumstances which is sometimes adduced as testimony to our ' genius for empire '. It is really attributable to the fact that our empire was got by an unconnected series of private adventures, mostly engineered by business men who had the cunning and the opportunity to enlist other more reputable motives in their gainful service. So came about that amalgam of trade, religion, and philanthropy, adventure, pride of territorial size and dominion, that goes into the composition of Imperialism. That the policy and sentiment should have acquired a predominantly political significance is due, partly, to the formal impressiveness of the political aspect of the policy, partly, to the convenience which the business motives find in screening their private aims behind the imposing façade of Empire. For more recent imperial policy no longer proceeds in fits of absence of mind. Modern imperial Governments know very well what they are doing, when they place their particular applications of imperial power at the disposal and determination of the favoured interests within their nation. When strong imperialist measures are called for, a hot glow of patriotic sentiment is pumped up by the bellows of the public Press, in whose confusing vapours the pushful groups of business men and their political confederates may reach their goal.

There are, of course, in every country numbers of men who, living in the fumes of this exalted patriotism, will see in this analysis nothing but cynical falsehood. But a closer examination of the actual forces at work before any recent act of territorial expansion will bear out its accuracy.[1] Where statecraft has placed itself most consciously and consistently in co-operation with organised trade and finance, as in the modern policy of Germany and France, the nature of the ' power ' which goes into Imperial policy is more clearly discernible than in the case of Britain, whose longer and more varied imperial career has taught the economy of taking each proposition upon its own merits and ' letting events take their own course ', with a confidence based on long experience that the Empire will emerge with enlarged frontiers and new exploitable resources. Moreover, our empire is so large that we do not now suffer from the nervous disease called Kilometritis which infects the new and too self-conscious patriotisms of Italy, Poland, and other recent aspirants. British Imperialism, therefore, stands as the subtlest and most adaptable of modern political practices.

§ Imperialism in practice, then, is mainly the expression of two dominant human instincts, self-assertion and acquisitiveness. To the former the primacy may be accorded, in the sense that individual or collective self-assertion, or lust for power, which inspires men to take or enforce rule over others, uses the arts of acquisition both as means to the

[1] In our own recent history the efficient causation of the Boer War and the Occupation of Egypt are perhaps the most instructive instances of the utilisation of national force by private business.

furtherance of this end, and as instruments for the direct satisfaction of positive self-feeling. The imperial-minded statesman realises his personal craving for a large, distinguished, and active career, and carries along with him the patriotic sentiment of his class or nation in the collective realisation of this national ' destiny ', by an expanding rule over lands and peoples outside the national area. To him and to his nation the gain-seeking of traders or investors, or the humanitarian or religious sentiment pressed into the imperial service, rank as subordinate considerations. It is indeed an unsettled point in the modern foreign policy of most advanced nations, how the interplay of distinctively political and economic forces operates, as regards the initiation and conduct of the lines of policy which aim at, or result in, imperial expansion. A closer study of the facts, were they fully available, of recent British policy in Egypt, South Africa, China, and the German colonies during the war settlement, would throw useful light upon this interplay of politics and business. The general body of evidence, however, seems to support the view that power-politics furnish the largest volume of imperialist energy, though narrow economic considerations mainly determine its concrete application.[1]

§ This analysis, assigning the energy of imperialism to an instinctive reaching after power in individuals and groups, co-operating with displays of the acquisitive and certain other instincts, must not be regarded as necessarily carrying a condemnation of all imperialist action. That would involve too hasty an assumption that what are termed the instincts of leadership and submission are devoid of social value. It may be urged that the assertion

---

[1] Woolf, in his close and able study of *Economic Imperialism in Africa*, however, cites interesting cases of conscious trade policy avowed by imperialist statesmen.

of leadership, or domination, in the head, and the acceptance of this by the rank and file, are instinctive actions
fraught with survival value. The self-assertive leader has
more strength, initiative, and intelligence, and the prestige
which they win for him secures the voluntary obedience or
subjection of the herd. The abuse of such power may not
be a full offset against its herd or social value, where
discipline and quick unquestioned co-operation are needed.
That is why there are extremities in which any nation will
resort to a dictatorship. Now if this free self-assertion of
leadership is valid within a single group or herd, may it not
possess a legitimate collective application. Though
imperial aggression may carry no conscious purpose of
benefiting either the people subject to this aggression, or
the world at large, and though it may be easy to expose its
hypocritical parade of a mission, to Christianise the
heathen, to teach the dignity of labour, or the arts
of government, may not this collective assertion of an
instinct of leadership be accredited with a social or human
value ?

Is there a real or even rudimentary society of nations, in
which a value may be assigned to the natural selection of
leader and follower corresponding to that acknowledged
among the members of a group ? The affirmative contention is, I think, *au fond* the case for imperialism. Some
nations, it is urged, are fitter than others to exercise rule
and to teach, and the fact that they can successfully impose
their power is some testimony to their fitness. The submission of the weaker peoples is a sort of consent.

Nor is this theory disposed of by dwelling upon certain
unverified assumptions it contains, and certain dangers
that attend its application. The contentions that might
gives or attests right, that successful self-assertion implies
fitness to rule over another, and that such rule will be
exercised in the interest of the world at large, and not in

the exclusive interest of the ruler, are not, indeed, easy to maintain. For History is rife with the abuses which attend the application of these doctrines. But, if it be true that in a single group some men are naturally fitted to rule, others to obey, the principle may plausibly be extended to the relations between groups themselves. The objection, that no nation can properly be regarded as a safe judge of its own fitness to rule, may be overridden by contending that in default of any impartial testimonial (and such does not exist) the self-assertion of a ' leader ' nation is *prima facie* evidence of its capacity.

This, I think, is the half-conscious doctrine of imperialism, as soon as it comes to require a doctrine to satisfy the qualms of its more sensitive practitioners. A born ruler, whether individual or nation, will thus seek to reconcile his own personal craving for power with the claims of genuinely human service. It is idle and wrong to arraign him for selfish greed of power, even if that be the chief impelling motive, provided he ' delivers the goods '. We may have gone into India, Egypt, or elsewhere, prompted consciously by considerations of our own power or gain, but our capacity for rule has operated to the advantage of the ' governed ' and contributed to world welfare ! This implicitly serviceable conduct is adduced as a justification of the policy. So we seem to carry about with us in our loose, pushful career of imperial expansion an alembic which transmutes our leaden instincts into golden conduct !

Critics of imperialism point out that it is *we* who attest alike our fitness to rule, and the success which accompanies its practice. And it may well be admitted that such self-recommendation is not satisfactory proof. But, on the other hand, it is not disproof, and since no impartial tribute exists to pass upon the policy, imperialists rely upon a rough general consensus of outside opinion, together with an acquiescence of the subject peoples in favour of the forceful acquisition and the peaceful rule of a Roman or a British Empire.

This is the most specious case which the group of interests figuring as national policy have been able to make out in support of Imperialism. Two particularly audacious assumptions underlie it. The first is that the failure of a subject people successfully to rebel against their imperial rulers is equivalent to a consent of the 'governed'. The second is that the *ipse dixit* of an imperial power in testimony to its good government is valid so as to cancel the presumption in favour of self-government.

§ It is significant that the transparent absurdity of the claim of an imperial power to be a just judge in its own case should have evoked the quasi-internationalism of the mandatory principle set forth in the Covenant of the League of Nations for the governance of certain groups of subject peoples taken over from the conquered empires. If the League contained the substance of a government for the Society of Nations, some such mandatory principle might be applied most serviceably to safeguard the world against obvious abuses of the doctrine of absolute national self-determination. For no nation can rightly claim to refuse to other nations fair access to its natural resources and its markets, or to block some natural convenience of transport. In the relations of civilised countries it might seem that intelligent self-interest supported by ' the comity of nations' would suffice to secure these elements of international co-operation. But some coercive provisions might be required in order to bring backward countries into conformity with such requirements of world-welfare. The exercise of this limited coercion might reasonably be vested by the Society of Nations in one or other of its members best qualified by situation, race, or other special faculty. Here is the theory of the Mandate which the

Covenant of the League pretends to put into application. There are, however, four conditions needed to validate the principle in its application. First, the Mandate should issue from the full Society of Nations. Secondly, it should involve a minimum of interference with the self-government of the mandated territory. Thirdly, the priority of native rights and interests in the development of the country's resources should be adequately safeguarded. Fourthly, the Mandatory Power should occupy no preferential position in trade, or other economic opportunities, over other nations.

The failure of most of the Mandates allotted under the Covenant to conform to any one of these conditions indicates the measure of insincerity attending this pretence to oust imperialism by equitable internationalism. The Mandates actually operative did not issue from a full Society of Nations, or even from the self-chosen little group of Governments who constituted the Council of the League. They proceeded from a division of the territorial spoils of victory, passing to the several conquering Powers by virtue of the right of conquest. With certain ill-guarded provisions for native rights, the mandated areas pass under the rule of the Mandatory Power as Colonial Possessions or Protectorates. One group of Mandates expressly recognises the administration of these areas as 'integral portions' of the territory of the Mandatory Power, thus abrogating all priority of native rights and customs in favour of the policy and interests of the Mandatory. In these latter cases the Protective Tariffs and other preferential or exclusive economic rights of the Mandatory offend against the principle of equal economic opportunity, while in other cases the full provision of such equality is confined to Members of the League. Apart from these defects in the character of the Mandate, experience has already shown how incompetent the League is to enforce even the most elementary safeguards against the abuse of Mandatory Powers,[1] and how impotent is the permanent Commission to secure full and reliable information in the annual reports from the Mandatories. In view of the facts, the reference in the Covenant to " the principle that the well-being and development of such peoples form a sacred trust of civilisation " may be held to establish a new record in political rationalisation.

§ I have drawn out at some length the implications of the psychological doctrine of instincts of leadership and submission, as illustrating the tendency of the practitioners of power to invoke intellectual support from the science of psychology.   You cannot argue with an instinct ; you may repress it, at your peril, or you may sublimate it, i.e. put it to some higher biological or social service.   But, manifestly, if ' Nature ' has implanted in man strong and fixed propensities to leadership and submission, all forms of crude political equality, and the sort of democracy which implies some capacity for self-government in the ordinary man, will go by the board.   True that, under modern conditions of life, the ' instincts ' will work more indirectly and in sublimer ways, but none the less inborn fitness to rule in the few, and corresponding fitness to obey in the many, must stamp themselves on all successful institutions.   In such ways does political practice evoke theories and principles of State Sovereignty and Empire which shall furnish intellectual and moral support to these operations of the will-to-power in self-assertive individuals and groups.

This will-to-power is, as we see, primarily engaged in two related tasks, the reassertion of effective oligarchy within the national State, controlling or ignoring the earlier forms

[1] The deliberate defiance by France in her mandated areas of the prohibition of " the military training of the natives for other than police purposes " and the acquiescence by the League in that defiance tell us all that is necessary on this score.

of equalitarian democracy, and the assertion of the right of 'imperial' peoples to rule inferior, backward, or inefficient peoples in the name of law, order, and progress. Revised conceptions of sovereignty and expanding internal functions of the State help in the performance of the former task.[1] The earlier Absolutism, adopted in the relations between sovereign states, which led to a naked policy of imperial aggression, as a naïve exercise of the will-to-power, and a Hobbes-Machiavellianism for its political philosophy, is now in course of transformation. For that political and moral isolation and self-sufficiency, only qualified by agreements or conventions of no final validity, has, under conditions of modern intercourse, given place to an ever closer and more intricate internationalism. This compels the will-to-power, in its aggressive aspect as instinct of leadership, to weave fresh theories for its free action in the new situation. Under the old political philosophy there was no 'society of nations'. States moved 'like dragons of the prime' or like stars in their courses. Now the new facts of intercourse have brought into being a rudimentary Society of Nations, and it has become necessary for the national will-to-power to find some theory or intellectual scheme for the conduct of that society inside which nations with an instinct of leadership can exercise this propensity.

[1] Cf. Laski, *Authority in the Modern State*.

CHAPTER II

RACE EUGENICS AS A POLICY

§ THIS brief account of the submergence of older democratic and equalitarian theory under the new political psychology moulded by the requirements of dominant classes and peoples would, however, be incomplete without reference to some recent contributions from the fields of eugenics and anthropology. That certain stocks and strains are intrinsically superior to others, yielding persons with stronger bodies, better brains, and finer ' characters ', may be taken as a true popular account of the first contribution from these biological sources to the new doctrine of Aristocracy. This doctrine is closely linked up with that of the non-transmissibility of acquired characteristics, ' good ' stock enjoying a double advantage as contributors to human progress, first by their inborn superiority, and, secondly, by the superior ability thus conferred for using and improving the natural and social environment in which they find themselves. Under such circumstances it is the right and duty of the better stocks and races to secure for themselves the best opportunities for physical survival and increase, and for the exercise of their superior powers of leadership and government in the arts of life. By serving themselves they will be best serving the true interests of humanity. The white races of European origin are superior to all coloured races, Mongolian, American-Indian, Negroid, and others, the latter varying among themselves in their intrinsic human values. Among the European whites the ' Nordic ' race stands out pre-eminent in its intrinsic superiority and

survival value, as compared with the Alpine and Mediterranean races. Long heads, blond hair and skin, blue eyes,
are the physical indices of the Nordic race with a predominantly northern habitat. As fighters, rulers, thinkers,
creative artists, a primacy is claimed for them. Nations
which have most of this blood form a natural aristocracy.
Inside the different white peoples of the world the Nordics
have furnished the leaders in all the more strenuous movements. As conquerors they have seized the seats of power
—generals, statesmen, territorial rulers, explorers, and
adventurers, not only in the physical but in the intellectual world.

Unfortunately these Nordics have fallen upon evil days.
Everywhere they are in danger of extinction, unless they
devise effective methods of protection against their
' enemies '. One of their chief virtues, the fighting propensity, has even told against them. For though they have
been conquerors, when fairly pitted against Alpines,
Mediterraneans, or coloured peoples, they have through
long ages suffered heavily from losses in these struggles.
Worse than this, they have sinned against Nordic solidarity,
fighting among themselves. Here is the gravest charge
brought by anthropology against the Great War, that the
nations engaged in it were largely Nordic, and that the
Nordic strains, being represented disproportionately to their
numbers in the several belligerent nations, suffered greater
losses than the other races.

But under modern civilisation this failure of the Nordic
strains is accelerated by the prevalence of industrialism and
city life. Mediterraneans and Alpines are better accommodated to selection and survival under the conditions of
factory and tenement. So a dysgenic selection is taking
place among the white civilised nations.

" If England has deteriorated, and there are those who think they
see indications of such decline, it is due to the lowering proportion

of the Nordic blood and the transfer of political power from the vigorous Nordic aristocracy and middle classes to the radical and labour elements, both largely recruited from the Mediterranean type." [1]

So also in America :

" In America we find another close parallel in the Civil War and the subsequent granting of citizenship to Negroes and to ever-increasing numbers of immigrants of plebeian, servile, or Oriental races, who throughout history have shown little capacity to create, organise, or even to comprehend Republican institutions." [2]

It is, however, not only internecine warfare and the degrading selection of town life that tells against the free outdoor living Nordics. Partly owing to these conditions, partly to other physiological or social influences affecting their ability or will to reproduce their kind, their birth-rate everywhere is lower than that of the intrinsically inferior stocks with whom they live. Hence :

" It would appear that in all those parts of Europe outside of its natural habitat, the Nordic blood is on the wane from England to Italy, and that the ancient, acclimatised, and primitive populations of Alpine and Mediterranean race are subtly reasserting their long-lost political rule through a high breeding rate and democratic institutions." [3]

The responsibility of democracy for this collapse is manifestly due to the fact that democracy is a process of levelling down.

" If equality cannot be obtained by lengthening and uplifting the stunted of body and of mind, it can be at least realised by the destruction of the exalted of stature and of soul." [4]

Now this may well seem a doctrine of despair. You cannot stop Nordics from fighting (for ' it is their nature to ! '). You cannot stop the growth of city life. You cannot force Nordics to produce large families ! Some alleviation of these dysgenic influences might perhaps be

[1] *The Passing of the Great Race*, by Madison Grant, p. 210.
[2] *Ibid.*, p. 218.   [3] *Ibid.*, p. 190.   [4] *Ibid.*, p. 191.

attainable if we could rid ourselves of the ' equalitarian '
sentiments and the democratic institutions they inform.
For Europe there may seem little hope, this ferment of post-
war Fascism and other assertions of autocracy being manifestly short-lived and desperate experiments. But for
America and our Dominions this racial eugenics may help
to mould a policy, in which the will-to-power of the ' Nordic '
elements (or those who claim this rôle) may assert itself.

§ In the modern ferment of mind, when new fields of
research stimulate imagination, a great variety of theories
are continually presenting themselves for selection and rejection. In the social sciences, as we have seen, this process of
selection is peculiarly liable to bias from the side of interested
policy. This Nordic ' myth ' has greatly thriven from this
source. Derived from a slender body of verifiable facts, it
offered just that sort of popular appeal which made it
suitable for intellectual and moral boost. The egregious
Houston Stewart Chamberlain furnished a grotesque form
of the doctrine as propaganda for the great mission of
Pan-Teutonism. Now we find reputable anthropologists
and their popular exponents serving out a slightly more
specious presentation of the theory which they endeavour
to endow with the authority of ' Eugenics ', a study of a
seriously scientific order, employing close laboratory and
statistical methods and generally careful in its practical
judgments.

The reason why America just now is the forcing bed of
these doctrines is that the political and economic masters
in that country and their intellectual and spiritual mercenaries have required these ' scientific ' supports for their
defence against the dangerous excesses of an equalitarian
democracy, continually fed by large hordes of unassimilable
foreigners from South-Eastern Europe and elsewhere.
This had to be stopped. A stringent selective immigration

policy must be applied. Here, of course, the 'Nordic' principle must be supplemented by a wider criterion of racial values, which shall effectively exclude all further penetration by Asiatic or other coloured races, and shall sanction the practice of social, political, and economic discrimination against those members of the coloured races already settled in America and too servilely useful to be expelled or segregated. The determination of the ruling and possessing classes, who run, or finance the running of, the political and economic, the intellectual and spiritual machinery of America, to keep firm control of these instruments of power, without any formal abandonment, unless as a last resort, of the equalitarian forms and traditions inherited from their ancestors and needed for the earlier stages of plutocracy, derives a serviceable confidence from the new doctrines of racial values. No more striking example of 'rationalisation' is to be found than the discovery of these intellectual buttresses of the established order. For the policy of Americanisation, to which it makes so valuable a contribution, will serve, though with naïve unconsciousness, to use the self-made standards of the ruling class so as to maintain convenient inequalities under the specious banner of national solidarity. By the standardisation of American institutions, conduct, ideas, sentiments, in accordance with a 'Nordic' evaluation, all the special characters and values of other races are repressed, and, instead of contributing their proper share to a highly varied and complex civilisation, their repression obstructs the mental and moral channels of activity among these new elements of population and thus helps to keep them inferior 'Americans'. A 'disinterested' solution of the great American problem would endeavour to find standards that would discover, educate, and bring into play, the countless variations from the earlier American traditions which the later immigrations have introduced, so as to select from them contributions that would enrich

American life, and supply new seeds of a higher and more plastic civilisation. To stifle these seeds of progress by refusing them food and freedom of growth, in the interests of an accepted order of values, attested by racial self-esteem dressed as Anthropology or race Eugenics, is the most injurious, as it is the most ridiculous, example of the havoc which the 'will to power' can make when a social science prostitutes itself to its paymasters. But the latter-day exponents of Americanisation hold that America cannot afford these dangerous experiments in liberty and progress. Order and stability come first!

§ But wider implications of this racial eugenics are to be found in the new internationalism. It is of deep significance that the first draft of the new constructive internationalism incorporates a policy of Mandates and principles of control for dominant white peoples over backward races. The earliest applications of these principles and policies are naïvely suggestive of the realistic motives of the formulators. While Mandates purported to be 'trusts for civilisation' created under international sanctions by which the Mandatory Power exercises government over a backward people for its own and for the common good, the allotment, acceptance, and refusal of Mandates everywhere exhibited the cloven hoof of economic imperialism, each Power marking down for itself the most succulent joints upon the supine carcass. This, of course, was not exactly how the process appeared to its executants. The Power nearest in position, or in prior intercourse, to the mandated area claimed to be the 'natural guardian', best capable of the fulfilment of the international will. Any selfish interest he might appear to have in the undertaking of the Mandate, was, so the theory ran, compatible, even harmonious, with the fulfilment of the wider humanitarian purpose. It was, at worst, a necessary inducement to the performance of a serviceable task.

But the real significance of this mandatory system is that inter-Imperialism here first finds its formal expression : [1] As in the competitive business world competition gives place to combination, when each competing unit sees larger and securer gains in co-operative action, so with the competition of national imperialism which the last half-century has evolved. Indeed, to many this inter-Imperialism figures merely as an aspect of international capitalism, a partition of areas of exploitation between powerful financial groups, using their respective Governments as instruments. But if, as I have indicated, this purely economic interpretation of national Imperialism is inadequate, the same inadequacy applies to the wider application of the doctrine. Imperialism, as the politics of power, contains various ingredients, and though conscious economic motives often direct its action, the play of other less ' materialistic ' considerations supplies the main current of effort. While, therefore, this inter-Imperialism serves, and is partly designed for, the partition of the supplies of raw materials and profitable areas of economic development among organised groups of business men in the imperial nations, it has a deeper significance from the standpoint of world-order. Here it figures primarily as a vindication of white supremacy by virtue of racial superiority. To the white peoples—or some of them—is vouchsafed the opportunity, and the obligation, to impose good government upon the world, and to protect the lives and civilisation of the white races. In the practical policy of inter-Imperialism, as thus developing, there are two essentials ; first, to keep white countries free from forcible or pacific penetration by coloured peoples ; secondly, to secure the reliable development of natural resources in non-white countries for the use of white peoples. As an important adjunct to this policy is the insistence upon a direct and

[1] The Berlin Convention of 1885 for the allotment of African Protectorates was an early and partial anticipation of this policy.

dominant control over the government of non-white countries, partly for the insurance of these two essentials, and
partly as a scope for adventurous members of white races in
their capacity of rulers, and exploiters, missionaries, scientists, sportsmen, explorers, and philanthropists. In inter-
Imperial, as in national-Imperial policy the more reputable
of these subsidiary motives will naturally act as protective
colouring to the dominant instinct of power. To the racial
eugenist, however, all motives and activities alike are
subordinate to the instinct of racial protection. For the
highest human values are thus alone conserved and
developed. The white peoples secure full play for their
creative and ruling genius, while the servile peoples gain
by their submission such advances in the arts of industry
and politics as they are capable of attaining.

§ Though modern psychology has done so much to destroy
the earlier democratic doctrines of the equality of man, it has
so far failed to apply adequately to the wider art of government one of the most salient features of its inequality, viz.
the distinction between positive and negative self-feeling, to
adopt M. Ribot's terminology. Professor McDougall distinguishes these as primitive instincts, emphasising their
opposed nature as Self-assertion and Self-abasement. Presumably all men, or normal men, possess both of these
dispositions, but in very different degrees. Those whose
self-assertion is strong, impose themselves upon those whose
self-assertion is weak (or self-abasement strong), and in any
group the former assumes a leadership which is accepted by
the latter. But though it is easy to base upon this distinction a theory of natural oligarchy, a defence of a Government
expressing the self-assertion of the few and the submissive
' consent ' of the many, nowhere in his *Social Psychology*
does Dr. McDougall unfold this implication. Yet it would
come in extremely handy for the practical eugenics to which

he commits himself in *Ethics and Modern World Problems*,
For this natural self-assertion ought surely to have due
consideration in the caste-system there advocated. Instead
of the feeble expedient of literary requirements, in distin-
guishing his classes for citizenship and representative
democracy, it would seem far preferable to apply some test
of leadership, initiative, and risk-taking, which will have the
advantage of drawing on the primitive instinct of self-
assertion. For evidently Nature ' intends ' the two instincts
of self-assertion and abasement to have due satisfaction, and
a sound policy should furnish that satisfaction ! It is
presumably for the good of the group-life that the self-
assertive shall have full opportunity for self-assertion and
the submissive for submission. If this seems to partake too
much of the *Realpolitik* of power, one can only say that
human nature, as Dr. McDougall sees it, appears to give a
strong endorsement to this right of might. Still more
valuable to the cause of intellectual reaction would be the
application of this same instinctive differentiation on the
wider plane of international relations. Some nations, to
wit, the Western white nations, clearly display high degrees
of collective self-assertion, while others, to wit, the peoples
of Africa and of Asia (with one exception) are submissive.
It is thus for the benefit of all that international relations,
expressed in politics and economics, should establish the
world order upon this basis, assigning sovereignty to those
with the instinct of rule, subjection to those with the instinct
to obey. A power-politics in the widest sense, no doubt !
But why should we seek to escape Nature's decree ? It is
the more strange that Dr. McDougall should have failed in
this simple application of his roll of instincts, in that, when
he turns as a practical statesman to concern himself with
the construction of the International Authority, he frankly
accepts the power-basis of representation. " Let each
nation ", he holds, " be represented in the International

Authority (whether court or league) to an extent propor-
tional to its annual budget. The justification for this
arrangement is the fact that the annual expenditure of a
nation corresponds roughly to *the extent of its power* and to
the magnitude of its interests in the economic world-order.
It would thus be an approximately just arrangement and
one which all nations might be expected to accept." [1]

There are, however, two flaws in this psychological
support for oligarchy. The first is that there is no warrant
for regarding negative self-feeling or submission as a primitive
instinct at all. The mere fact that some persons submit to
the self-assertion of others, who are stronger, fiercer, or more
capable, may be attributed to fear, admiration, laziness, or
stupidity. The second flaw consists in the assumption that
self-assertion is a sound warrant for good, or just, rule.
What confronts us in such reasoning is nothing other than
a rationalisation of the self-assertive instinct itself, which
invents an instinct of submission or abasement to justify
its aggressive behaviour. What the classical economists
have done for capitalist rule in industry, certain psychologists are prepared to do for oligarchic rule in politics.

§ Thus we find that, as within each nation, so within the
Society of Nations, the dominant classes and peoples break
away from the earlier loose theories of equality of stocks
and races, and resort to theories of inborn and ineradicable
distinctions which stamp with the authority of scientific
law the positions of political and economic superiority
they hold. But before we consider how far this narrow
class or group interest necessarily invalidates the ' science ',
we must note the emergence of a scientific defence of the
older equalitarianism. Just as in economics the socialists
put up an intellectualism of their own, to counter the classical
and neo-classical theory, so here the class and racial eugenists

---

[1] *Ethics and Modern World Problems*, pp. 175–6.

are confronted by equalitarian democrats who reassert inborn equality, finding in environment and social heritage a full explanation of differences of aptitude and attainment. This issue between Nature and Nurture is of crucial importance. For the eugenists furnish a powerful support for oligarchic rule in politics and industry, and for imperialism in world government. The strength and worth and progress of a nation, on their hypothesis, depend upon the maintenance of a selective process by which strains endowed with strength, intelligence, and character assert their 'natural right' to success and leadership and transmit these qualities to a sufficiently numerous posterity. Similarly on the wider scale of humanity, the maintenance and progress of world civilisation will depend upon the selection, survival, and domination of the superior white races. The eugenists need not deny that environment, social heritance, and education, make a large contribution to superior capacity for rule. It is, indeed, part of their case that children with superior native endowments will get more out of the common opportunities, and so increase the measure of their superiority. Their quarrel with equalitarian democracy is that, by claiming equal opportunities in the exercise of power for all alike, regardless of their natural differences, a sort of Gresham's Law prevails, whereby the 'fit' are ousted by the 'unfit' from the seats of power, and ultimately from the earth itself.

'Race Suicide' is the sensational designation of this process. It is worth attention in any disinterested attempt to assess the facts. For the eugenic claim is that certain intrinsically superior strains and races which, in the interests of humanity, ought to rule, are threatened with extinction. Now, as we have seen, this natural right to rule, derives from the alleged instincts of leadership and submission in the herd, the activity of which is endowed with survival value. A few are born to rule, the many to obey. This is asserted to be a law of Nature, securing the survival and progress of the herd. ' Yes,' say some eugenists, ' and it is precisely the defiance of this law that to-day imperils humanity.' But how, it may be asked, can a law of Nature be violated in this way ? How can those with an inborn propensity to rule, fail to rule, and those born with an innate propensity to submit fail of submission ? This could not happen in a herd of buffaloes, a hive of bees, or in a savage tribe of men. Has civilised man somehow broken away from this sound instinctive direction, yielding to some ' misdirection ' of his ' reason ' ? This, I think, is the implication of the eugenic argument. But it is not easy to reconcile it with the teaching of modern psychology, which imputes no such independent potency to ' reason '. Indeed, we may go farther and convict these eugenic pessimists of a contradiction in terms. Creative initiative is the prime character of the natural leader and ruler. He not only makes good his ' natural right ' to rule, but stamps his virile impress on a large posterity. Is not race suicide, or class infertility, itself a confession of a fatal flaw in the claim of the superior right to rule ? Can the sort of ' fitness ' which includes a deliberate refusal to breed, and to transmit its claimed superiority, be accounted racial fitness ? And how came it about that the natural rulers permitted the making of political and economic institutions which cramp their initiative and frighten them from reproduction ? Such happenings seem quite out of keeping with the natural play of the instincts of leadership and submission.

§ No conclusion, however, is reached by following these considerations. I therefore suggest another line of explanation. May not all these theories of the failure of superior stocks and of race-suicide, be part of the defensive-offensive tactics of the dominant groups in each white nation and in the ' society of nations ' ? Current history furnishes no

evidence that oligarchy and autocracy are seriously threatened as ruling forces in industry and politics, though some
shifting of their centres of gravity and changes in methods
of government take place.   Strong men continue to exercise
dominion over us.   But part of their strength consists in
ability to persuade the governed that their rule is based on
the consent of the governed, and is directed to secure the
general welfare.   For this purpose they must make good
their natural claim to fitness, on the ground of success in a
struggle for wealth and position according to the current
rules in the game of life.   Hence the service rendered by
the eugenists in representing the current economic struggle
as one in which inborn strength, ability, and character, tend
to rise to the top.   How this is compatible with the ' Nordic '
contention that modern conditions of life favour the survival
of the older Mediterranean and Alpine stocks, I cannot
comprehend.   For it would seem that ' leadership ' in the
sense of Nordic virtue must have been displaced by Mediterranean ' leadership ' attested by a conquering power in
what rank from the Nordic standpoint as the low arts of
commerce and adaptation to town life.

Thus we are brought round to the essential vice of all
this inter-racial and racial eugenics, viz. that it furnishes no
admittedly disinterested standard of human fitness.   This
did not matter under the primitive conditions of an animal
struggle and selection, for the strugglers could not appreciably affect the conditions of their struggle, and an ' absolute '
standard of fitness was thus prescribed by Nature.   But
when man came to be able in an increasing measure to
control and alter his environment, he got a corresponding
power to make the conditions of his struggle, and to lay
down his own standards of fitness.   Now how far are the
' artificial ' environments he has created and the standards
of fitness in that environment so satisfactory from the
' disinterested ' human standpoint as to warrant us in

accepting the judgment that the men, the classes, and the races, which have achieved the most success under these conditions of the human struggle are intrinsically superior, and by virtue of that superiority are entitled in the interests of humanity to exercise masterhood in the arts of industry and politics ? Some considerable *prima facie* case can doubtless be made out for the identification of current success with certain valuable human qualities. Apart from any reliance upon the transmission of ' acquired characters ', there is some ground for holding it likely that the older rich families in most countries were founded by persons of physique, energy, or ability, above the common, who, marrying into families of similar grade or into the energetic *nouveaux riches*, have transmitted some of this physical and even mental superiority to their offspring. Most recent rich or well-to-do families, established by men of superior ability, grit, cunning, and initiative, containing the pick of these business qualities during the past century and a half out of the large middle and lower social strata, may be accredited with a more than average measure of these physical and mental characters in their present representatives, notwithstanding the admitted tendency of a reversion to the mean. In the ' new ' countries, settled by successive waves of immigration, while the whole population may be deemed to consist of stock with more than average health, energy, and enterprise, these qualities should be generally higher in the descendants of the earliest settlers, in whom political or religious heterodoxy was combined with the physique and spirit of adventurers. Since in nearly all countries these upper-class families are failing to reproduce themselves as fast as the lower-class families, there is some ground for supposing that for the population as a whole there is a decline in these physical and mental qualities.

But before concluding that this implies a definitely dysgenic selection, a survival and growth of inferior stock, we ought to take account of the arbitrary assumption of an absolute standard of human values contained in this argument. Is it even certain, or reasonable, to suppose, that because physical health and energy of a superior sort went into the composition of the founder of a family, that superiority will normally be retained in later generations ? Here death-rate, not birth-rate, is a chief determinant. Among the rich and secure classes the low mortality of infants and children, as compared with that among the lower classes, enables their weaklings in body and in mind, to survive, grow to maturity, and transmit offspring, while the more rigorous elimination of weaklings among the poor contrives to raise the average of their stock. It is, indeed, a charge made by many eugenists against humanitarian legislation that it reduces the efficacy of this selection, though with curious inconsistency they refrain from urging the advantages of high infant mortality and dangerous living as selective agencies among the rich. It may well be true that the reckless breeding of the poor, with the improved protection accorded to their offspring by more humane legislation and other social conditions, does let down the rigour of the physical survival test. But it still remains a much severer test for the poor than for the rich, and *pro tanto* refutes the general contention in favour of the superior inborn physical and mental qualities of the higher social grades.

It may, however, be contended that the children of the higher social classes in spite of this weakening of the selective process, are, on the average, superior in certain qualities of physique[1] and intelligence[2] to the children of the lower

---

[1] "There can be little doubt that on the whole the most fertile sections of the population are the less physically fit section " (Carr-Saunders, *The Population Question*, p. 379).

[2] " In place of natural selection, group selection, and sexual selection, we have had at work, within each public in increasing degrees, various forms of social selection—military selection, selection by the towns, selection by the Church, political selection with its exiles and its colonial system, and lastly economic selection, which has become exceedingly influential in recent years among ourselves. And all these, as far as can

classes, though the difficulties of eliminating the influence of environment and nurture have invalidated most actual tests. Granted that this be so, can we assert, or assume, that these physical and mental qualities constitute the true and sufficient tests of desirable personality ? Certain truly vital powers of personality seem to survive and flourish better in simple, hard surroundings. Stephen Reynolds, writing from intimate acquaintance with Devonshire fisherfolk, says :

" The more intimately one lives among the poor the more one admires their amazing talent for happiness in spite of privation, and their magnificent courage in face of uncertainty ; and the more also one sees that these qualities have been called into being, or kept alive, by uncertainty and thriftlessness. . . . The Man matters more than his Circumstances. The poor man's *Courage to Live* is his most valuable distinctive quality. Most of his finest virtues spring therefrom. . . . The poor and the middle class are different in kind as well as in degree. Their civilisations are not two stages of the same civilisation, but two civilisations, two traditions, which have grown up concurrently, though not, of course, without considerable intermingling. . . . The civilisation of the poor may be more backward materially, but it contains the nucleus of a finer civilisation than that of the middle class." [1]

It is perhaps even permissible to question the confident assumption that the more lively and adventurous stock, which always presses from the traditional rural life into cities or into foreign lands, is intrinsically superior to the more sluggish, conservative, and home-loving types. It might be maintained, at any rate, that this slower-witted, more conservative majority, rooted by physical assimilation and affection to their native soil, and there entrenched in

be seen, have operated mainly, among some peoples and in some ages very powerfully, to diminish the fertility of the best elements of the population and so to produce actual retrogression of the average intellectual capacity of peoples, and especially to deprive them of eugenic stocks, the stocks which were most fertile in individuals of exceptional capacity on whom the progress of civilisation and the relative power of nations chiefly depend " (McDougall, *The Group Mind*, p. 261).

[1] *A Poor Man's House*, pp. 262, 267, 270 (quoted, H. Wright, *Population*, p. 159).

strong and tried traditions, forms the permanent staple of a national life, at least as important for collective survival and progress as are the variant elements which carry into the bustle of a wider life the seeds of change. But be this as it may, it can hardly be denied that the conditions of the social-economic struggle by which ' success ' is attained in modern times are calculated to overstress certain intellectual and moral, perhaps also physical, characteristics, and to depress others of equal or greater intrinsic human worth. Successful acquisitiveness, under modern conditions either of competition or of combination, usually requires an extremely persistent selfishness, an habitual disregard of the interests of others, that is incompatible with high qualities of sympathy and imagination. The self-assertive and fighting instincts are given excessive play, and the personal will-to-power finds expression in the crudest command of men and money. If in some cases there is large scope for constructive ability coupled with a passion for improving the conditions of life for large bodies of workers, or for the wider public, the normal career of money-making under existing circumstances involves a narrow concentration of intelligence and a hardening of heart not favourable to the selection for success of the highest types of human character. Men of the finest intellectual character and of the most delicately sensitive nature are apt to fight shy of the business life. Great thinkers, creative artists, lovers of mankind, are not usually successful men of business. These fine qualities are defects in the process of selection for the successful classes. For this reason it is inherently probable that the world loses the most precious services of its greatest offspring, whose nature does not fit them

> " To grasp the skirts of happy chance
> Or breast the blows of circumstance "

in the rude and degrading struggle for wealth and economic security. So far as this is true, the case of the eugenist, founded mainly upon the test of financial success, is false. Its falsehood lies in the wrong identification of qualities of successful money-making with those of desirable humanity. The anti-human determinants for success in the struggle stamp their character upon the stock that succeeds, and, so far as the character is retained intact in its posterity, these defects continue to war against the service of humanity. It may not unreasonably be urged that the inability to get peaceable conditions into Europe after the Great War is directly attributable to the determinant power exercised in nearly every nation by men whose position has been won by forceful selfishness in political or economic struggles, either on their part or on that of their ancestors.

§ The same criticism applies to our race eugenists with their Nordic and other hypothesis. The claims for innate superiority on behalf of the white races, and the Nordic race in particular, and for such national and world policies as shall help them to survive and rule, rest on the same rickety foundations as those disclosed by class eugenics. Indeed, the Nordic case is perhaps the best of all examples of what I may call selective reasoning. The existence of a long-skulled, tall, blond, blue-eyed race, issuing from some ill-defined original habitat in North-East Europe, and spreading west and south by forceful conquest, may be a valid hypothesis. But the identification of elements of this race with classes or other segments of modern nations, by virtue of the survival of these physical characters, is a very dubious process, having regard to the admitted blends from inter-marriage to which all European nations have been so long subjected, and the difficulties which attend the reliable tests for most of the Nordic characters. When we pass from physical to intellectual and moral characters, the difficulties thicken for the Nordic champion. For, granting that a conquering and ruling race combines some superior powers of intellect and will with their physical vigour, is it clear that their descendants, could they be safely identified, would still retain intact these conquering traits evolved presumably by the harder struggle in their earlier habitat? Would these not have been largely eliminated by many generations of easier living in which they had no survival value? Or, if it be alleged, that the ruling classes in our white nations do in fact present the physical and mental characters of the Nordic ancestor in a distinguishable degree, how far would this carry us towards the admission of a policy directed to maintain the survival and dominance of these Nordic elements on grounds of human superiority and human service? For the Nordic champion claims that conservation of Nordic strains is doubly desirable, first, because the Nordic is in effect the superman, the highest sample of humanity, and secondly, because capacity to rule over others for their advantage as well as for his own, makes this conservation a disinterested human policy. The Nordic, in a word, is shown us as the natural leader not merely in the arts of war but in those of peace, the inventive and creative intelligence is particularly his, and his superior initiative and commanding personality mark him out for every sort of organisation and command. How far history bears out these claims, whether it does not normally present the conqueror as the destroyer of civilisations more advanced than his own, how far the political and social organisations established by conquering Nordics are stable and progressive, these are questions to which modern researches into early Greek, Assyrian, and Egyptian civilisations, as well as reflections upon the course of more recent events, give answers not generally favourable to Nordic claims. How is it even specious to suggest that qualities of group leadership in the ruder arts of rule and conquest, serviceable in primitive times for the survival of certain hardy stocks, and for their useful infusion into softer stocks, entitle the alleged descendants of this conquering race to sustain to-day national and imperial policies designed to maintain their racial purity and to make them dominant in political and economic government over inferior white strains in their own nations, and over all the coloured races of the outside world ? For no less than this is the logical and actual claim of the Nordic eugenist. The valuable Nordic strain is dying out, partly, because (as we have seen) the course of modern civilisation has taken a turn unfavourable to his survival, partly, because he is threatened by a hybridisation under which (so runs the biological contention) the higher and more recent Nordic characters are bred out by the lower and the older characters of Mediterranean and other inferior stocks.[1]

A full-blown American theory of Nordic rights would be an interesting statement, nowhere yet presented adequately. We gather, however, from various sources that it would run along these lines. Until the recent immigration from Southern and South-Eastern Europe, the white stock of America was Nordic to a predominant extent, partly because the original settlers were from countries, England, Holland, and France, where Nordic strains are numerous, partly, because immigrants from these, and later from Scandinavian and German sources, as carriers of adventurous qualities, were selected on a Nordic test. But later waves of immigration threaten to swamp this Nordic stock, both by numbers and by political and economic competition based on numbers. Under these conditions Nordics refuse to breed, and even the seats of power which they still hold in politics, industry, and ' society ', are threatened by the lower racial elements. The older American stock must protect itself against this free incursion of inferior white stocks, and against the

---

[1] There is something curiously vague about this breeding-out theory. In what sense is it maintained that the Nordic is a more recent ' race ' than, for example, the Alpine or the Mediterranean, or that the later-evolved characters are intrinsically more valuable than those developed in the earlier biological struggle ?

excessive demands of the worse white elements of the existing population for 'control' in government and industry. While retaining all the traditional forms and sentimental appanages of democracy, a strong hand must be kept upon the political and economic levers of power by 'good Americans' who have inherited the blood which carries the right to rule. As the entire resident white community must be mobilised for refusing entrance to coloured outsiders, and for maintaining the segregation and political and economic servitude of coloured insiders, and for a rigorous restriction and selection of new white immigrants, so a skilful policy must be devised for repressing inside America all assertions of liberty and equality likely to hamper political and economic government by 'the better elements', predominantly Nordic.

§ I have dwelt upon this Nordic theory and its loose, half-disclosed policy in America, as the ripest and most audacious example of the racial eugenics, upon which ruling classes and ruling nations everywhere rely, when they desire to support their will-to-power by quasi-scientific authority. Presented in this form, what stands out most conspicuously is the humour of the intellectual procedure. From the fact that *we* have managed to conquer some other people by force of arms and to compel their submission, *we* deduce our superior fitness to govern them and the consequent benefits *we* confer upon them and the world at large. As presumably disinterested judges, we assign to ourselves the prize for good conduct ! We support this claim by adducing all sorts of evidence of the concrete benefits of our forceful rule, ourselves being the valuer of each item of this benefit. Similarly with the 'Nordic' rulers in national life. They convert their own alleged superior characters into the standard of absolute 'fitness' or social efficiency, and then, trying others by this standard, find them failures, thus assigning to themselves the right to rule as an obligation to assist their weaker brothers. What we have in effect is a revival of ' divine right ', Nature posing as divinity, and right as the naïve endorsement of our will-to-power.

At present, however, the attitude of convinced eugenists is one of deep despondency. They see the inferior stocks in their nation multiplying faster than the superior, the latter sometimes exhibiting a positive decline. Their world-survey shows the white Western peoples, and their Nordic strains in particular, slowing down their vital output, while the coloured races, black, brown, and yellow, continue to multiply. Imperialism and other white contacts have not merely helped this increase of the lower races, by reducing internecine wars, and stimulating more productive uses of the soil, but have sown seeds of knowledge and stirred instincts of adventure, impelling many of these peoples to seek outlets for their redundant population in some of the large territories which white men hold but fail to occupy. This pressure of population from the densely occupied into the thinly occupied countries has always been a chief impelling motive in the larger historic drama. Conscious superiority in scientific equipment has until lately, however, served to give a sense of security to the white peoples. The pressure of ignorant, unorganised numbers could not prevail against the monopoly of scientific force and discipline. This security, however, is now seriously undermined by the proved capacity of certain coloured peoples to assimilate white men's science in the arts of peace and war. Indeed, the deliberate arming and training of coloured troops, African and other, by white Governments with the avowed intention of using them in white men's warfare, may well appear to racial eugenists the deadliest menace which the future holds in store for the white races. For when the impelling motive of migration into white men's unused lands is backed by training in the use of white men's scientific force, how can this steady increase of pressure be resisted ?

CHAPTER III

THE STRUGGLE FOR A FREE ETHICS

I

§ THESE studies in Economics and Politics, with the not
infrequent excursions into Psychology which they have
involved, have brought us inside the territory claimed for
Ethics, or Moral Science par excellence. For, holding as
we do, that these social sciences are demarcated, in their
subject matter and the questions which they put to it, by
the requirements of their corresponding arts, we have been
driven to the recognition of standards of values, concepts of
human well-being, and motives or incentives to activity,
which clearly fall within the domain of Ethics. Now,
though the theory, or principles, of Ethics is sometimes
claimed as a branch of Philosophy, rather than of Science,
the sharp insistence upon this distinction will generally be
rejected as an inconvenient pedantry. Philosophy will
rightly be recognised as *scientia scientiarum*, mainly concerned with the nature of knowledge and the presuppositions
of the sciences, as well as with the underlying unity required
alike to give order to them and to their subject matter, the
phenomenal Universe. Whether, therefore, Ethics be formally classed as a branch of Philosophy, or as a science, its
devotees claim for it a field of ordered knowledge in the
conscious behaviour of man. The distinction sometimes
made between Ethics and other ' Sciences ' viz. that the
latter deal exclusively with what is, whereas the former
deals also with what ought to be, is wrongly taken to dis-
qualify Ethics as a claimant to the term Science. For an

' ought ', i.e. some fact weighted with a ' moral ' value, is none the less an ' is '. From the standpoint of science, an ideal, as also an illusion or a fallacy of reasoning, has evidently as much right to be taken for a subject of scientific study, as a piece of rock or a plant.

But it is needless to pursue this metaphysical inquiry. It suffices to our purpose to recognise that ethical principles, laws, bodies of doctrine, are set up which have an important bearing upon the arts and practices of human conduct. It is therefore worth while to consider how far and in what sense these principles, laws, doctrines, are the product of thinking that is ' disinterested ', in our accepted meaning of the term, and how far and in what ways special interests mould, influence, or warp, the thinking. A science of ethics cannot pretend to be advancing towards quantitative exactitude. If there was a time when a determinist utili-tarianism seemed to be heading in that direction, with the assistance of a doctrine of conservation of energy and a hedonistic calculus, that time has long gone by. The dismissal of the law of efficient causation, or indeed any causation, from the service of ' science ' on the one hand, the repudiation of the pleasure and pain motivation of behaviour on the other, are held to have played havoc with the Benthamite utilitarianism and most of its later revisions.

§ But while modern psychology has broken with the older determinism, so far as even to reject the concept, it professes to furnish a scientific substitute in the shape of an evolution of morals, " a continuously graded series " of " modes of purposive striving " " from the pursuit of its prey by the Amœba to the moral struggles of Man ". Professor McDougall distinguishes seven stages in this evolution :

(1) The vague, almost undifferentiated striving of the animalcule in pursuit of his prey :

(2) The striving of animals in which the instincts are sharply differentiated and directed towards specific goals that are vaguely anticipated by the creature :

(3) The instinctive strivings of primitive man towards goals more fully imagined and anticipated ; the strivings of instinctive desire :

(4) The strivings of man prompted by desire for instinctive goals, but directed also to goals which are conceived and desired only as means to the instinctive goal :

(5) Conduct of the lower level ; that is, instinctive desire regulated and controlled, in the choice of means, by anticipation of rewards and punishments :

(6) Conduct of the middle level ; that is, the same instinctive impulses regulated in the choice of goals and of means by anticipation of social approval and disapproval :

(7) Choice of the higher level ; that is, striving regulated in the choice of goals and means by the desire to realise an ideal in character and conduct, a desire which itself springs from an instinctive disposition whose impulse is turned to higher uses by the subtle influences of organised society embodying a moral tradition.[1]

Now, disregarding for our purposes the earlier stages as pre-ethical, and confining our attention to those which are dignified by the name ' conduct ', it is interesting to consider how far and in what sense the study of the ' conduct ' and the ' ought ' which it embodies can be ' disinterested '. First, regarded from the distinctively moral standpoint, these three stages differ not primarily as regards code of conduct, or moral contents, but as regards sanctions. Conduct at the lower level is regulated and controlled " by anticipation of rewards and punishments ", whether imposed

[1] *Outline of Psychology*, p. 449.

by law or custom, an external objective sanction. Conduct at the middle level still rests upon a sanction mainly external to the individual, the approval of others, but it involves a sympathy with that approval which acts as an inducing or co-operating influence. Conduct of the higher level places the sanction in the interior of each personality as " a desire to realise an ideal of character ". Now, as regards the levels of conduct controlled and sanctioned by external rewards and punishments, or social approval or disapproval, it will hardly be disputed that these sanctions and controls cannot be ' disinterested ', in the sense of a single-minded devotion to the general welfare, but will carry the pressure of the interests of the ruling and more influential members of the community. The greater part of what is often represented as the inherent and instinctive conservatism and submissiveness of ' the herd ' is fear, not of change in itself, but of the repressive hand of the ruler or ruling caste playing on the ignorance and induced superstitions of the multitude. Customary canons of conduct, though perhaps laden with some ' survival value ' for the herd or tribe, carry large disabling burdens of interested oppression, whether imposed by legal penalties or by public opinion. What is more to our point, such thinking of a general order as is applied to conduct on these levels, whether by the more reflective members of such a community, or by later outside students, will not be adequately disinterested but will be weighted by various personal valuations and notions of the observer and thinker. It is not possible for distinctively ' ethical ' students of anthropology to avoid importing into the values they assign to the customary life of a community something of their own feelings and beliefs about the inherent rightness of certain attitudes of mind towards such institutions as marriage, slavery, and property. Since ethics is a science and art of values, this interestedness is unavoidable.

Can it be otherwise when we deal with conduct at its

higher level, involving the setting up within the shrine of a personality of " an ideal of character and conduct ", with " a desire to realise it " derived from " an instinctive disposition whose impulse is turned to higher uses by the subtle influences of organised society embodying a moral tradition " ? How far on this higher level, will this ideal, as an internal operative influence, be one and the same for different persons ? i.e. how far can it be erected into an absolute and objective standard ? What is this ' instinctive disposition ' which furnishes the impulse to realise a moral ideal, and how far is it identical in different persons ? And these ' higher uses ', what is the standard of height ?

No great reflection is needed to teach us that an ethical theory which seeks to get away from the ' utilitarian ' conception of human welfare, as end of action and standard of values, and to fall back on some ' instinctive disposition ' rising somehow to ' higher uses ', is likely to lose itself in a fog of mystical language.

But that is not the only step towards irrationalism taken by this psychology. Not only is utilitarianism of the modern enlightened order to be scrapped in favour of this mysterious conation, but determinism even of the elastic form that incorporates all the ' real ' advantages of ' freedom ', is also dismissed. For Professor McDougall it is not enough that " organic evolution is a creative process and that Mind is the creative agency ". Into this process he imports the strange dogma that " The belief in a certain creative power of *original determination* [1] is a necessity of our moral nature ". Now, that some power, producing changes, and in this sense creative, operates in all organic evolution may well seem a reasonable working hypothesis. But the term ' original determination ' is void of intelligible meaning. If I am provided with an urge towards lines of conduct which harmonise my personal ' good ' with that of

[1] My italics.—J. A. H.

' mankind ', and if each fresh act of choice is personal to me, so that I can and must utilise my latest experience to help in the ' determination ' of my next act, so making me a 'new' man for every ' new ' action, what earthly need have I of some ' original determination ' ? A ' creative ' urge of instinctive co-operation towards attainment of the welfare of mankind, operating with a growing measure of consciousness and intelligence in an ever-widening interpretation both of ' welfare ' and of ' mankind ', is surely the most ' rational ' as well as the ' highest ' setting of the ethical problem.

§ Why is there a disposition to shirk and confuse this determinist utilitarianism by the retention of vague notions of ' freedom ' and the introduction of new nebulous ideals ? The answer to this question is, I think, to be sought in the feeling and belief that certain vested interests, material and moral, can be served by this intellectual procedure. There are two distinguishable ways in which, it is deemed, this service can be rendered. One is by an authoritative intellectual endorsement of the accepted doctrine of personal responsibility, the other by the establishment of a scale of moral values favourable to economic and political conservatism. Though these two intellectual services are in a measure interdependent, they require separate consideration.

The doctrine of responsibility is the more fundamental, inasmuch as its emotional import underlies and helps to form the scale of moral values. To many men of scientific training, acustomed to believe that there are no limits to ' the reign of law ' in any department of observed phenomena, the attempts of moral scientists or philosophers, to withdraw certain critical acts of the human mind from the field of orderly and calculable sequence, by the introduction of some special creative function of a central personality, seems mere obscurantism bred of loose thinking and moral cowardice. But that judgment does not go deeply enough into motives.[1] The collapse of definite Theology has always bred alarms, lest, the divine sanction to a divinely appointed code of conduct having disappeared, no adequate human sanction would take its place. So long as the divine will, operating either from its supreme centre, or by delegation, through the personal conscience, was acknowledged to be a law unto itself, there was no real danger of any refractory instinct heading a successful revolt against the established moral order. However difficult it might be to furnish a satisfactory account of the way in which the personal responsibility of man co-operated with the overruling will of God, a sort of accepted ' balance ' had long been reached which for practical purposes reconciled divine authority with personal accountability. When the belief in external divinity weakened or disappeared, it became more important to secure and strengthen the stronghold of the human conscience. The modern cult of irrationalism, so far as it is not a natural reaction against the dogmatic excesses of nineteenth-century hard-shell rationalism, has this object prominently in view. Modern science, it was believed and felt, denied or disparaged the power of self-control in man, and by the utterance of this denial or disparagement, actually weakened that self-control. In certain teaching this disparagement of rational control was accompanied by something like a glorification of the primary instincts and a demand for a ' free life ' whose freedom would consist in furnishing large opportunities for the naked play of these several instincts. Now, holding, as I do, that the danger of a decentralised determinism, in which conduct was explained wholly in terms of a conflict between opposed motives of given strength, was real and of considerable dimensions, the reaffirmation of a central rational control, exercised in

[1] By ' motives ' here and elsewhere I signify not conscious end or object but impelling power.

the interest of the entire personality and involving freedom of the will, in the sense to which I have referred, was an entirely legitimate step. Unfortunately, it was inevitable that behind this assertion of personal control, and using it as a cloak or screen, the vested interests of reaction should advance towards new lines of defence. Their keener-minded representatives were quick to realise that the demands for social justice, involving uncomfortable changes in the economic and political order, could best be countered, not by direct refutation of the rationality or even the ' abstract rightness ' of the demands, but by stressing the paramount importance of personal character. A positive and a negative principle and policy of social conduct were erected on this basis. Reforms of economic or political structure we were told, were of no avail for bettering the members of the depressed classes, unless they were preceded, or at least accompanied, by a strengthening and improving of the rational will of the individuals. Nay, these reforms could not be brought about in true conformity with modern democratic principles, until and unless intellectual and moral education had gone far enough to evoke in the masses an intelligent and real demand for them. Even so, there remained the lasting danger lest these structural reforms should, so far as they brought improved material and moral conditions of life to ' the people ', weaken their moral fibre by slackening the incentives to effort which existing difficulties and hardships brought into play. Proposals for effective relief of poverty have been met by the insistence that such relief would be a premium on idleness and in-efficiency. Free education was, by the same philosophy, subjected to constant criticism as sapping the sense of obligation in parents to make sacrifices for the education of their children. Reasonable facilities for divorce are met by the setting up of the integrity of the family as a desirable end, irrespective of the nature of that integrity. Old Age

Pensions evoked a howl of virtuous alarm lest the habit of thrift, with its attendant forethought and sacrifice, should be uprooted. In England the leaders of the Charity Organisation Society assumed the rôle of defenders of working-class character against the attempts of philanthropic sentimentalists and political demagogues to corrupt it by free public services, doles, or other benefactions. State or collective action meant a loss of personal responsibility, substituting a mechanical compulsion for a voluntary exertion. A curious significance was given to this protest against socialistic measures by the fact that some of its ablest exponents were committed to the philosophic doctrine of a ' general will ', which required for its political expression the activities of that very State which was the enemy of personal morality ! It is difficult to understand how these thinkers can have failed to realise the contradiction between their political philosophy and their social ethics, unless we take account of the subconscious pressure of the conservative interests. For, however defective the structure and working of the existing State might be as an instrument of the general will, it would seem to be self-evident that these defects could only be removed by a strengthening of the general will,[1] and this required a larger and more vigorous use. This faith in and practice of the general will our ' moral individualists ' insist upon withholding, until, by some slow process of personal education, the individual constituents of that general will have attained such powers of wisdom and of self-restraint as to make collective action safe. On the one hand, they fail to realise that, precisely on account of the defects of the present social-economic order, the personal education, on which they rely, is made impossible ; and on the other hand, they reject the wholesome influence which participation in acts of collective conduct, however imper-

---

[1] It does not matter for our argument whether the term ' general will ' involves group-consciousness or not, whether it is *volonté générale* or *volonté de tous*.

fectly administered, brings to bear on the personal character of the participants. This misrepresentation of the separate moral personality as the sole source of genuine social progress is inspired by the ' rationalising ' need of the vested interests.

§ As might be expected, the institutions of criminal and civil law furnish examples of a similar conflict between modern psycho-physics and established legal theory. Here the issue often turns upon the fact and meaning of *mens sana*. Though law, as embodied in statute or precedent, and interpreted by men steeped in the spirit of this law, must take a conservative position on matters of responsibility, this need not involve a harsh or unjust view of abnormal or borderland cases. Indeed, in matters where no fears of dangerous laxity arise, as in the question of the degrees of intelligent understanding and intention involved in the signature of a will, or the entering of a contract, the law may usually be trusted to hold the balance fairly. But in certain types of conduct falling under criminal jurisdiction, acts relating to sex, property, and life, there are many signs that legal justice refuses to give fair consideration to the results of modern psychological researches into the nature and limits of personal responsibility, because it is affected by considerations of social safety irrelevant to the matter on which judgment is invoked. The inherent difficulty of reading the mind from the record of external behaviour operates with peculiar force in certain cases of alleged mental abnormality. Kleptomania, or homicidal mania, regarded as lasting states of mind, though still encountering much prejudice in the conservative mind of jurists, have effected a definite lodgement in the administration of justice. The same is probably the case with some forms of sexual aberration. Such concessions are not felt to involve any serious derogation from the doctrine of personal responsibility. These are cases of lasting moral insanity, the victims of which ought to be kept in permanent seclusion, with other defectives. But where an anti-social action, whether crime or folly, is attributed not to a lasting condition of mind but to an ' uncontrollable impulse ', there exists a strong legal and lay bias against the acceptance of this plea, as a reason for withholding conviction and punishment. That certain social risks are involved in the acceptance of the plea may be readily admitted, seeing that the act of control is the most delicate and recondite operation of the personality. It may also reasonably be urged that uncontrollability is a matter of degree, and that the expectation of punishment, or of immunity, may determine whether a particular impulse is controllable or not. The value given to this argument will chiefly depend upon whether we believe that in an ' uncontrollable impulse ' the normal control is absent, or is overborne. But here, as in other cases, I am not concerned with the validity of the position, but with the question how far an equitable and disinterested consideration is given to it. A useful illustration of the difficulty is furnished by the commentary of a *Times* leader-writer [1] upon the recommendation of a recent committee, to the effect that the Macnaghten rules in legal recognition of irresponsibility should be extended, so far as to include uncontrollable impulse among the conditions rendering a person irresponsible. *The Times'* comment that this recommendation is " calculated to undermine our whole system of justice " well presents the panic mind which established ' law and order ' offers to an inconvenient conclusion of disinterested science. Nobody acquainted with the deep conservativism of Medicine can seriously impute the medical acceptance of this form of irresponsibility to any rash spirit of innovation. *The Times* writer manifestly is not concerned with evidence or truth, but with the feeling that this position, true or not, should be refused admission because of the disturbing

[1] November 27, 1923.

consequences it invokes. It is felt that a firm insistence upon personal responsibilty for breaches of public law is of such paramount importance to the maintenance of ' social stability ' as to warrant the ignoring of any scientific judgments which might undermine our confidence in this responsibility.[1]

§ A disinterested ethics, dedicated to the discovery of sound rules of human welfare, finds itself, as we have already seen,[2] in constant trouble in dealing with three institutions or spheres of conduct, the family, property, and the State. The inquirer discovers that free discussion upon the origin, nature, and utility of these institutions is taboo, and that any proposal which contemplates the possibility of radical reforms affecting them is regarded, not merely by the multitude, but by the intellectual class, as wicked.   These institutions are in a peculiar sense ' sacred ', and as such ' untouchable ' even by thought.   The peculiar horror in most societies of incest, sacrilege, and treason, is attested by the terrible penalties attached to these acts.   This abhorrence of ' the unclean thing ' dates back to the most primitive mentality of man.   Rooted in fears of a mysterious nature, it was stamped upon the dawning mind of man with such intensity of feeling that centuries of ' rationalism ' have availed little to weaken its hold.   Superstition is the term best conveying to the modern mind the mitigated form of this primitive horror.   But it survives in a more attenuated form wherever ' the sense of sin ' prevails.   Among bad actions deliberately anti-social, those only are ' sins ' where a breach of the divine law, or of a human law with its presumed divine sanction, occurs.   We may condemn

---

[1] The discussion in the House of Lords upon the Second Reading of the Criminal Responsibility Bill (May 15, 1924) makes very clear this rift between the legal mind and the medical.
[2] Part I, Chapter IV.

the selfishness, callousness, or cruelty of many acts which yet do not evoke in us this sense of sin.

Now there are good ' reasons ' why the sheltering influence of the sentiment of ' sanctity ' has attached to ' the family ' ' property ', ' the State '. For these institutions have in their several ways been of prime importance as conservative factors in civilisation. That the family was often a nest of despotism and cruelty is ignored in virtue of the education which close family life gave to the associative instincts and emotions. The abuses of private property in all times have similarly been condoned on account of the incentives to industrial progress it affords. The organised community, the City-State, or its head, were serviceably sacred in that they sheltered the growing arts and institutions of human society. A heavy cost for these services is still paid in the exploitation of these sanctities by the powerful and privileged classes defending their powers and privileges. The claims of modern science to open up for close and fearless scrutiny the instinct of sex and the structure of the family, the historical basis and the ethical limitations of private property and industry, the sovereignty of the State in relation to its individual members, other institutions, and other States, are subject to much obstruction, mainly from the secret or avowed fear lest the primitive taboo, improved and sublimated for modern conservative uses, should be weakened or dissolved by subjection to impartial criticism. The maxim " To understand all is to forgive all " does not recommend itself to those who value the sense of sin and the just hatred of offenders against the purities, sanctities, respectabilities of the established social order. Science they fear may sap the emotional roots of personal responsibility on the one hand, and on the other, by suggesting large new rational measures of social reconstruction, may hustle in a dangerous way the slow processes of adjustment to new situations which have hitherto enabled the vested interests and controlling classes in each community to safeguard their essential interests.

Professor McDougall makes an inspiring claim for social science when he tells us : " In many directions—by the historians, the biologists, the anthropologists, the statisticians—data are being gathered for a Science of Society whose sure indications will enable us deliberately to guide the further evolution of the nation towards the highest ideal of a nation we can conceive ".[1]

But how is this ideal itself determined ?   What conception or composition of national, or human, welfare does it embody ?   This question opens up the nature of the struggle that is taking place to subjugate the social sciences to the requirements of those in a position to impose a ' highest ideal ' which expresses the valuations of institutions and conduct which they approve.

§ This consideration links on the first great ethical issue, viz. that of the nature of moral responsibility, with the second, viz. that of a standard and scale of moral values. Now the contribution of social science towards the formation of a ' highest ideal ' and a standard of values is chiefly critical.   The projection, or imaginative seizure, of a social ideal is properly regarded as a work not of science but of art.   The ordered information of science checks the play of the creative art by shedding light on the attainability of ideals and the modes of advancing towards their attainment.   Nay more, the valuation of the several factors in a vision of social welfare will be affected by knowledge of the part these factors have played in human history.   The informed idealist will thus not easily be led to set his aspiration upon the ideal of a society economically motivated by the single sense of social service, or the delight in work for its own sake.   Nor will he accept a vision of political democracy

[1] *The Group Mind* p. 300.

which sees a common will issuing equally from all members
of the body politic, and expressing itself fully, clearly, and
without deflection, through chosen representatives and their
controlled executive. But the same body of accessible
knowledge will yield widely divergent ideals for men of
different native temperaments and different interests. What
Mr. McDougall somewhat naïvely styles " the highest ideal
we can conceive " cannot emerge in any solid substance from
a social science. The common constant factors in our
inherited equipment and our ' social heritage ' will not
suffice to place a single ' highest ideal ' in charge of social
aspirations. Our ' conception ' will largely reflect the
preferences, or scale of values, rooted in our instinctive
make-up, as modified by our personal experience and
traditions, and the more or less strong and definite ' interests '
thus formed. A man of dominant nature and eager initiative will form a widely different social ideal from that of a
gentler and more easy-going man. An ' average ' American
of any social status would require in his ideal society a much
larger measure of ' sociality ' and more quick happenings
than the ' average ' Englishman of any class. And when
we come to the assessment of material, intellectual, and
moral values in an ' ideal ' or a standard, no acceptance of
social science would go far towards merging into one ' highest
ideal ' the racial, class, and individual divergences. English-
men, perhaps less than other civilised persons, are given to
the conscious formation of ' highest ideals '. But in no
other people has history disclosed plainer divergences of
human valuations, or subconscious ideals, than that presented in the struggle of Cavaliers and Puritans which, with
modifications of form, has continued up to the present day.
Had the seventeenth-century Cavalier been capable of formu-
lating his latent pattern of a social ideal, it would have been
rooted in the maintenance of a free-living, sporting, idle,
high-tempered, showy-mannered country gentry, sustained

by a subordinate but not too servile body of merchants and
workers, whose ways of living would be a coarser imitation
of his own high life. The tough persistence of the Puritan
spirit and its valuations in the modern political, and still
more the economic, history of modern England (and I may
add America) is a theme that has attracted much attention
in social psychology. We need not here discuss the insoluble
problem, how far this Puritan spirit originated in a religious
revolt of the individual conscience against the collective
authority of a Church, or how far the sentiment of political
and economic liberty seized and exploited for more ' practical ' purposes the spiritual resources of the Reformation.[1]
The special importance of a study of Puritanism is that it
affords the most striking example of the part played by
definitely material interests in the selection and spiritual
boosting of a particular standard of morals and scale
of values. The opportunity for the play of its extraordinary rôle was afforded by a set of happenings having
no direct or close causal connection with Puritanism,
which, transforming rapidly the industry and commerce of
this country, formed a natural home for the Puritan spirit.
Industry, thrift,[2] sobriety, honesty, chastity, the regulation
of life in all departments, the close association of like-
minded persons with the same social and business standards,
abstinence from all interests and occupations that interfered
with profitable business on week-days and profitable religion

[1] For an interesting historical study of this problem, see Laski's Introduction to *A Defence of Liberty against Tyrants*.
[2] " The morals, the politics, and the religion of the age joined in a
grand conspiracy for the promotion of saving. God and Mammon were
reconciled. Peace on earth to men of good means. A rich man could,
after all, enter into the Kingdom of Heaven—if only he saved. A new
harmony sounded from the celestial spheres. ' It is curious to observe
how, through the wise and beneficent arrangement of Providence, men
thus do the greatest service to the public when they are thinking of nothing but their own gain ',[3] so sang the angels " (Keynes, *A Tract on Monetary
Reform*, p. 7).
[3] *Easy Lessons on Money Matters for the use of Young People*, published
by the Society for Promoting Christian Knowledge, twelfth edition, 1850.

on Sundays—this combination of attributes was finely accommodated to the requirements for success in the new forms of business enterprise that were opening out towards the full-blown capitalism of our time. The concentration upon personal salvation in this world and the next was itself a sound business economy. For stressing, as it did, the factor of personal character and individual effort as the method of achieving success in both spheres, it threw upon everyone the full responsibility of his own fate. Moreover, by the accepted view that this world was but a stepping-stone to eternity, it led to a disparagement of poverty and economic oppression as negligible ills, or perhaps not ills at all but trials providentially designed to educate and brace the character. If it be said that this tenet seems inconsistent with the devotion of so much energy to one's own personal success in business, it can only be replied that this sort of inconsistency is widely prevalent in the rationalisation of our selfish motives.

§ Though I am far from adopting the rigorous doctrine of economic determinism that regards all politics, religion, and morals, as instruments by which economic forces conduct their struggles and achieve their aims, there is a sense in which it may be held that, in the reciprocal interactions of social forces and institutions, those which express the dominant business-trend exercise a disproportionate power to mould and direct the others towards the realisation of their special ends. This is not because man is primarily an economic being but because at certain times the economic purposes are more clear-sighted, skilful, and persistent, in executing their designs. It is neither chance nor reasonable justice which determines that property is better protected than life, not merely by legal enactments but by the general ethical sentiment of the community. Not merely is theft more surely and severely punished in most countries than assaults upon the person, but, more significant, the moral reprobation of theft is far keener and more general than that for personal violence, save in extreme cases of brutality or cruelty. As regards minor infractions of law and morals, property is more ' sacred ' than life, a stronger sense of ' sin ' attaching to its voluntary injuries. The Great War has demonstrated how much easier it is to effect a levy upon life than a levy upon property.

A significant testimony to the dominance of propertied interests is furnished by the ethical attitude towards the acts of force, fraud, and cunning, by which big businesses extract large quantities of wealth from weaker private owners or from the public purse. Though most persons are aware that large lucrative privileges, in the shape of concessions, franchises, subsidies, tax-exemptions, protective tariffs, obtained by favour or corruption from persons purporting to represent the public interests, are acts of plunder, no sense of ' sin ', no keen moral repugnance, is felt, even by those who perceive the nature of these acts and disapprove them. This deficiency of moral feeling may be due partly to the indirectness of the injuries inflicted upon the unseen persons who are sufferers from these policies of plunder. But it is largely explained by the fact that no drastic legal restraints have been allowed to be imposed upon modern methods of big business. Most of the plundering by monopolies or combines, in which the sufferers are weaker businesses, workers, or consumers, where the plundering takes the shape of superior power of bargain, or ability to dictate prices, or other conditions of sale, is conducted within the protection of the law. But even where legal restraints exist, and are successfully set at defiance by big business, as in the case of some of the ' trust-busting ' legislation of the United States, little moral indignation is aroused among those who see what is going on. Such reprobation as is evinced is tepid when compared

with that accorded to some petty act of pilfering. I would
go farther and aver that, even when a big business firm is
convicted of positive fraud, in its relations with another
firm, or with the Government in its capacity of taxing
authority, the nature of the reprobation is affected by the
high regard in which big business is held by the common
mind.[1] Some allowance, no doubt, must here be made for
the impersonal character of most big businesses. But the
obstruction offered by organised business to legislative
interferences with the malpractices here named, and the
prejudice aroused against effective State control over
monopolies and combines, attest the success of the business
interests in stopping any clear understanding of economic
equities. Even the sufferers from these forms of economic
oppression are often softened in their indignation by a
sense, not perhaps of condonation, but of admiration for the
ruthless power wielded against them. For big business
has succeeded in imposing a wide acceptance of the view
that success is a sound test and measure of a socially serviceable fitness or ability, and that large profits, even when
visibly resulting from price-fixing monopoly, are a natural,
a necessary, and a just incentive to the exercise of high
business qualities from which the general community draws
great though indirect advantages. By inculcating this
view through their press and other organs of public opinion,
they stave off close scrutiny into the complicated processes
of big business, and so avert the moral condemnation which
an accurate analysis of these processes might bring home to
their own and the public conscience. In cases where
conscience breaks this boycott, and, aided by an unusually
keen and impartial understanding, arouses in big business

[1] Compare in the field of high politics the naïve expression of indignation from Signor Salandra, the Italian representative at the meeting of
the League of Nations, when it was proposed to interfere with the Italian
outrage upon Corfu. "It was never contemplated that such restraints
should be imposed upon Great Powers."

men a feeling of social compunction, damaged self-esteem is commonly repaired by voluntary concessions in the shape of co-partnership, profit-sharing, workers'-welfare schemes, pensions, and other good conditions of employment. Principles of chivalry are invoked, property and business administration are treated as ' trusts ' in which all factors of production and the consuming public figure as rightful beneficiaries. This acceptance of the idea of property as a moral ' trust ' is the specially favoured device by which reflective philanthropists can ' rationalise ' their persistent craving to keep the ' power ' that attaches to large ownership and administration. The social philosophy closely identified in England with the intellectual leaders of the Charity Organisation Society based its defence of the present system of industry and property mainly on the need of every man to express his moral personality through the acquisition and administration of property regarded as the natural reward of individual industry and thrift. By this doctrine of moral individualism they avoided disturbing inquiries into the methods of obtaining property, which would have disclosed on the one hand the glaring disabilities which beset the poorer and weaker members of the community in the attainment of this condition of the good life, and, on the other, the part which inheritance, chance, force, and anti-social cunning play in the acquisition of large means wherewith to fulfil this moral duty. No more insidious and humorous handling of ethical philosophy by the root-instincts of acquisitiveness and self-assertion has been exhibited than this ' trust ' view of property and business power, well summarised in the pregnant saying, which delivers the *coup de grâce* to ' philanthropy ' : " These people will do everything for us except get off our backs ".

§ Property as a moral ' Trust ' is, of course, no novel doctrine of ethics. It is only an enlargement of the practice of private charity, which has always operated, frankly, as an assuagement to the distress of the rich when the painful conditions of the poor are thrust too closely upon their vision, partly as a parade of generous self-assertion, partly as a way of buying off dangerous discontent and a demand for economic justice from the have-nots. Most churches, and among them the Christian Churches, have cultivated charitable practices, not merely because they recognised these personal and social gains, but for two other diverse reasons. Lavish charity fitted in with the formal disparagement of material prosperity and luxury that belonged to the spiritual life, while the administration of such charity was usually a chief instrument of ecclesiastical power. The sense of property as a ' Trust ' seldom, however, came out clearly into consciousness, until the development of great soulless modern capitalism, on the one hand, and organised proletarian sentiment upon the other, ripened the issue of economic justice, disclosing wholesale charity as the only specious alternative.

Modern psychology has done no greater service than its ruthless exposure of such rationalisation of the egotistic motives, which cloak their craving under the sublimation of the social instincts with which they associate themselves.

I would here guard myself against the appearance of imputing hypocrisy to many honourable business men and property owners who are genuine believers in the ' gospel ' of a moral ' Trust ', and are prepared to sacrifice their personal material interests in its cause. Many of these gospellers are manifestly keener for the social gains which they hold will follow the adoption of the economic schemes than for any personal prestige or other private satisfaction that may accrue to them as pioneers in social reform. But it is no less evident that the sudden new disposition of large numbers of employers to look favourably upon schemes which a few years ago they would have scouted as unworthy of consideration, is attributable to a feeling or conviction that, in the new dangerous world, rife with menaces of revolution and class war, concessions of a specious order, involving even some substantial derogation of powers and privileges hitherto enjoyed, are necessary and desirable, in order to retain intact the main substance of economic dominion, the freedom to wield control of business enterprise and to obtain large profits.

§ This ethics of moral individualism, alike in its strength and in its weakness, is an amiable substitute for the pre-established harmony of the classical economists. As the latter held that the intelligent selfishness of all members of an industrial community would bring about the most advantageous use of their joint productive resources and would distribute the wealth thus created in substantial conformity with the just deserts of all participants, so these moral individualists hold that, if every person engaging in a common business enterprise, as worker, employer, or share-holder, were actuated by a spirit of comradeship and mutual service, each giving out the best of his capacity to help in the success of the enterprise, and seeking for himself only ' a fair share ' of the gains accruing from it, all indi-vidual discords would cease, and industry as a whole would be established on a basis of lasting peace and equity. This appeal to individual good will as a sufficient source of social harmony owes its vogue, partly to the higher business ethics, it propounds, partly to the relief which it affords, alike from injurious friction between capital and labour within the business and from State interference. Its fatal defect is identical with that discernible in the earlier economic *laissez-faire*, viz. the failure to recognise that value is a social product, and that the sociality which determines it is something far wider and more complex than any sense of comradeship, or mutual good will, within the several little

co-operative groups that constitute a business. This
attribution of social determination to values is no barren
abstract doctrine.   It signifies that the amount and nature
of the human wealth, or welfare, attaching to the work done
in a department of a factory or store, and the human contribution made by that work to the satisfaction of human
needs, depend upon the interplay of needs and activities of
the entire community of producer-consumers, and respond
to the innumerable stimuli that come from all parts of the
economic system.   If it were true that the human value,
or even the monetary value, of the particular product of a
factory, the stock of boots, or yarn, or cocoa, were separately
attributable to the productive energy given out in that
factory, it would be plausible to argue that a sound and
satisfactory distribution of that value among the producers
of each factory would solve the economic problem.   But
since, in point of fact, the value, human or monetary, of
any such stock of boots, yarn, or cocoa depends, first,
upon the quantity of similar products turned out by
other businesses contributing to the same market,
secondly, by the quantity of other products of innumerable sorts with which the product in question ex-
changes in the intricacies of commerce ; and since behind
those objective determinants stand the ever-changing
subjective valuations both of work and of commodities, in
accord with the changing arts of industry and the changing
tastes of men—the notion of harmonising industry and
securing peace and economic justice by particular arrangements within the several productive units is false, alike in
theory and in practice.   Taking one or two practical issues,
there is no rational or equitable basis for determining how
the so-called profit of a business, over and above the necessary wages and interest on capital, should be apportioned
among the members of the business.   There is no ground
for holding that the whole, or any measurable proportion of

the surplus profit of a business, directly due perhaps to a conjunction of many causes, ability of management, superior facilities for marketing, lowering of transport costs, greater energy of certain workers, a new trade treaty, a general trade revival, and a variety of other factors, mostly outside the direct area of the business, should be absorbed in higher dividends or wages by the members of this particular firm. Such surplus means that prices are kept higher than they need have been, and that the consumer, whose demand is a main support and condition of high value, gets no share. If, on the other hand, as in certain semi-public services, his claim is taken into consideration, how much should he get in price-reduction ?

§ To none of these questions can the prophets of co-partnership, or any other scheme of separate business harmony, give a satisfactory answer. So long as the ' social good ' is conceived in terms of an aggregate of individual goods, and the social will as an aggregate of individual or group wills, the notion of appeals to individual character and motives as the sole and morally sufficient source of economic harmony will continue to enjoy the patronage of moralists and philanthropists who eschew a scientific analysis of industry. All these modes of rational-isation of the instincts supporting existing forms of property and economic power will continue to refuse acceptance of the doctrine of social value. " What is society, anyway ? Nothing but its individual members ! Stick, then, to individuals ! Improve them, induce them to act properly and cultivate good will in their immediate relations with those around them, and all will be well ! " So runs the popular form of this moral individualism. Why must the social nature of value be refused acceptance ? For two plain reasons. First, because the analysis of economic distribution which would flow from its acceptance would disclose the flagrant iniquity, inhumanity, and irrationality of all processes of actual distribution. The condemnation, alike of wealth and poverty, could then no longer be dismissed as a sentimental attitude, but must rank as a scientific judgment of supreme importance. Secondly, because with the realisation of social determination of value there would emerge a reasonable sense of the necessity of a conscious organisation of all the factors of social value, as a sound economy of human resources for the production and distribution of wealth. In other words, either the political State, or federation of States, or else some economic State or super-State, would assume a conscious government of industry, either undertaking the direct organisation of the correlated functions of that industry, or exercising a guidance or suzerainty over all processes of private industry.

It is therefore to the avoidance of this distinctively 'socialistic' theory and practice that all these arguments and experiments in moral individualism are subconsciously directed. Moral individualism rests on a wish to believe (1) that everybody tends to get as much as he is worth, (2) that the only just and feasible way of enabling him to get more is to induce him to make himself worth more, (3) that improvement can only come from the reasonable wills of individuals who will wisely confine their improving zeal to themselves and their immediate associates, leaving the general benefit to follow. It is successful just so far as it shuts its eyes to the organic nature of the economic world, and the social implications of that organic nature.

§ But if the 'Haves' use ethics for their defence, so do the 'Have-nots' for their attack. The socialistic and other revolutionary movements have wallowed in a moral sentimentalism of their own, in which elements of genuine feeling for the general good are intertwined with greed, envy, pugnacity, and self-assertion, the whole complex being rationalised by loose and hasty reasoning brought to bear on ill-collected and ill-assorted facts. The democratic formula of Liberty, Equality, Fraternity, still claims to stand as the social ideal. It presents a great spiritual image of a social order in which comradeship shall operate as the associative principle, bringing men together into a free union upon an equal basis of common humanity. Democracy itself, the instrument and expression of a common or general will in which all members equally take part as their right and duty, thus figures as a distinctively moral concept. It relies for its efficacy upon certain virtues of human character which it assumes to be effective in social conduct. Are these qualities effective in any type of democracy known to history ? Do revolutionary movements exhibit this humanitarian idealism in practice ? Or are less worthy motives always masquerading under these elevated concepts ? Let history answer. A self-protective or even a constructive, instinct of the group-mind may be assumed to work towards the substitution of a wider and more fully representative Government for narrower forms of autocracy, or class dominion. But such movements, whether gradual or precipitate, when reflected in the conscious desires or policy of the individuals or groups engaged in operating them, do not in fact exhibit as their prime impelling motives any of these democratic ideals and aspirations. If they are, indeed, to be regarded as the real creative forces working secretly in the background of the general movement, they are carried on waves of self-seeking, self-glory, adventure, and combativeness, blended with some sense of comradeship and pity, which utilise the pious formulas as conveying some quasi-magical virtue. The trinitarian flag of democratic principles is waved with confident enthusiasm by revolutionists upon the march, or by popular Governments in power, who are engaged in stamping out liberty of speech and press for their opponents,

in disenfranchising their enemies or gerrymandering elec-
tions, while every step they take, or speech they make,
breathes forth class sentiments of hate, suspicion, fear,
contempt, and other separatist passions. The psychology
of revolutionism, as propounded by Sorel, centres around
the propaganda of stimulating and explosive ' myths ',
bright visions of violent achievement and triumphant
proletarianism, designed to evoke a concentration of
popular effort and sacrifice among the worker-citizens.
The analysis contains a considerable element of truth, but
it errs in failing to recognise that an essential factor in the
power of these ' myths ' is the spontaneity and low
consciousness of their appeals. Once draw them out
from the recesses of popular subconsciousness to stand in
the foreground of assessed, calculated motives, a sense of
artificial dupery and doping will soon spoil their efficacy.

Moreover, as a reflective mind and temper appear among
the ' proletariat ', the instinctive disposition to use their
class-force in a class war for their own personal and class
advantage is crossed and modified by a feeling that their
cause is just and reasonable, and by a reflection that in the
ordinary course of human affairs justice and reason prevail.
Hence a genuine impulse to interpret the existing social-
economic structure in terms of injustice and unreason
which need to be redressed by exhibiting their nature. So
we get an extreme ethics which condemns all ' property ' as
theft, with a variety of modifications naïvely designed to
justify the small acquisitions of workers, to maintain the
right of ' the workers ' to ' the whole product of labour ',
and often the right of any class or group of workers to the
whole product of their particular trade or business. Even
the milder doctrines of the rights of labour generally assign
to the workers in a trade a wage which comprises the whole
of any surplus-profits in excess of charges for the maintenance of capital, thus depriving the general community

of all share of new economies of industry or other favourable trade conditions. Most working-class socialists waver between this narrow class allegiance, which would absorb all the gains from improved industry in wages, and the wider claims of the community as an organic whole with its demands for public revenue.

The glow of moral indignation, evoked by the 'inhumanity' of capitalism in treating 'labour' as a mere commodity and an instrument for grinding out profits, signifies, no doubt, a right sense of the dignity of man, and the success which the labour-movement has achieved in winning so wide an acceptance for the idea of standard minimum conditions may be held to attest the fundamental soundness of this ethical appeal. It is, indeed, a comforting reflection that this, the most important achievement of 'practical socialism', has been at least as much the fruit of social compunction among the well-to-do classes as of organised working-class force. Those who read the revelations of the almost incredible callousness of 'social conditions' which prevailed among 'good people' of early Victorian times [1] will recognise here the most remarkable of modern advances in social ethics. It is doubtless true that the economic doctrine of 'the economy of high wages' and of other good conditions had some influence in inducing more intelligent and humane employers to abate sweating and generally to humanise conditions of employment. But accessibility to these enlightened views must itself be taken as implying an emotional attitude that would have been scouted as weak sentimentality by the earlier and harder generation of employers.

§ This union of force and rational ethics, alike by labour in its attack and capital in its defence, is symptomatic of all social movement. But the growing use of ethical appeals

[1] Cf. the Hammonds' *Town Labourer* and *Life of Lord Shaftesbury*.

testifies to a growing consciousness in the process of social evolution, especially in the economic sphere, where the concreteness of the issues exhibit the procedure most clearly. The efficacy of such appeals is continually advancing. Personal liberty, equality, justice, and humanity, are more evidently effective as watchwords among wider areas of population, whether as bonds of comradeship, or as standards of revolt. We have seen how this perception of their efficacy leads on both sides to abuses, envisaged mainly in terms of ' rights '. Political, and still more economic, cravings for property and power, come easily to dress themselves in these spiritual garbs. In support of their moral claims they seek, not only to construct new scales of values, but often to distort or exaggerate scientific facts or laws. A noticeable example in the proletarian case is the use of an excessive ' environmentalism ' to meet the claims put forward for the superior productivity of men of ability as a justification for their high rewards. The democratic doctrine that ' men are by nature equal ' finds useful support in the biological doctrine of reversion to a mean, and in appraising nurture above nature. Educationalists are easily drawn to the support of a doctrine which magnifies their office, so that quite a respectable body of intellectual authority is committed to this depreciation of innate qualities. Proletarian propaganda takes advantage of the situation and utilises ' science ' to promote a policy of ' equality of opportunity ', and the public provisions required for its achievement, as a rational vindication of practicable socialism.

So the secular struggles, through which and behind which humanity advances towards a larger, fuller, more complex, and perhaps a better social life, are dramatised by opposing forces which brandish more vigorously than ever their self-made weapons of reason and justice. Each side exposes and denounces the illogic, the perversity, and

ill-will that disfigure the pretensions of the other side.
The loudest of these denunciations on the part of socialists
is directed against the general body of bourgeois ' ethics '
with its taboos and scale of moral values. Com-
munists make the same charge against socialists. Not
only is the sacredness of property the object of their
animadversions, but the whole body of that Puritanism
which, as we saw, was so serviceable in building up the
capitalist system. It is not merely that thrift, regularity,
abstemiousness, and other personal virtues, are less esteemed
among the workers because they would cost too much to
practise and yield too little in near and certain gains.
There is a certain coldness, rigour, and austerity in the
Puritan life and character alien from the ordinary attitude
towards life prevailing among most workers. Gambling,
risk-taking, some recklessness and adventure, some foolish-
ness, constituting a certain *joie de vivre*, are incorporated, I
will not say, in their standard, but in their way of living.
This attitude has perhaps a ' survival value ', helping them
to bear up and confront the immediate future and to under-
rate the dangers that await them. Their socialistic thinkers,
who theorise on these valuations, find in them a spontaneity,
a craving for the adventure of life, partly in reaction against
the mechanical drudgery of their work, partly from resentment at the character and standards of the exploiters. As
revolutionary fervour tends to the overthrow of all the
respectabilities and sanctities of the oppressor, even his
ethics of the family and his useful religion must be scrapped !
Hence in socialistic circles, even in Britain, the contempt
for bourgeois ethics makes for a conception of a free life
whose freedom is prone to reject, not only the authority of
priests and churches but the restraints of morals, especially
in sex relations. Free love is conceived as belonging to this
free life.

This so-called ' realism ', indeed, accepted as a principle

of thought and conduct among intellectual revolutionists in certain countries, often repudiates morality altogether as a guide of life, regarding it as a capitalist contrivance for the maintenance of the existing social order. Sometimes a ruthless egoism of individual or class, a forceful imposition of the will to live, a spontaneous play of impulse, qualified and directed by some sense of a distinctively æsthetic propriety, will take the place of morals.

§ In either case revolutionary realism takes issue with current morality in denying all validity to the sense of the sinfulness of sin. For this reason it concentrates its attack upon religion and sex morality as the centres of sanctity and sin. Its attitude on sex has been thus summarised : " The sexual act being a fulfilment of a natural instinct, it will no longer be regarded as a sin ". Here the battle is joined between the two conceptions of the conduct of life. To the naturalist, or realist, the sexual act is *per se* ' good ', as a realisation of a natural impulse ; to the religious moralist it is *per se* bad—a sin, but the badness may be abated or removed by sacramental magic. " It is better," wrote St. Paul, " to marry than to burn," the most instructive declaration of the asceticism which is the core of this whole ' sense of sin '. It is not a recognition of the anti-social bearings of free love that inspires the Puritan repudiation of its sinfulness, but the craving ' to keep under the body ' which has found its most exuberant expression in the zest for suicide and martyrdom among certain religious communities. This craving for low-living has appealed to the austerity of priests and elders who derive a personal and sadistic satisfaction from the policy of regulation and repression of full-blooded instincts it places in their hands.[1] The genuinely social value of many of

[1] Some social reformers annex it under the caption " A Return to Nature," or " The Simple Life ".

their laws and taboos, a survival value which has given them origin and lasting support, has never figured consciously either in the Puritan morality or in the revolutionary realism that rejects it. The theories of this latter movement are just as much a ‘rationalisation’ of the instinctive cravings for free life as the theories of bourgeois morality are for repression employed in the service of conservatism. The dangers of a revolutionary realism which would scrap the uses of morality because of its abuses are, however, probably exaggerated by those who tend to over-estimate in general the influence of theories upon conduct.

Such loosening of personal morality, as has spread with the spread of communist, socialist, and other revolutionary propaganda in Continental countries, has not perhaps much affected the ‘advanced’ movements in Britain or America. For in these countries standards of conventional behaviour respond very slowly to the impact of ideas, and respectability has great resistance-power. The interests, desires, and valuations of the organised workers in England are strongly formed and kept in place by half-conscious imitations of the bourgeoisie, into which their more energetic members have some chance of rising. Where opportunities of leaving the wage-earning ranks are so frequent as in America, this aspiration carries no such taint of snobbishness as is everywhere descernible in England, where the ladder is sufficiently narrow to give great social distinction to the successful climber. Taken in conjunction with the feeble hold of theory and idealism upon the general mind, this explains why the extreme doctrines of the modern gospels of revolt have had so little influence upon the practical ethics of the most powerful labour movement in the world. The Russian taunt that English working-class aspiration is directed, not towards the domination of the proletariat, but towards the attainment of a bourgeois standard of life, contains thus a large element of truth.

This is partly due to the feeble pulsation of class-consciousness in general, but mainly to the intensely 'practical' character of an Englishman and his innate distaste for the close guidance of ideas. This practicality is linked up with a dislike of regimentation and close regulation, even, perhaps especially, by members of his own class : he is instinctively against bureaucracy, and could never become ' a good socialist ' in the accepted use of that term. His tendency, however, is not towards anarchism : he wants laws, customs, and agreed arrangements, but wants to move among them with some freedom, especially in matters of personal habits and home life. In fact, he displays that spirit of unreasoned compromise in his private ethics that is discernible in all the wider processes of his collective policy.

II

§ While this unreasonable way of going on has its advantages, it has also clearly marked defects. It gives great opportunities to the subtle play of interested influences. This is particularly applicable to the theories and practices of public conduct where private business interests mask themselves under public policy in the guise of patriotism and imperialism. The ethical doctrine which they find most serviceable in these operations is that of collective responsibility. Loose modern conceptions of the group-mind, national consciousness, a general will, easily play into the hands of those who desire to use the public resources of their State for their gainful ends, transfigured into national trade, or who desire to hold a foreign people responsible for some private action of its individual rulers. It is hardly too much to say that the surprising degradation of the laws of war in two respects, viz. the planned starvation of the civil population and the confiscation of enemy private property, manifested during the late

war, was in large part attributable to this spread of conceptions of collective responsibility used in hostile
propaganda. The passionate desire to hate the whole
enemy nation and to injure it in every way was the real
incentive to these indiscriminate abuses of the ' laws of
war '. But this craving rationalised itself under the
attribution to the enemy of a single guilty mind. To the
Allies a collective Germany was responsible for all the sins
of its rulers and its war-lords. Those who knew least
about any particular Germans could most easily make an
abstraction of ' the German mentality ' and so spread the
wickedness evenly over the entire nation. The fact that
they could entertain this sentiment of equal collective
responsibility simultaneously with the separate denunciation of Junkerism and popular servility is but one more
example of the easy terms on which contradictories consort
in times of passion. As the group-mind of the enemy
nation is centralised for purposes of effective hate, so that
of one's own country for purposes of effective co-operation.
Instead of regarding a nation as an interaction of minds for
certain definite co-operative purposes, Dr. McDougall tells
us that " the nation alone is a self-contained and complete
organism : other groups within it do but minister to the
life of the whole—and when the nation is regarded from an
enlightened point of view, the sentiment for it naturally
comes to include in one great system all minor group-
sentiments and to be strengthened by their incorporation.
. . . Loyalty to the nation ", he adds, " is capable of
exalting character and conduct in a higher degree than any
other form of the group spirit ".[1] Now, if the attribution
of the term ' organism ' to a nation be permissible, the
epithets ' self-centred ' and ' complete ' are not, nor is
there any intelligible meaning in the statement that other
groups ' do but minister to the life of the whole ', or that

[1] *The Group Mind*, p. 180.

the national sentiment 'includes' all minor group sentiments. The suggestion that loyalty to the nation is a more potent and a higher educative influence upon personal character and conduct than loyalty to a religious or an ethical code, or to the interests of one's family, is one that could hardly seem specious to anyone except when caught in the blinding heat of ' the great war '.

Such employment of the gregarious instinct, group mind, or common will, in order to glorify the State and inflame the combative passions of peoples, is an instructive illustration of the most insidious abuses of ' social psychology'. Comparable with it in mischief is the fallacious habit, fed by Government statistics, of representing the trade done by the members of one nation with those of another, as if the nations, as such, were trading firms. This habit is responsible for much ill-feeling towards ' nations ' who are said to be trading to our disadvantage because ' they ' sell to us more than they buy, or ' dump ' on our shores their cheapened goods, or ' steal ' our foreign markets. Since the progress of humanity, if not its survival, depends upon an increasing realisation of the community of interests and need for a corresponding co-operation among all mankind, doctrines which thus glorify single nations and represent them as complete and self-sufficing, must be accounted inimical to mental sanity.

§ Everywhere in our investigation of social conduct among persons and groups we have traced the intricate patterns of the rationalisation with which purely personal or narrow group instincts have sought to cover their nakedness. These instincts and their accompanying passions and interests everywhere throw up defences for their free expression. We have inspected some of the elaborate edifices of science and philosophy, erected by the instincts of greed for property and power. Now the most subtle of

these theories takes shape in the doctrine of the supremacy
of private conscience. This is the core of moral anarchy,
in an individual as a nation. If an individual claims to
overrule and disobey the laws and regulations of the
society in which he lives by virtue of his private judgment
in matters which are not purely self regarding, he is a
declared anarchist, repudiating the authority of the
organised society.[1] If a group within a nation, a trade
union, or a combine, acting in its own interpretation of its
own rights, plunders the community or holds up the entire
operation of industrial life, for its own gain, even though
the action may be within the law, its action is anarchistic
in defying an authority which ought to override its own.
In each case the unreason and injustice is the same, namely
an insistence upon being a judge in your own cause and
executing your self-made justice by your own force.

The processes of rationalisation and justification which
the interested parties employ in these spheres of conduct
have been so fully explored as to require no further attention here. But the self-esteem of nations still exercises so
powerful a hold upon group-sentiment as to prove the
greatest and most urgent peril to society in its widest
sense. The assertion of the absolute sovereignty of a
State is not yet realised as the supreme anarchy, the sin
against the holy spirit of humanity. Indeed, so far is it
from awakening this sense of sin that it carries to most
hearts a throb of righteousness.

We are the best judges not only of our interests but of
our obligations in our dealings with others. In fact, we
accept no binding obligations : our conduct towards others
will be directed by our own good will and our own judgment
of what we ' owe ' to others. It seems nobler to be good to

---

[1] He may, however, recognise a higher court than the State, e.g.
Divine Commandment. This is, strictly speaking, the position of the
conscientious anarchist.

others of our own will than on compulsion. If others
complain that we wrong them, we will consider their com-
plaint, but we will not submit the issue to any outside
judge. This is, and has been, the policy of international
anarchy to which all sovereign states still adhere. The
ethics is conveniently set forth in a recent message of
President Coolidge. " The United States sees no reason
why it should *limit its own freedom* and independence of
action by joining it " (i.e. the League of Nations). " We
attend to our own affairs, our own strength, and protect the
interests of our own citizens, but we recognise thoroughly
our obligation to help others, *reserving to the decision of our
own judgment the time, the place, and the method.*" In
speaking of the Permanent Court of International Justice,
he adds : " The Court is merely a convenient instrument
of adjustment to which we could go *but to which we could
not be brought*".

Does a nation limit, in the sense of diminishing, its freedom by entering into a Society of Nations ? Is an
individual less free as a member of a national society ?
The necessary result, if not the prime purpose, of a society
is to enlarge the real freedom of its members. This should
be as true of a society the membership of which consists of
nations, as of one where the members are individuals. An
' obligation to help others ', with the reservations here
named, amounts to a substitution of collective charity for
justice. It stands as a second mortgage on the moral
resources of a nation, only ranking when the first charge
of national self-interest has been fully met. Here again it
differs from the theory of a national society, where the
general welfare is placed by all good citizens as rightly
overriding personal interests. Finally, the proud declaration, that the nation will only consent to submit to an
international court such issues as it chooses, is a repudiation
of the first principle of justice. It is the express reservation

of the right to be a judge in one's own cause, when the issue touches honour, vital interest, or some other matter in which strong feeling is most certain to bias judgment in the court of our own interested conscience.

Such an appeal to the pride and dignity of absolute sovereignty is the great stumbling-block to-day to the peace of the world and the progress of humanity. It is the collective survival of the ethics of duelling in private affairs of honour. Its advocates commonly adduce in its support ' *Republicæ salus lex suprema* '. But is this maxim any more valid for a nation than for an individual, resting, as it does, on the unwarranted assumption that the right of private war makes for the safety of nations ? Faithful analysis will disclose the truth that in the sentiment of absolute sovereignty the plea for security is but one and a minor ingredient in an emotional complex where collective pride, self-assertion, combativeness are dominant factors, and where a tight group of professional and business interests operates upon the complex for personal power, profit, or prestige. Until the control of statecraft by ancient diplomacy, professional fighting castes, and the armament trades directed by the keen business interests which seek to utilise the force of their State to win, hold, and improve their foreign markets for goods and invest-ments, has been effectively replaced by some methods of international adjustment and co-operation, the world will remain as insecure as ever. The pretence that sovereignty rests on the right of security with its auxiliary right of self-defence, is seen to be an impudent falsification of the real content of that concept of autocracy.

§ The fundamental distinction between a functional and an acquisitive policy, so powerfully applied by Mr. Tawney to the industrial system of a nation, has also its wider appli-cation to the politics, economics, and ethics, of the Society of

Nations. It is clearly recognisable how many movements are working together for world-organisation in every sphere of human intercourse, economic, scientific, hygienic, artistic, educational, recreative; and more or less effective arrangements are made for the best conduct of these co-operative enterprises. In the carrying out of these arrangements, Governments for the most part play a minor, though an increasing part. Here two salient points are visible. The first is that, regarded as a gradual evolution of world control, this movement proceeds by a growth of special organs and functions, each seeking to enlarge, strengthen, and improve, the performance of its particular task in the general economy of human relations. The second point is that, in the beginning of these international or inter-group arrangements, the self-seeking, or acquisitive, motives of the several nations, or groups, are paramount in consciousness. Even in the more cultural aspects of the movement it may be admitted that, in the earlier stages, it is the desire to get rather than to give, or to participate, that evokes the will to co-operate with foreigners. In other words, there is an initial tendency, not only to feel, but to think, these organisations in terms of separate group-gains—a replica of the individualism which envisages both industry and politics as elaborate balances of powers and self-interests. Only by actual experience of co-operative arrangements do this feeling and this conception gradually change. As an *esprit* enters the *corps*, the acquisitive gradually gives place to the functional consciousness. So an international mind is formed inside the frame of a League of Nations, just so far as the members realise from actual experience the genuinely corporate activities of the League. Just so far as the form and policy of the League are designed and operated in partisanship, or for the separate ends of stronger States or groups of States, this international mind is injured or retarded.

It is idle to expect that, either in the individual or the nation, the self-seeking, and acquisitive impulses can quickly, wholly, or even generally be displaced by sentiments and aspirations for the welfare of the whole. But neither can it be maintained that human nature in individuals, or groups, is immutable and intractable. Still less is it evident that government of great spheres of conduct can best be conducted by the secret interplay of selfish motives, with a total disregard in the consciousness of participants for the general ' purpose ' that is served.

A great new peril to human society arises from the tendency of peoples to persuade themselves that an international mind already informs and governs the inchoate frame of a Society of Nations. For this tendency will certainly be pushed with every art of persuasive propaganda by interests, economical or political, which seek to establish confidence in this new international society in order to abuse it. A crude example of this method is afforded by the recent ' Guarantee Pact of Mutual Defence ' where, under the guise of a pacific instrument fully international in scope and activity, special enmities and antagonisms were to be maintained and furnished with military resources which must destroy all effective movement towards a general appeasement. It is evidently a point of cunning for the statesmen of a country which under cover of defence desires to retain the liberty to aggress, or to safeguard her past aggressions, to do homage to the League of Nations as a potent pledge of international security, thereby encouraging a general disarmament, while guarding their country against equal participation in such reduction by means of secret pacts designed to supplement their national forces by those of allies upon whose armed assistance they have secured a call. This utilisation of the machinery of the League of Nations, in order to break up the beginnings of an international mind, by substituting smaller and tighter group-minds, is a piece of perfidy so gross that it ought to have deceived nobody. The fact that it has succeeded in winning the approval of men genuinely devoted to the welfare of the League proves once more how difficult it is for a disinterested moral purpose on the loftiest plane of conduct to preserve its chastity against the wiles of the tempter.

§ Both law and morals permit an individual the ' right ' to lie, steal, or even kill, when his life is closely jeopardised under conditions which preclude effective appeal to public protection. But there is no moral obligation on him to use such modes of self-defence. When, however, the honour or vital interests of our country are imperilled, collective ethics imposes on the nation as a body and upon its several members, an absolute obligation to perform any act of violence and undergo any personal risk of loss, including life itself, held serviceable for the defence of the country. It is true that in theory, and even by common usage, certain acts of violence are proscribed, but such proscription is riddled with inconsistency and is always set aside in a strong emergency. The ethical distinction in the case of the individual and the nation is a double one. The individual *may* ' break the Commandments ' in the defence of himself or his family : the nation, and the individual as a member of a nation, *must*. Again, the interest which justifies the former violation is a genuinely ' vital ' one. That which justifies the latter is seldom ' vital ' in the same literal sense. Even the successful invader of a country can seldom be said to destroy that country, or its people. He can only subject them to loss of political independence and material damage. To patriotism, no doubt, these injuries are represented as so dishonouring as to justify any amount of killing or being killed. Now, it may even be contended, that a man or woman is justified in killing in the defence of

' honour ', in cases where no legal protection is afforded. The duel is capable of defence upon these grounds. But a patriot, it will be said, is one to whom the honour of his country is as dear, or dearer than his personal honour. But on points of honour the national consciousness is far more sensitive than the individual : on some alleged violation of a treaty, some injury to a nation's property in a foreign country, some affront to the ' sacred ' flag, the ' nation ' is eager to take the law into its own hands and prides itself upon quick, impulsive violence, unchecked by delay and calm inquiry. This ' high spirit ' in a nation is esteemed a noble quality. When such a case of national honour arises, it is very difficult for a pacific statesman to get the public mind to wait, adopt an impartial inquiry into the facts and merits of the case, and accept an impartial judgment. Honour calls for immediate action by our own force upon our own partial judgment, reckless of truth or equal justice. It is the ethics of this patriotism, with its sense of national dignity and honour, that offers the stoutest resistance to a genuinely international mind. The spirited foreign policy, prescribed by honour, is, partly, a collective pride, self-assertion, combativeness : partly, a keen-eyed, pushful, business man's acquisitiveness, exploiting the national honour as an economic asset.

§ The success of constructive internationalism thus hinges partly upon the setting up of instruments of international justice, to which the ' honourable ' practice of each nation, executing self-made justice in its own cause, will yield place ; partly upon devising within each nation adequate checks upon these abuses of the national honour and vital interests by trading, financial, or professional groups.[1]

---

[1] In the modern world, oil, iron ore, rubber, cotton, and other natural resources are everywhere hampering the endeavours for international security. Every disturbed or contested area has its trouble in one or other of these coveted commodities.

Economic psychology could do no greater service than in rescuing national honour from this degradation and abuse. It could drag into clear consciousness the secret conspiracy of passions and interests which feed with new temptations the sentiment of national honour. It could harness this stream of collective feeling to the task of active international co-operation, by diverting it from contentious and destructive exercises into a wholesome self-assertiveness and rivalry in common enterprises for the welfare of humanity. No task of sublimation is so urgent.

It is not now difficult to obtain a large assent to the demand for the application of psychology to the sciences and arts of politics and economics, as of ethics. Human welfare, the formal end of all these arts, though no longer presented in measurable comparable blocks of pleasure and pain, is found to be realised in terms of the harmonious satisfaction of natural urges and activities evolved for the protection and enlargement of human life, and welded into an effective 'spiritual union', through natural selection, tradition, and the pressures of a changing environment. Hence the necessity of resolving all political and economic systems into terms of collective and personal feeling, thinking, willing. Their efficiency is seen in terms of psycho-physical incentives, their utility or productivity in terms of the harmonious satisfaction of psycho-physical needs. So Politics and Economics and other social arts present themselves as groups of problems of the interaction and co-operation of minds in the conscious handling of physical environment.

CHAPTER IV

THE SURVIVAL POWER OF FREE-THOUGHT

§ It is one thing to win acceptance for the statement that more conscious social organisation is essential to the security and advancement of civilisation, quite another to translate that acceptance into terms of practice. There is something in the natural man recalcitrant to conscious organisation. He has a double objection, first to being organised, secondly to having to think about it. In England this refractoriness perhaps is more marked than elsewhere. For, on the one hand, all regularised compulsory group-action is more apt to be resented as an oppressive interference with individual liberty. On the other, the call to think upon social conduct, in politics, economics, or otherwise, irks us. We are temperamental anarchists, and the jibe that " When an Englishman finds himself thinking, he thinks he is sick " has a bite of truth about it. We feel that we are not very good at thinking, and, perhaps just because thinking is disagreeable, we feel that we can get on better without it. Psychology may even put up a rational defence of this unreasoning attitude, by positing a common sense of the herd whose good guidance is spoiled by individual attempts to think it out. Hence a case for a tactics of ' muddling through ' as against meticulous planning. Our loose, unwritten constitution, for example, is felt by us to provide, not only a better political guarantee for safety, but a more pliable instrument for large organic movements of reform than any written constitution. Hence also our clinging to the ' somehow good ' in our economic arrangements, a conviction that, by each of us feeling his own way, guided by some short-range and often dim recognition of his own advantage, the wealth and welfare of the whole community will be better served than by any attempts at central guidance consciously directed to the general good.

If, therefore, we are to envisage, as I think we must, a clearer understanding of what we are doing in economic and in political life, and a common, agreed rational will to do it, we must recognise and try to surmount the obstacles which thus stand in our path. It will take an earnest and persistent education of the individual intelligence to overcome the recalcitrance to conscious organisation, and especially to win acceptance for the large part which Governments must undoubtedly play in the actual work of conscious guidance.

§ On this, as upon other burning questions, our immediate concern, however, is not so much to discover answers, as to consider their bearing upon political policy and thinking. The new defences of class-power and property which are throwing up biological and sociological defences of aristocracy, within the group-nation and in the Society of Nations, have important reactions upon the structure and functions of the State. So far I have touched briefly on the reinforcement of the sentiment of Sovereignty, for the exercise of internal and external power. The experience of recent years has brought into play two apparently opposed tendencies of thought and feeling about the State. State control or interference with business or other ways of life, are *prima facie* disliked by every class in the community. This is due only in part to irritation at the burdens of taxation and the failure of Governments to make a sound peace. There is also a widespread resentment against official meddling and a wide-sown criticism of bureaucratic incompetence. These sentiments and opinions are not confined to business men, they are shared widely, though less intensely, by all other classes, except Government employees. Regarded from this standpoint, the State is unpopular.

On the other hand, every weak or threatened interest, and every interest with some axe to grind, is more clamorous than ever for State aid. State protection or subsidies for private benefit are urged as salutary policies by landowners and farmers, manufacturers and traders, and for imperial development, emigration, housing, unemployment. Speaking generally, it is recognised that the State must and will play a new positive and constructive rôle in the defence of the national economy and the development of national and imperial resources. The definite committal of the modern ' democratic ' State to a public guarantee of a minimum standard of living is, on the whole, accepted by the ruling and owning classes as a wise and not too expensive concession to ' democracy '. But it impels them to a clearer and more energetic policy of managing the State, so as to obtain through it fuller financial assistance for the profitable conduct of their business at home and abroad, and an immunity from effective interference with the new arts of combination which are the crowning discovery of modern capitalism. On the whole, there emerges everywhere a more or less conscious intention of the master-class to hold and operate the State for the defence and furtherance of their interests presented as elements of the national welfare. The dramatic exaggeration of this movement is Fascism. But the open seizure of supreme power in the State by a dictator or a ruling junto is probably a passing extravagance. In such countries as England, America, and France, any extreme break with the forms and traditions of popular government would seem unwise and unnecessary. It is far simpler and safer to make public opinion, and control representative institutions, than to repress them. Even in more primitive times it was always dangerous for a tyrant or a close oligarchy to cut loose from all formal contacts with the people. In these days it is necessary to dope the intelligence and massage ' the great heart of the people ', so as to get the right popular opinion coursing through the customary channels. Press, platform, pulpit, library, schoolroom, cinema, can all be handled by their business-end for this work. We are here concerned with the necessary implications of the process upon political thinking and its theories. For a formal adhesion to old democratic doctrines has to be combined somehow with a growing sense of their unreality, and with the conscious adoption of opposing principles of aristo-plutocracy. In the ' thick, warm mental fog ' thus induced the sharp-eyed interests find an atmosphere conducive to success.

§ The stress I have been compelled to lay upon the modern development of the intellectual defences of aristo-plutocracy has tended to some over-emphasis of the biases to which political science and art have been subjected. For these doctrines derive part of their acceptability from the reason-able criticism which modern psychology and sociology have brought to bear upon the crude liberalism that has exercised so wide and so arrogant an influence during the past two centuries in the Western world, and has recently spread to Asiatic and other backward countries ; posing as the accepted theory of government. Absolute individualism, complete equalitarianism, mechanical ration-alism, the ruling principles of the liberal politics as of the liberal economics, have been justly discredited by the closer modern study of human nature in its individual and collective behaviour. The discovery of the wide differences of mentality even among members of the same stock, the larger number of variations constantly presented in a wider group or nation, the effect of strongly marked natural environment and social heritage in forming racial character in whole populations, taken in conjunction with the flood of light which modern democratic experiments have shed, have made havoc of the whole body of the accepted liberal presuppositions, and have rendered necessary a complete recasting of the theory and art of government.

If modern psychology and sociology have gone too far and too fast in their disparagement of human equality on the one hand, and reason as an instrument of government, upon the other, their criticism of the older democratic doctrines has been very salutary, and their contribution towards the reconstruction of the theory of representative government, and of international relations, from the stand-point of a clearer conception of human welfare, is of conspicuous value. By this I mean that these studies have succeeded in doing the work of disinterested science better than the general course of my analysis, purposely directed to display their defects, would suggest. A partial explanation of this fact has already been indicated by reference to the place of disinterested curiosity among the instincts. It makes no difference whether this instinct be really primary, in the sense of an independent urge for knowledge, or auxiliary to the other instincts as furnishing them with better and more complex modes of operation. In the latter case ' disinterested ' signifies impartial in its service to the interests of our instincts, and, indeed, involves the active study of our environment as a related whole, for the furtherance of some purpose, or conation, in which the activities of all our instincts are co-ordinated, i.e. the harmonious co-operation of all the instinctive impulses which make up the character of the individual, of all the members in a social group, and finally of all the groups that constitute humanity, present and to come. This itch for knowledge, curiosity, incipient ' reason ', helping every instinct in its efforts to get expression, evolves, in the performance of this practical task, methods of investigation and reasoning that gradually transforms its blind fumbling with the dangerous unknown into accurate methods of handling and adapting it to human uses. The satisfaction, or pleasure,[1] if that term be preferred, attached to the successful operation of this work becomes a strong habitual need to the performer. The scientific spirit, thus engendered and rising into ever clearer consciousness, comes to value more and more highly the freedom and integrity of the truth-seeking processes, and to resent more strongly, and defend itself more stoutly against, attempts, either to bias its reasoning, or to subject it to the short-range pragmatism of early tangible utilities. This satisfaction of free-thinking, or resentment at ' outside ' interference, is finally inseparable from the central urge in every organism or organisation towards that harmonious working which in the case of man we term human welfare. This wider pragmatism, indeed, belongs to the play of ' curiosity ' from the very beginning, converting its apparent ' idleness ' or ' disinterestedness ' into the higher service of man. For this very reason the scientific spirit maintains its active defence against every interference with the free performance of this service.

The pride of every workman in the exercise of his skill is the best guarantee of good workmanship. A sense of the paramount importance of that skill as the first condition of all human improvement, appeals to self-esteem so keenly as to evoke in the scientist a passion for making truth prevail that is stronger and steadier than in any other type of man.

---

[1] Modern psychologists who, in their anxiety to cut themselves loose from nineteenth-century hedonism and utilitarianism, endeavour to present instinctive activities as working, in the first instance, quite independently of the pleasure motive, by some *vis a tergo*, seem to me to introduce needless difficulties about the meaning of a ' motive '.

It is on this conscious pride and passion for exploring the nature of man and his environment, so as to evolve an understanding and a control which shall give the fullest, finest, most successful scope to man's instinctive outfit, that we must rely for keeping the operations of the social sciences disinterested. The attempts of vested interests to capture these sciences, and set them to furnish intellectual supports for policies of power and private gain, evoke in disinterested science a quite elaborate cunning of defence. Here, as in all organic defence, three instinctive methods may be employed : the attacked may fight, run away, or lie low. For disinterested science the last is incomparably the best defence, though necessity may sometimes compel resort to the others. By lying low, however, I do not signify concealment of thought or opinion, or suspension of free inquiry or speech, but an ignoring of the attempts at interference and a ' carrying on ' as usual. This meekness is more baffling than any encounter. It presents to the assailant the awkward situation of an apparent submission which, though its unreality may be suspected, cannot be closely scrutinised or effectively impugned.

§ Though psychologists like Mr. Veblen [1] appear to me to overstrain the separation between disinterested science and pragmatism, or specific utilitarianism, both in origins and in later evolution of the sciences, and to overrate the primacy accorded to the former in the current cultural scheme, with him I pin my reasonable faith to the ability of disinterested science to win through in the long run, chiefly from its capacity for a resistance which, though seemingly passive, is only so in the sense that its forward urge is gradual, quiet, persistent, and broad-fronted. Intellectual craftsmanship, with the personal pride or satisfaction in good work which it evokes, is so alluring and dominating a

[1] *The Place of Science*, p. 19.

force in most of its regular practitioners that, though they may sometimes weakly yield to narrower pragmatic or emotional biases, they will normally return to the more disinterested course, helping to get out truths irrespective of their immediate utility or popularity.

It is this tendency that is so baffling to the attempts of the vested interests, in economics, politics, or religion, to control, direct, or dope, the teaching of controversial subjects in the seats of learning or the churches. Heresy-hunting, the imposition of orthodox tests, the index of dangerous books, the proscription of scientific doctrines, and other open tampering with intellectual craftsmanship, arouse a deep resentment even among a majority too timorous to risk their career and livelihood by open protest or rebellion. This majority will furnish a protective cover for the undetected free-thinkers and heretics. Here is the permanent truth in the saying that ' The blood of the martyrs is the seed of the Church '. There is a curious body of testimony in America to the efficacy of this stimulus to freedom, in the notorious failure of recent attacks on liberty of teaching in history, economics, politics, and biology, in schools and colleges, to purge these institutions of dangerous doctrines and dangerous teachers. Those intimately acquainted with those universities where attempts of trustees or powerful outside interests to ' doctor ' teaching have been rife, attest the keener valuation of academic liberty resulting from this interference. This applies with special force to faculties of economics which have drawn the fiercest fire from the vested interests. Business men all over the States are given to grumbling about the ' radical ' teaching they are sure is going on in their universities, but they admit that ' they don't know what to do about it '. They are quite aware that ' firing ' a dangerous professor here or there, does not make the teaching safer. This may seem at first sight inconsistent with the general trend of my argument relating to the abuses of economic science in Great Britain, where authoritative teaching has been bent into submission to the intellectual requirements of the ruling and owning classes, with considerable success. This temporary success is attributable to the subtler and more secret modes of influence that there go to the selection of teachers and the moulding of authoritative doctrines. There is no superficial interference with liberty of teaching, no such proscription of heretical teachers or doctrines as often occurs in America ; every teacher and writer feels himself quite free to state whatever he holds true. There is even a pharisaical parade of intellectual freedom, a sincere pretence that no teacher would stoop to misrepresent or dissemble, or could fail to detect and reject any bias of sentiment or interest that might assail his virtue. I have already demonstrated the unsubstantial character of this defence, by examples from the history of economic theory, which show how disinterested science can be bent to the service of vested interests or class feeling. But, whereas the cruder interference in America with disinterested science has awakened powerful resentment which has acted as a stimulus to free-thinking, in England the discovery that her authoritative science is less ' disinterested ' than it seems and claims to be, is only beginning to dawn upon our intellectual world, and the indignant disclaimers of scientists are still accepted as if they were the cool judgments of an impartial tribunal, instead of the self-exculpation of the suspected.

The result of this super-subtilty and indirectness of the moulding influences has been to make economic science in this country furnish plausible defences for vested interests of property and power, not by the rude expulsion of opposing doctrines, but by a finesse of irrelevant exactitude of reasoning directed to material which is either selected as

18

amenable to this sort of treatment, or is manipulated so as to remove whatever is intractable to it.   This mishandling is, of course, far too subtle to arouse popular suspicion, and has attractions that win over many students trained in abstract reasoning.   Hence the damage and the danger to free-thought in this, as indeed in other social sciences to which the same intellectual economy applies, are graver here than in America.

§ But the resources of disinterested science, so far from being exhausted, are only beginning to be exploited effectively by means of psychological analysis.   For the disclosure of the nature and the method of the inimical forces must liberate new powers of resistance on the side of ' idle curiosity '.   Indeed, this must be regarded as the first among the many services which the disinterested study of the mind of man can render, the disclosure of better ways of keeping clean the intellectual instruments, especially for service in the sciences and arts of human government. For only by the patient study of man's animal make-up and social heritage is it possible to discern accurately the trend and purpose of disinterested curiosity on the one hand, and the interferences of other powerful individual and group instincts, emotions, sentiments, interests, upon the other.   Until the relations and the interplay between this disinterested and integrating urge and these interested and ' special ' urges are clearly understood, the sudden or secret persistent power wielded by the latter cannot be curbed effectively.   The shallow psychology of the age of rationalism played into the hands of the enemy by an excessive appraisal of the directive power of reason.   If the new psychology has seemed to plunge to the opposite extreme, by disparaging reason as the mere tool of the full-blooded instincts, there are already signs of the recovery of a juster balance.   For whether curiosity be regarded as a prime instinct of independent origin, value, and activity, or as a part of the procedure of each several instinct in working out the plan of its activity, the necessity of effecting some harmony or co-operation among the instincts will endow it with a constantly increasing importance as a co-ordinating and controlling power. The sciences of man and his environment will be evolved as intruments of this co-ordination and control. Curiosity, thus raised to reason, will not be a merely distributive machinery, devoid of power or sanctions. Reason, in its most developed form, will retain the conative energy derived from its origin, whether as a separate instinct or as a common element in all instincts. This view asserts for reason a real and a rightful mastery, attested throughout human history in the 'progress' of every civilisation. If, as some think, the collapse of a civilisation must come with time, and that our Western civilisation already shows signs of breaking up, such collapse or break-up will seem to indicate the successful revolt of some group of powerful prime instincts against the delicate machinery of adjustment and controls which reason had set up and operated. Should this come about, the revolt, we might expect, would largely consist in the capture by the 'rebel forces' of the very sciences which reason had elaborated for her rule. The fighting, self-assertive, acquisitive instincts might, by separate or joint action, so enslave the physical sciences, and mutilate the social sciences, as to make them fit tools for the execution of their will. There can be no absolute security against this happening, and some of the evidence cited in preceding chapters appears to indicate the approaching success of such revolt. As Lord Bryce put it in his arresting phrase : " Another ice-age may be settling down upon the human mind ". But even these dismal forebodings do not dispose of reason as a guarantee for progress. For the instinctive energy of curiosity, and the function assigned to it in the evolution of society by the orderly co-operation of the instincts, cannot perish so long as the human race endures. Even were the breakdown so complete as to involve in the ruin all our social heritage, humanity reduced to its lowest terms of precarious subsistence would press unceasingly towards a revival of the rule of reason as conservator and economiser of the various specific modes of the urge of life.

§ But before accepting as seriously probable the breakdown of Western civilisation by this perversion of the sciences, it would be best to consider how far that psychology which has disclosed the nature of the diseases to which those sciences are exposed can indicate and help to apply a remedy. May not the very discovery of the perils which beset humanity from the degradation of the sciences and the enslavement of the mind itself liberate fresh resources to the cause of reason ? A large part of the danger lies, as we have seen, in the secrecy and indirectness of the assault upon the virtue of the sciences. If psychology can drag the whole skein of this cunning into the light of day, if the various devices of the vested interests and the pressure of their will-to-power can be exposed, the virginal integrity of the scientific spirit will be roused to self-defence, personal pride will reinforce the claims of free-thought, and only cowards and avowed worldlings will consent to wear the livery of intellectual lackeys.

But, it may be said, ' You are making a high claim for what you call psychology when you suggest that it will be able to liberate effectively the social sciences from enemies so powerful as you have shown. You look to the youthful science of psychology to liberate, cleanse, and nourish with fresh vigour the damaged or endangered theories of economics and politics. But who shall guarantee the integrity and competency of psychology ? *Quis custodiet ipsum custodem ?*' And, indeed, it may be taken for certain that, as psychology extends its claim to give authoritative advice in all the arts of individual and collective conduct, the vested interests—economic, intellectual, and moral—will seek ever more urgently to defend themselves by canalising psychology into safely serviceable channels and by putting obstacles in the way of all inconvenient and improper revelations or innovations which its free speculation and teaching may involve. As yet, I think, there is little appreciation or apprehension of the disturbing influence psychology is destined to exercise upon many of the beliefs, sentiments, customs, and institutions which are most sacred because of their obscurity of origin. At present the halo of sensationalism, enveloping the more extravagant applications of psycho-analysis and psychical research, acts as a protective medium. Psychology is not yet taken quite seriously as an authoritative science. But, as it makes good its claims to explain the psycho-physical origins of the human actions, beliefs, and institutions, hitherto regarded as sacred and untouchable, and to expose the obstructive superstitions which have grown around them for their protection, the vested intellectual and spiritual interests will set themselves to tame the ' wildness ' of psychology and keep it in its proper place, as a guardian of spiritual and political authority and a promoter of industrial efficiency. Inconvenient explorations into religion, sex and the family, acquisitiveness and property, combativeness and self-assertiveness, particularly in their larger fields of national action, will be frowned upon. Especially will the free play of psychological analysis into the nature of those sentiments of sacredness, reverence, respectability, submission, and herd feeling, which are the spiritual pillars of the existing institutions, meet with strenuous opposition from the interests controlling the machinery of education and of scientific research. The battle of free-thought and free-speech, formerly waged in the fields of religion and of the physical sciences, will be fought out most bitterly in this arena of human self-knowledge. A 'safe' science of psychology will be the prime educational desideratum in all our seats of learning. Chairs will be founded, professors appointed, textbooks written and selected, with this supreme end in view.

§ Psychology, left free, is busily undermining the rotten foundations of a civilisation which has proved itself at many points incapable of adaptation to the vital needs of humanity. Religion, the State, Internationalism, Education, Industry, Poverty, Crime, Lunacy—turning the light of disinterested science on all these departments of conduct, it exposes ignorance, brutality, falsehood, injustice, and demands, first, a revaluation of all values by standards of ordered knowledge and humanity ; and, secondly, a correlated application of this social science in revised arts of personal and collective conduct. Insincerity is perhaps the word which comes nearest to expressing the radical disease from which all these institutions, and the beliefs, sentiments and theories relating to them, are suffering. That insincerity is deep-seated in the language, the popular conceptions, and the formal thinking upon all these topics. I have spoken of the external pressures and obstructions set up by vested interests that fear the disturbances which free psychology may bring about. But this insincerity, conveyed in the conventional language and feelings that encircle and claim to express social phenomena, is an inner bondage more difficult to escape. A free-thinker in the social sciences may, by personal integrity, bid defiance to all external interferences. His real difficulty is first to recognise, and then to shake off, the hampering bonds of accepted terminology and ways of thinking. For the insincerity, which I here cite, is not a conscious dishonesty of reasoning in the individual student but an accretion of falsehood or deceit in the collective character of the common thoughts and sentiments that form the spiritual nature of a social institution and therefrom affect the embryonic social science. This sort of insincerity blocks disinterested inquiry at every stage. It sets a student looking for the wrong facts, by imposing on him wrong questions to put to the stream of phenomena before him, it leads him to wrong classification and barren generalisation. It carries false valuations and false tests of relevance. It causes him to find what he has been taught to look for, the laws and judgments which conventional thinking conducted in conventional language puts over him.

§ This double bondage to external interests and accepted ways of thought may well seem fatal to the progress of disinterested social science. But it is not. Even in the more objective sciences of economics and politics where interested bias operates most powerfully, it has not been possible to bind free-thought successfully in the long run. The subtler and more definitely subjective study of psychology will prove even less amenable to interested control. The perpetual advantage which truth possesses over falsehood is not, I think, as J. S. Mill insisted, its greater persistency or tendency to reappear. For errors also tend to reappear. It is that seeing facts and thinking straight are more attractive to the mind than seeing falsehoods and thinking crooked. Accurately observing similarities and differences, building general truths out of them, fitting those truths into harmonious correlations, and so creating the architecture of a science, these processes feed the mind with a sense of creative power which grows ever stronger in the student until it becomes a passion that defies every attempt at corruption or subjection. A good argument is more pleasing than a bad argument. It satisfies better alike the sense of power and the æsthetic feeling, both of which are deeply implicated in the processes of original thinking, and in the application of such thought to the conduct of life. While, therefore, it may remain an open question whether there is a separable instinct of curiosity or whether curiosity is part of the *modus operandi* of every separate instinctive process, appearing in the experimental play or strategy of search for food and shelter, combat or escape, courtship and protection of the family or herd, or in whatever other instincts seek their ends by dealing with and overcoming difficulties, it remains true that this curiosity and cunning form the prime scientific urge in man. Its successful activity involves resistance to all attempts to harness it to the yoke of some special instinct or interest, with the inevitable degradation of the processes of observation and of reasoning this subjection will involve. To place this human curiosity and cunning under the exclusive dominion of religion, property, the State, or any other section of humanity, would be not only to imperil all that has been won in the secular struggle towards a fuller personality and a stronger community, but to stop or injure that delicate and continuous readjustment in man's relations to his material and spiritual environment that constitutes human progress. That this delicate balance of the forces making for human safety and advancement can be upset disastrously for considerable periods of time and over large portions of the habitable earth, admits of no dispute. And it is possible that the stroke of some such disaster may be now upon us. But history also bears plain testimony to some natural power of recovery, deep-seated in the constitution of man, a power to resist and ultimately to overcome the temporarily successful sedition in the member instincts. No small part in the emergence and stimulation of this recuperative power belongs to psychology itself. For psychology simply means a finer self-knowledge, enabling man to learn more accurately and more quickly what is wrong in human conduct and how to set it right. In other words, the instinctive processes of recovery, readjustment, and fresh creative activity, formerly performed as loose, low-conscious movements, now admit of clearer perception and understanding, and of much short-circuiting and other economies which it belongs to reason to achieve. As psychologists become increasingly aware of the critical importance of keeping their instruments clean for this supreme service, they will put out increasing forces of resistance against the attempts of the vested economic, political, and intellectual interests to set their Samson to turn the wheels of the Philistine mill.

§ In expressing the conviction that truth prevails in the long run because it is more pleasing than falsehood, I may seem to end upon a note of pragmatic hedonism. But this is not really the case. For this human preference upon which I dwell signifies that man likes to use his mind to seek as much order and harmony as he can find in his own personal life, his relations to his fellows and the universe. It is this ultimate adjustment between human motive and what we term the facts of life that furnishes our guarantee for every advance of ordered knowledge. This preference for truth and sound reason is, therefore, an affirmation of the disinterested search for truth. The true strength of science thus lies in its contribution to the life of reason as the ultimate instrument and guarantee of human values. This disinterested motive, working quietly and persistently in our Universities and other places of learning, will in the long run not merely resist successfully the attempts of interested outsiders to enslave it to the ends of immediate utility, but will even subdue to its own ends the fetters sought to be put upon its liberty. Sometimes it may stoop to conquer, by the arts of conciliation, compromise, and concealment. But conquer it will. While vested interests may sometimes imagine that they are guiding and controlling the intellectual life, the latter will be utilising the resources intended for these arts of management in order to further and sustain its free career of intellectual discovery.

How surely, rapidly, and fruitfully this natural preference for free-thinking and truth-seeking can operate for progress in the social sciences must, however, be conditioned largely by opportunities which are, in part adventitious, in part the result of purposive provision. By the former I signify the stimulus or lack of stimulus to individual minds furnished by the intellectual and moral atmosphere in which they exist. " Historians tell us that the great periods of intellectual activity are apt to follow the coincidence of the discovery of important new facts with the wide extension of a sense of personal liberty." [1] Are we living in such a great period ? Discoveries of important new facts in the several branches of physical science crowd upon us, and transform the material apparatus of life at a pace that seems to threaten nervous sanity. It is, indeed, a common plaint that these new commands of the physical powers of Nature have so far outridden the arts of social control as to threaten the very existence of our Western civilisation. Hence the cry for better human government. Hence the eager rush of attention towards the new claims of psychology offering to repair and transform the arts of government in every department of conduct, so as to enable man to cope with, and apply to his progressive welfare, the rich new provisions of the physical sciences. How far this attempt is likely to succeed must, however, depend primarily upon the accompanying condition named above, viz. " the wider extension of a sense of personal liberty ". Now this extension is not assured. Certain important tendencies in the swift progress of the material

[1] G. Wallas, *The Great Society*, p. 206.

arts are adverse to this sense of personal liberty. The standardisation of mass-production carries with it a tendency to standardise a mass-mind, producing a willing conformity, not merely to common ways of living, but to common ways of thinking and common valuations. The worst defect of patriotism is its tendency to foster and impose this common mind, and so to stifle the innumerable germs of liberty. The tendency of all strong Governments has always been to repress liberty, partly in order to ease the processes of rule, partly from sheer disbelief in innovation. When vested economic interests ' stand in ' with Governments, the sacredness of property converts all innovation into sacrilege. The endeavour to brand loyalty to existing institutions upon a common mind is incompatible with free-thinking. Most rulers and some educationalists appear to think that free-thinking can be safely canalised into channels of loyal social service, and denied access to dangerous courses. Here is a fatal error. The creative spirit is one and indivisible. It cannot live and work under servitude or external control. Disinterested thought cannot be drawn into the physical sciences and kept out of politics and economic theory. If we are right in holding that the most urgent business of our age is to devise better laws of conduct in the arts of human government, within and beyond the limits of nationality, success depends upon stimulating in as many spots as possible the largest number and variety of independent thinkers, constructing and maintaining among them the best conditions of free intercourse and co-operation and finally enabling their creative thought to play freely in criticism and in reform upon the existing modes of political and economic life. Those who in vague rhetoric dwell on education as the substitute for force and revolution often mean a doped, standardised, and servile education. But such education affords no safety in this dangerous world. Free-thinking alone can furnish the energy and the direction to human government, helping to bridge the chasm between physical and moral progress. Safety does not lie in standing still, but in marching with 'the times'. And these times require a quickening of the march. If marching quick appears to be dangerous, safety does not lie in marching slow, but in knowing where you are going and in keeping a good look-out. This is the task of disinterested thinking.

INDEX

Printed in Great Britain by
UNWIN BROTHERS, LIMITED, LONDON AND WOKING

T - #0051 - 160425 - C0 - 216/138/16 [18] - CB - 9780415578561 - Gloss Lamination